UNEASY AT HOME

Uneasy
at Home

ANTISEMITISM
AND THE AMERICAN
JEWISH EXPERIENCE

Leonard Dinnerstein

Columbia University Press

New York

1987

Columbia University Press
New York   Guildford, Surrey
Copyright © 1987 Columbia University Press
All rights reserved

Printed in the United States of America

Library of Congress Cataloging-in-Publication Data

Dinnerstein, Leonard.
  Uneasy at home

  Includes bibliographies and index.
    1. Jews—United States. 2. Jews—Southern States.
3. Antisemitism—United States. 4. United States—
Ethnic relations. 5. Southern States—Ethnic relations.
I. Title.
E184.J5D495 1987   305.8'00975   87-521
ISBN 0-231-06252-4

This book is Smyth-sewn
Book design by J.S. Roberts

To Rita and Levon Kabasakalian

Contents

Preface

The essays in this collection were written over an eighteen-year period, from 1968 to 1986. In rereading them, I see that I no longer have all of the same opinions. In fact, were I writing some of these pieces today, I would question some of my earlier conclusions. I am not certain that Jews have been absorbed into the dominant culture to as great a degree as I thought in the early 1970s. I do not think that antisemitism is a thing of the past in the white community as I suggest in some of the earlier pieces. The commitment to Israel and to the cause of Soviet Jewry have emerged as much greater factors uniting Jews than I had originally believed. And the disappearance of the most rabid forms of anti-semitism has not led to mass assimilation. Another significant occurrence on the Jewish-American scene has been the establishment of political action committees which have united business-men and philanthropists in a new type of Jewish alliance. Finally, I had not anticipated the growth of strong Jewish communities outside of the major cities in the East and Midwest aside from Miami and Los Angeles. Thus, I have new perspectives which are not apparent in reading some of my earlier work.

Let me hasten to add, however, that I am not distancing myself from what I wrote years ago. To be sure, some of my opinions have changed, but, in the main, I still firmly believe that anti-semitism as a factor in American Jewish history has been to a considerable extent overlooked by other historians (more so when I first began writing in the 1960s than the 1980s). This history cannot be understood unless people have some knowledge of the antagonism and hostility that Jews in America have faced since they first arrived in the American colonies in 1654.

Inevitably in a collection of this kind, there is bound to be some repetition and stylistic variation. Also, there are different spellings and ways of citation. I spell antisemitism as one word, all in lower case; many publications, however, prefer the more conventional anti-Semitism. Gentile is sometimes capitalized but other times the ''g'' appears in lower case. Dates are sometimes cited as 1960s without an apostrophe or as 1970's with an apostrophe depending on the style of the publication in which the article first appeared.

Leonard Dinnerstein

Tucson, Arizona
January 12, 1987

Acknowledgments

My editor at Columbia University Press, Kate Wittenberg, suggested the assembling of this collection and has been consistently supportive during the entire production process. Leslie Bialler, the manuscript editor, has an unerring eye and saved me from many potentially embarrassing and awkward expressions.

Over the years the essays in this collection were read and improved upon by a large number of people. Although my memory is not good enough to remember everyone who commented upon early drafts my debts to the following people are enormous and I list them in alphabetical order: Seymour Drescher, Fred Jaher, David Reimers, Michael Schaller, Robert Schulzinger, and Richard Weiss.

My greatest debt is to my loving wife, Myra, who is always there. She reads everything that I write and her astute observations have often forced me to rethink early assessments and reevaluate the conclusions that I have reached.

Leonard Dinnerstein
Tucson

UNEASY AT HOME

Introduction

Interest in American ethnic and immigrant history grew in the 1960s as the burgeoning civil rights movement confronted traditional American prejudices and social arrangements. Stimulated, if not actually spawned, by concern for blacks, historians and other scholars displayed a renewed interest in the experiences of people largely omitted from major chronicles of the American past. Books and articles appeared not only about blacks but also about Mexicans, American Indians, and European and Asian immigrants, whose experiences in America have been glossed over and whose lifestyles had all but been ignored. Although historians had written about minorities in scores of filiopietistic works showing how their compatriots had fit into the United States, these books, under the influence of the melting pot tradition, minimized the distinctive cultures of immigrants and focused instead on their alleged acceptance of existing traditions upon arrival in the United States. Such writings served the purpose of promoting ethnic pride by demonstrating how much each group contributed to American development but they failed to grapple with the stubborn complexities of ethnic adaptation in the United States. Nor did they shed much light on American nativistic reactions to the newcomers.

Some scholars in the late 1960s began to ask different questions about American minorities and many of them, second or third generation ethnics themselves, did not avoid exploration of either why or how the immigrants of yesteryear coped with problems of adjustment, and how Americans reacted to foreigners in their midst. Although I was not aware of it at the time that I wrote my doctoral dissertation in the mid 1960s,[1] I was part of a movement of historians involved in reexamining aspects of an ethnic past in a country whose rhetoric and traditions glorified the concept of the melting pot and whose people rarely, if ever, took note of the persistence of minority cultures.

The impact of the civil rights movement and a chance encounter with another graduate student who suggested to me that Jews had been involved in the area for decades nudged me into the direction of an ethnic topic for my doctoral dissertation. After preliminary inquiries I learned about Leo Frank, a Jew who had been lynched in Georgia in 1915 under extraordinary, but little known, circumstances and I found out that there were extensive materials on the case at the American Jewish Archives in Cincinnati.

What I discovered during this investigation of the Georgian Jew who, for a brief period of his life, made national headlines was that there were few background studies about southern Jewish experiences. I found snippets about Jews and their "contributions" to southern and American life but no analysis which would help me understand why Leo Frank, as a Jew, aroused the intensity of passion that he did, and why, contrary to racist southern mores, a prosecuting attorney would build his case on the bizarre testimony of a lone black man.

Thus, I was forced to look for material that would give insight into the history of southern Jewry and found that those who wrote about American (and southern) Jews (almost all Jewish themselves) were in the tradition of minority writers whose central interest was to show how well Jews blended into American and southern society and how much they had contributed to the growth of their communities and the nation. Unpleasant, or antisemitic, episodes were almost always ignored. Jonathan Sarna brilliantly summed up these accounts in 1981 when he wrote: "The portrait of early America in many American Jewish history textbooks is an alluring one. No anti-Semitism mars the Eden-like national landscape; religious freedom spreads over the face of the

country, expanding with the frontier; Jews luxuriate in the bless-
ings of justice and liberty." (Bertram Korn's chapters on anti-
semitism during the Civil War were singular exceptions).[2]

These chronicles provided most of what we knew of American Jewish history because American graduate schools were not
training students in the field before the 1960s even though several
distinguished scholars were qualified to do so. Oscar Handlin, for
example, knew of and had written about, the immigrant experience but his most brilliant work covered Boston's Irish immigrants
before the 1870s;[3] his approach to the tercentenary commemo-
ration of American Jewish history, published in 1954, is revealed
in its title, *Adventure in Freedom*.[4] A student of Handlin's, Moses
Rischin, made a major impact in 1961 with *The Promised City*,[5] a
study of New York's immigrant Jews on the Lower East Side at
the turn of the century, but his emphasis was on the adjustment
of the East Europeans to New York and he did not dwell on the
hostility they encountered.

The dean of American Jewish history, Jacob Rader Marcus
of Hebrew Union College in Cincinnati, probably influenced more
rabbinical students to write about American Jewry than did any
other person but his own work, as well as that of most of his
students, emphasized how Jews had acculturated.[6] Rarely did
Marcus or his disciples scrutinize the agonizing process of adaptation and adjustment to the host culture in Christian America.
But to write almost exclusively about the positive experiences of
Jews, while minimizing or ignoring the negative aspects, did not
give a comprehensive view of the past.

That does not mean, of course, that no one explored American antisemitism. In the 1950s a number of scholars embarked
upon a serious examination of the topic but most of their studies
were limited in either time or perspective. Bertram Korn was a
student of Jacob Marcus, and he showed for the first time how
pervasive antisemitism was in the North and the South during the
conflagration. Morris U. Schappes edited a marvelous collection,
A Documentary History of the Jews in the United States, 1654–1875, that
revealed, as he put it, "that anti-Semitism in our country has a
much more ancient history, a more persistent continuity, and a

wider dispersion than even liberal opponents of anti-Semitism have hitherto dreamed."[7] But Schappes' book stopped before the advent of the major East European Jewish migration to this country and other scholars showed little interest in pursuing what he started.

The most serious and important historical analysis of American antisemitism came from John Higham, who originally started writing on American nationalism and wound up with a classic on nativism, *Strangers in the Land*.[8] He followed that with two studies of American attitudes toward Jews, one from 1830–1930, and another during the Gilded Age.[9] Higham concluded that Americans held contradictory views: they both liked and rejected Jews at the same time. Religious and economic stereotypes included the opinions that Jews were the "people of the book" yet they had rejected Jesus; and in the economic sphere, praiseworthy observations about Jewish industry, thrift, and business accomplishments were accompanied by beliefs in the Jewish shylock who exploited others for pecuniary gain. These conclusions remained the standard interpretation for more than a generation.

Oscar Handlin and Richard Hofstadter also made attempts in the 1950s to explain the development of American antisemitism. They both concluded that its seeds lay in the agrarian protest movements of the late nineteenth century.[10] This stimulated several other historians to reexamine the Populist movement of the 1880s and 1890s. Several of them—Norman Pollack, Walter T. K. Nugent, and Frederic Cople Jaher[11]—disputed the connection between Populism and antisemitism but their conclusions received far less attention than the charges made by Higham, Handlin, and Hofstadter.

Not until the late 1960s did any other aspect of American Jewish history receive the concentrated attention of chroniclers and scholars. Then, in 1967, Arthur Morse published *While Six Million Died*, showing that Franklin D. Roosevelt and his administration had done shockingly little to prevent European Jews from being killed during the Holocaust of World War II. Historians like David Wyman, Henry Feingold, and Saul Friedlander followed shortly thereafter with trenchant analyses of the same subject, carefully expanding Morse's original arguments. Fifteen years after his original effort, David Wyman concluded his analysis, which he published under the title *The Abandonment of the Jews*.[12]

Although the Populist era and the failure of the United States to come to the aid of European Jews during World War II were the only two areas of American Jewish history that attracted the attention of several historians before the 1970s, the emergence of another approach to historical analysis, the new social history, began to affect examinations of the American Jewish past. Historians of this school focused upon ordinary people—immigrants, women, children—and the nature of their daily lives. No longer did leaders, contributions, or the assimilative process dominate immigrant studies. Local, rather than national, trends were examined. And new questions were asked. How did kinship networks and community institutions contribute to stability and adaptation? Which members of the family worked, and under what conditions? What kinds of activities did individuals engage in and how did they spend their leisure time? Which factors brought prestige to members of the community and which contributed to the continuing secondary status of women? Often the authors who asked these questions buttressed their arguments with statistical analyses. Some of them also utilized Marxist interpretations of ethnic groups by emphasizing immigrant responses to and confrontations with capitalism.[13]

More specifically in tune with the values of the new social history and its emphases on ethnic strengths, urban development, and occupational choices was an explosion of books on American Jewish history. Among them were Arthur Goren's study of New York City's Jewish quest for community—the Kehillah experiment during the Progressive Era; Naomi Wiener Cohen's history of a major Jewish defense agency, the American Jewish Committee; Melvin Urofsky's examination of American Zionism, and Ronald Bayor's inquiry into the relationship among Jews and several other ethnic groups in New York during the 1930s.[14] In other urban analyses Jeffrey Gurock detailed the days *When Harlem Was Jewish*, and Deborah Dash Moore's *At Home In America* concentrated on the lives of second generation Jews in New York

City. Several other monographs, and only a few can be mentioned here, highlighted *The Americanization of the Synagogue* in the nineteenth century, and on an occupational class, Jewish criminals, that had previously been ignored: *The Rise of the Jewish Gangster in America* and *Our Gang*. A literary critic, Irving Howe, wrote perhaps the best known and most popular treatment of any aspect of American Jewish history, *The World of Our Fathers*, a comprehensive synthesis of the people who lived in New York City's famed Lower East Side at the turn of the century.[15] Numerous accounts also appeared detailing the events leading up to President Harry S. Truman's recognition of the state of Israel in 1948.[16] The most recent analysis, Charles Silberman's *A Certain People*, retraces the American Jewish past, but emphasizes how well integrated Jews now are in the American scene.[17] These monographs not only broadened our understanding of the multifaceted American Jewish experiences but also sharply shifted the focus away from filiopietism and instant absorption of American cultural values.

Antisemitism is another topic that Jews showed renewed interest in during the past decade. Michael Dobkowski's *The Tarnished Dream* showed how pervasive animosity toward Jews was in this country between the 1870s and the 1920s, thereby suggesting that detailed studies of earlier periods might result in new insights about its prevalence at other times. In 1980 Jonathan Sarna wrote the first historigraphical analysis showing why historians had avoided the subject of American antisemitism, and in 1986 David Gerber's *Antisemitism in American History* brought together a collection of original essays on the subject. That same year, Dan Oren, a psychiatrist, wrote an absolutely scathing volume, *Joining The Club*,[18] which exposed the bigotry at Yale University during most of the nineteenth and twentieth centuries.

Despite these excellent contributions to the analysis of antisemitism, the study of the subject is still in its infancy. Neither Jewish, nor American Jewish, history can be understood without an extended analysis of how others have reacted to Jews and how Jews have interpreted these reactions. A great deal of what Jews have done and what endeavors they have avoided, as well as their behavior in both European and American society, has been dependent on both existing antisemitism and Jewish anxieties about possible antisemitic outbursts. Therefore, to separate American Jewish history from an analysis of American antisemitism strikes me as ahistorical.

Today there are no longer any limits to the study of American Jewish history. Any aspect of Jewish development in this country is open for inquiry but there are fewer graduate students now than there were in the late 1960s and there are still no centers of American Jewish history where younger scholars can go for training. That there is a broader contemporary interest in the field there can be no doubt. In 1984 Columbia University received money to establish a chair in American Jewish history and there was some talk that Yale might be equally endowed. If these universities begin to train American Jewish historians other schools will imitate their efforts. Then whole new areas worthy of serious historical scholarship will flourish. Works on Jews in the Sun Belt states, their professional experiences in the academic, governmental, business, legal, and scientific communities since the end of World War II, and on the expanded horizons and the blended cultural values of third and fourth generation Americans will prove fruitful topics for exploration. Imaginative historians of the future will no doubt unearth topics on American Jewry unthought of in our own day.

To a considerable extent many of the essays in this collection represent inquiries into subjects that scholars of a previous generation shunned. When politics, diplomacy, and military affairs were considered the essential historical concerns ethnic studies did little to advance one's standing in the profession. Although major figures like Marcus Hansen, Carl Wittke, and Oscar Handlin[19] received kudos for their works in the field of immigration, younger historians generally did not want to bring attention to their immigrant backgrounds. But the temper of the 1960s encouraged wider horizons and the greater tolerance spawned by the Civil Rights movement broadened the nature of historical inquiry. Thus, the pieces in this book constitute a search for answers to a number of historical questions that used to lie dormant.

Because I grew up in the 1930s and 1940s, the peak period

of American antisemitism, and then studied the ramifications of the Leo Frank case, it has been important for me to find out why so little had been written about the many Jewish-gentile tensions in the United States. Why were Jews so concerned with the opinions that others had of them? Why did their histories keep proclaiming how happy they were in this country and how well accepted they had been by others? Why were many Jews so reluctant to take public positions on controversial issues? Why had conflict with other groups been almost ignored in the study of the American Jewish past? These, and several similar questions, occurred to me during the course of my study into American Jewish history and attempts to answer them appear in the essays in this book.

The first part includes a disparate grouping of three pieces written for quite different audiences. An overview of the East European Jewish experience in the United States tried to capture the highlights of the past one hundred years for scholars at an international conference who wanted some insights into why Jews in the United States have been so extraordinarily successful (in the conventional use of the term). The article on Franklin D. Roosevelt was prepared for a general retrospective on the New Deal fifty years after its inception. Written after exposure of Roosevelt's shocking indifference to the fate of European Jews before and during the Holocaust, the essay explores the reasons why American Jews revered him. The last article in the first part, "Education and the Advancement of American Jewry," surveys the reasons for the Jewish commitment to education. These three items highlight a number of the positive aspects of American society which allowed Jews to prosper—emotionally and financially.

Parts II and III of this book concentrate on areas where I have done most of my research: Jews in the South and antisemitism. The inquiries into southern Jewish history extended logically from my doctoral dissertation on the Leo Frank case. Finding so little in the way of analysis of the southern Jewish experience, I set out to discover what life was like for Jews below the Mason-Dixon line. What I found suggested that a fear and tension existed among southern Jews that historians had all but overlooked. Jews did not want to stand out in society. They did not want to appear different from other southerners. They wanted their own Reform temples to seem just like another southern church. And they fretted constantly lest some Jews make an untoward remark, or take an unpopular stance on a public issue, which might bring the whole Jewish community into disrepute. At the same time, however, Jewish spokesmen in the South publicly ignored these tensions and stressed instead how happy they were and how well they fit into the communities throughout the region. I examined these attitudes in several essays included in this collection: "A Neglected Aspect of Southern Jewish History," "A Note on Southern Attitudes Toward Jews," "Atlanta in the Progressive Era: A Dreyfus Affair in Georgia," and "Jews and the Desegregation Crisis in the South." My conclusions were not as sanguine as the previous Jewish accounts. I concluded that southern and other American antisemitism was much greater than had previously been acknowledged, and that American Jews were much more ambivalent about their status in America than they had ever before been willing to articulate publicly.

The third part of the book contains essays concerning hostile attitudes of non-Southerners toward Jews. I was curious about why American Jewish historians had rarely examined conflicts with members of the dominant culture or with individuals of other groups, and undertook inquiries into this relatively unexplored area of antisemitism. The ramifications of the findings offered new insights into intergroup relations that broadened my own understanding of both ethnic and American Jewish history. The subject of the first of these analyses, which deals with events that occurred during the funeral of Rabbi Jacob Joseph in New York City in 1902, intrigued me ever since I read a mention of it in a essay that John Higham wrote in 1957.[20] The second article in this grouping, on Congressional antisemitism, is a direct outgrowth of the research that I did for my book *America and the Survivors of the Holocaust*.[21] So too, is the third piece, which covers the period 1945–1950, when American attitudes toward Jews started to become more tolerant. Finally, the study of black antisemitism has been a long time germinating. It first came to my attention in the 1960s when many blacks and Jews engaged in serious public conflicts with one another, and I have watched over the years how tensions between the two groups have waxed and waned. What I have written here are my preliminary findings; I still feel that much digging is necessary before attempting any definitive conclusions.

Thus, this eclectic collection represents some of my own views on aspects of the American Jewish experience. I think that together the essays give a somewhat different perspective than might result from reading other books on the topic. There is more concentration on antisemitism than other historians may have thought appropriate to emphasize. But after they read the articles I would hope that my audience will have some additional insights into why a great many American Jews remain uneasy at home.

Notes

1. Leonard Dinnerstein, *The Leo Frank Case* (New York: Columbia University Press, 1968).

2. Jonathan D. Sarna, "Anti-Semitism and American History," *Commentary* (March 1981) 71:42; Bertram W. Korn, *American Jewry and the Civil War* (Philadelphia: Jewish Publication Society of America, 1951).

3. Oscar Handlin, *Boston's Immigrants* (Cambridge: Harvard University Press, 1941).

4. Oscar Handlin, *Adventure in Freedom* (New York: McGraw-Hill, 1954).

5. Moses Rischin, *The Promised City* (Cambridge: Harvard University Press, 1962).

6. See for example, Jacob R. Marcus, *Early American Jewry* (Philadelphia: Jewish Publication Society of America, 1951), Marcus, ed., *Memoirs of American Jews, 1775–1865* (Philadelphia: Jewish Publication Society of America, 1955), and Marcus, *The Colonial American Jew, 1492–1776* (3 volumes; Detroit: Wayne State University Press, 1970).

7. Morris U. Schappes, *A Documentary History of the Jews in the United States, 1654–1875* (New York: Citadel Press, 1950), p. viii.

8. John Higham, *Strangers in the Land* (New Brunswick, N.J.: Rutgers University Press, 1955).

9. John Higham, "Social Discrimination Against Jews in America, 1830–1930," *Publications of the American Jewish Historical Society,* (September 1957) 47:1–33 and "Anti-Semitism In The Gilded Age: A Reinterpretation," *Mississippi Valley Historical Review* (March, 1957) 43:559–578.

10. Oscar Handlin, "How U.S. Anti-Semitism Really Began," *Commentary* (June 1951), 11:541–548; Oscar Handlin, "American Views of the Jews at the Opening of the Twentieth Century," *Publications of the American Jewish Historical Society* (June 1951) 40:323–344; Richard Hofstadter, *The Age of Reform* (New York: Knopf, 1955).

11. Norman Pollack, "The Myth of Populist Anti-Semitism," *American Historical Review* (October 1962) 68:76–80; Walter T. K. Nugent, *The Tolerant Populists* (Chicago: University of Chicago Press, 1963); Frederic Cople Jaher, *Doubters and Dissenters* (New York: The Free Press, 1964).

12. Arthur D. Morse, *While Six Million Died* (New York: Random House, 1967); David S. Wyman, *Paper Walls* (Amherst: University of Massachusetts Press, 1968); Henry L. Feingold, *The Politics of Rescue* (New Brunswick: Rutgers University Press, 1970); Saul S. Friedman, *No Haven for the Oppressed* (Detroit: Wayne State University Press, 1973); Wyman, *The Abandonment of the Jews* (New York: Pantheon, 1984).

13. See, for example, John Bodnar, *The Transplanted* (Bloomington: Indiana University Press, 1985) and Sherry Gorelick, *City College and the Jewish Poor* (New Brunswick: Rutgers University Press, 1981).

14. Arthur A. Goren, *New York Jews and the Quest for Community* (New York: Columbia University Press, 1970); Naomi W. Cohen, *Not Free to Desist* (Philadelphia: Jewish Publication Society of America, 1972); Melvin I. Urofsky, *American Zionism From Herzl to the Holocaust* (Garden City: Anchor Press/Doubleday, 1975) and *We Are One!* (Garden City: Anchor Press/Doubleday, 1978); Ronald H. Bayor, *Neighbors in Conflict* (Baltimore: Johns Hopkins University Press, 1978).

15. Jeffrey S. Gurock, *When Harlem Was Jewish, 1870–1930* (New York: Columbia University Press, 1979); Deborah Dash Moore, *At Home in America* (New York: Columbia University Press, 1981); Leon Jick, *The Americanization of the Synagogue* (Hanover, N.H.: University Press of New England, 1976); Albert Fried, *The Rise and Fall of the Jewish Gangster in America* (New York: Holt, Rinehart and Winston, 1980); Jenna W. Joselit, *Our Gang* (Bloomington: Indiana University Press, 1983); Irving Howe, *The World of Our Fathers* (New York: Harcourt, Brace, Jovanovich, 1976).

16. See, for example, Kenneth Ray Bain, *The March to Zion* (College Station: Texas A & M University Press, 1979); Zvi Ganin, *Truman, American Jewry, and Israel, 1945–1948* (New York: Holmes and Meier, 1979); Peter Grose, *Israel in the Mind of America* (New York: Knopf, 1983); John Snetsinger, *Truman, the Jewish Vote, and the Creation of Israel* (Palo Alto, Ca.: Stanford University, Hoover Institution Press, 1974); and Urofsky, *We Are One!*

17. *A Certain People: American Jews and Their Lives Today* (New York: Simon and Schuster, 1985).

18. Michael Dobkowski, *The Tarnished Dream* (Westport, Ct.: Greenwood Press, 1979); Jonathan D. Sarna, "Anti-Semitism and American History," *Commentary* (March 1981) 71:42–47; David A. Gerber, ed., *Anti-Semitism in American History* (Urbana: University of Illinois Press, 1980); Dan A. Oren, *Joining the Club* (New Haven: Yale University Press, 1986).

19. See, for example, Marcus L. Hansen, *The Atlantic Migration, 1607–1860* (New York: Harper Torchbook, 1961); Carl Wittke, *We Who Built America* (Cleveland: Press of Western Reserve University, 1939); Oscar Handlin, *The Uprooted* (Boston: Little, Brown, 1951).

20. Higham, "Anti-Semitism in the Gilded Age," pp. 577–578.

21. Leonard Dinnerstein, *America and the Survivors of the Holocaust* (New York: Columbia University Press, 1982).

Part I.
An Eclectic Overview

1

The East European
Jewish Migration

Jewish migration to the United States in the nineteenth and twentieth centuries may be divided into three groups: the German, the East European, and the Central European. During the first period of heavy Jewish immigration to the United States, mainly during the pre-Civil War years but roughly from the 1840s through the 1870s, about 50,000 Jews arrived from the German states. They engaged almost exclusively in trade and commerce, many starting off as peddlers and some moving up quickly into banking and department stores. The second and most important wave, from the 1870s through 1924, came primarily from Eastern Europe. Responding to the economic uprooting of society and the frequent pogroms of the late nineteenth and early twentieth centuries, more than 2,000,000 Jews left Russia, Galicia, Rumania, and Hungary for the great trek to the United States. These people included artisans, skilled workers, small merchants, and shopkeepers. They and their descendants have made the greatest impact of all the Jews in the United States and are the subject of this essay. The third group, from Central Europe, numbering about 365,000, came to America between 1925 and 1953, with approximately 132,000 in the years between 1948 and 1953. Some of these people emigrated for economic reasons, but the overwhelming majority were victims of Hitler's rise to power in Germany. In the 1930s Nazi persecutions and brutalities forced many German

Jews to leave the country, and after the Second World War some concentration camp victims and the displaced refugees were granted opportunities to resettle in the United States. This third group quickly moved into the Jewish mainstream in the United States. They made major impacts in the American scientific and intellectual communities.

Before the Second World War these Jewish groups were quite different and easily identifiable: by income, education, jobs, residence, and organized associations. In recent times, however, the differences have diminished considerably because of a vast leap in both educational and income levels of American-born Jews. It would be quite difficult, if not impossible, today to distinguish among the descendants of the previous generations of Jewish immigrants. In terms of life style, occupation, and income the overwhelming majority of Jewish families are in the middle and upper middle class and their breadwinners occupy professional, technical, and managerial positions.

Causes for Emigration

The Jews left Eastern Europe for much the same reason that most other peoples left their states—grinding poverty at home made them yearn for a decent life elsewhere. In Russia 94 percent of the Jews lived in the "pale of settlement," a huge belt of land in western and southwestern Russia and the Ukraine stretching from the Baltic to the Black Sea. Jews could live outside of this area only by special permission. Within the pale their population increased from 1,000,000 in 1800 to 4,000,000 in 1880 and this expansion constricted the possibilities of economic opportunities. In Rumania they were regarded as aliens, while in Galicia Jews suffered from economic boycotts and other manifestations of hostility.

During the 1870s the industrial revolution began to make a significant impact in Russia. That impact was greatest within the pale, where industrialization took place most rapidly. The Russian government, which had earlier set numerous restrictions on Jews, feared their influence, especially after industrialization began. Jews actively engaged in trade and commerce, which attracted many of the gentiles once they were forced off the land. Competition for positions in a tight economy heightened Christian-Jewish tensions. Industrialization also stimulated the movements of Jews and gentiles from rural to urban areas to seek employment. The city of Lodz, which had eleven Jews in 1797, counted 98,677 one hundred years later and 166,628 in 1910. Warsaw's Jewish population leaped from 3,521 in 1781, to 219,141 in 1891. Industrial expansion also led to a major flight of people to the west. Many Jews went to Germany, France, and England in Europe, and to Argentina, Canada, South Africa, and Palestine. More than 90 percent of the Jewish migrants, however, wound up in the United States.

Other factors also propelled the Jewish exodus. As in the case of emigrants from other nations, flight was impelled by specific items like the unsuccessful Polish uprising of 1863, the Lithuanian famine of 1867–69, the Polish cholera epidemic of 1869, and by the predisposition of young people to try their fortunes in a new world, and the developing political ideologies of Zionism and socialism which made traditional modes of thought and behavior too confining. Many Jews were outspoken socialists. They envisioned a new democratic social order with a more equitable distribution of the nation's wealth and resources. Antisemitism, which rose in intensity as Pan-Slavism gripped the Eastern Europeans, however, provided a unique reason for the Jewish migration. Jews were not Slavs and therefore stood as an impediment toward nationalistic unity. The assassination of Tsar Alexander II of Russia in 1881 by a group of socialists spawned a wave of pogroms against the Jews which continued intermittently until the First World War. Major pogroms occurred in 1881, 1882, 1903, and 1906, and hundreds of others have been recorded. These pogroms, often inspired by government officials, resulted in wanton and brutal assaults upon Jews and their property. Russia also codified and curtailed Jewish rights after Tsar Alexander's assassination. The May Laws of 1882 restricted the numbers of Jews that might attend Russian universities and the kinds of occupations Jews might pursue. They could not rent or own land outside of the towns and cities nor could they keep their shops open on the Christian sabbath or on Christian holidays.

American letters and money sent by earlier immigrants, along with the advertisements from railroad and steamship lines anxious to transport emigrants, further stimulated migration from Eastern Europe to the New World. Promising economic conditions in the United States, combined with increased persecutions and deprivations in Russia, Galicia, and Rumania, expanded the exodus to the West as revealed in the following figures:

    1870s: 40,000
    1880s: 200,000 +
    1890s: 300,000 +
    1900-14: 1,500,000 +

Patterns of Settlement

Over 90 percent of the more than 2,000,000 Jews who left Eastern Europe between 1870 and 1924 went to the United States. Unlike many other immigrant groups, the Jews mostly traveled with their families. During the years 1899 to 1910, females made up 43.4 percent of the total number of Jewish immigrants and children 24.7 percent, the highest figure for any arriving peoples. During the same period males constituted 95.1 percent of the Greek immigrants and 78.6 percent of the southern Italians. Only the Irish had a larger percentage of females than the Jews (52.1 percent), but it is believed that many of them came alone to work as domestics. Statistical estimates indicate that 71.6 percent of the Jews came from the Russian empire, including Latvia, Lithuania, and Poland; 17.6 percent from Galicia in the Polish area of the Austro-Hungarian empire; and 4.3 percent from Rumania.

Most of these people landed, and remained, in New York City. In 1870 the city's Jewish population had been estimated at 80,000; in 1915 almost 1,400,000 Jews lived there. The newcomers found friends, relatives, jobs, and educational opportunities in

New York City, and, in any case, few had the money to travel elsewhere. Moreover, the Orthodox knew that they could find kosher butchers which would allow them to maintain Jewish dietary laws, and jobs where they would not have to work on the sabbath. To be sure, those who landed in Boston, Philadelphia, or Baltimore, or even those who made their way to Chicago and other cities, found small Jewish communities in which they could settle. Chicago, in fact, had 200,000 Jews by 1912. But the major center, by far, for East European Jews was New York.

Most of the immigrants who chose to live in New York City settled originally in a small section of Manhattan Island known as the Lower East Side. The boundaries of this ghetto lay roughly within the blocks bordered by Fourteenth Street, Third Avenue and the Bowery, Canal Street, and the East River. The heart of the district, the tenth ward, housed 523.6 people per acre at the beginning of the twentieth century. In the 1890s Jacob Riis, an enterprising reporter, observed that "nowhere in the world are so many people crowded together on a square mile" as in the Jewish quarter. Within the Lower East Side numerous subdivisions could be identified as streets housing primarily Russian, Galician, Rumanian, or Hungarian Jews. The area contained 75 percent of New York City's Jews in 1892, 50 percent in 1903, and 23 percent in 1916.

The tenements where the Jews lived can be best described as dark, dank, and unhealthful. One magazine described the dwellings in 1888 as

> great prison-like structures of brick, with narrow doors and win-
> dows, cramped passages and steep rickety stairs. They are built
> through from one street to the other with a somewhat narrower
> building connecting them. . . . The narrow courtyard . . . in the
> middle is a damp foul-smelling place, supposed to do duty as an
> airshaft; had the foul fiend designed these great barracks they could
> not have been more villainously arranged to avoid any chance of
> ventilation. . . . In case of fire they would be perfect death-traps,
> for it would be impossible for the occupants of the crowded rooms
> to escape by the narrow stairways, and the flimsy fire-escapes
> which the owners of the tenements were compelled to put up a

few years ago are so laden with broken furniture, bales and boxes
that they would be worse than useless. In the hot summer months
. . . these fire-escape balconies are used as sleeping-rooms by the
poor wretches who are fortunate enough to have windows opening
upon them. The drainage is horrible, and even the Croton as it
flows from the tap in the noisome courtyard, seemed to be contam-
inated by its surroundings and have a fetid smell.

Two families on each tenement floor shared a toilet. In the summer
months the heat and stench in these places were unbearable and
the stagnant air outside provided little relief.

The first Jewish immigrants, despite their toil, earned barely
enough to subsist on. As a result it was not uncommon to find
parents, children, other relatives, and some boarders in a two-,
three-, or four-room apartment. The boarder may have paid three
dollars a month for his room and free coffee, but that came to 30
percent of the family's ten-dollars-a-month rent. Looking back,
the prices of four cents for a quart of milk, two cents for a loaf of
bread, and twelve cents for a pound of kosher meat may look
ridiculously cheap, but when one reckons this on an average
weekly income of less than eight dollars, the picture is quite
different.

Fortunately for the Jews, their earnings increased sufficiently after a few years in this country so that they did not have
to rot in the slums for an interminable period. "It was judged to
be a ten-year trek," Moses Rischin tells us, from Hester Street, on
the Lower East Side, to Lexington Avenue, in the more fashionable
uptown area. The tenements, of course, did not disappear, but
their inhabitants continually changed.

Most of the immigrant Jews from Eastern Europe resided
first on the Lower East Side and the Hebrew population in that
area of the city peaked at more than half a million in 1910; by the
1920s fewer than ten percent of New York's Jews still lived there.
The completion of the subways in the early part of the century
opened up vast tracts for settlement in upper Manhattan, Brooklyn, and the Bronx (other boroughs of New York City), and the
Jewish working class, anxious and able to take up residence in
better neighborhoods, moved away.

Jewish immigrants in Boston, Chicago, and other large cities had initial experiences similar to those who remained in New York. In most other places where Jews went, the tenement areas were smaller or nonexistent, the neighborhoods less congested, and the opportunities to live in more healthful surroundings considerably better. East European Jews who went south or west had experiences considerably different from their brethren who went to the urban areas of the Northeast and Chicago, but they constituted fewer than five percent of the entire migration.

Over the years the children and grandchildren of the newcomers moved out of these cities to surrounding suburban areas or flourishing new communities where economic opportunities beckoned. Most of the subsequent growth in the American Jewish population took place in the states closest to New York: Pennsylvania, New Jersey, and Connecticut, with two major and a few minor exceptions. After World War II job opportunities and a pleasant year-round climate drew hundreds of thousands of Jews to California, especially the Los Angeles area, and many older people first visited and then retired in Miami Beach, Florida. The growth of the Jewish population in California and Florida is primarily a postwar phenomenon.

Labor and Business

East European Jewish immigrants differed from most of the other foreign-born arrivals in the late nineteenth and early twentieth centuries in that 95 percent of them came from urban rather than rural areas. Their urban origins resulted in the development of skills and talents which would aid them greatly in the United States. An 1898 survey of the Russian pale of settlement found that Jews owned one third of all the factories in the area and that Jewish workers concentrated in the clothing (254,384), metalworking (43,499), wood-working (42,525), building (39,019), textile (34,612), and tobacco (7,856) industries. The skills they acquired there were also in demand when they reached the United States.

An American survey of the occupations of immigrants entering the United States between 1899 and 1910 listed 67.1 percent of the Jewish workers as skilled compared with a general figure of 20.2 percent for all newcomers. In his study *The Promised City*, Moses Rischin indicates that

> Jews ranked first in 26 out of 47 trades tabulated by the Immigration Commission, comprising an absolute majority in 8. They constituted 80 per cent of the hat and cap makers, 75 per cent of the furriers, 68 per cent of the watchmakers and milliners and 55 per cent of the cigarmakers and tinsmiths. They totaled 30 to 50 per cent of the immigrants classified as tanners, turners, undergarment makers, jewelers, painters, glaziers, dressmakers, photographers, saddle-makers, locksmiths, butchers, and metal workers in other than iron and steel. They ranked first among immigrant printers, bakers, carpenters, cigar-packers, blacksmiths, and building trades workmen.

In the United States the Jewish immigrants found jobs in distilleries or printing, tobacco, and building trades, while significant numbers of others started out as butchers, grocers, newspaper dealers, or candy store operators.

The majority of the Jewish immigrants, however, found work in the needle trades, which were—because of the increasingly efficient methods of mass production and the existence of a mass market—undergoing rapid expansion. The arrival of the East Europeans with their particular talents coincided with this vast growth. By the end of the nineteenth century Jews had just about displaced the Germans and Irish from the industry. In New York City the development of the clothing industry transformed the economy. In 1880 major clothing manufacturers numbered only 1,081, or 10 percent of the city's factories, and employed 64,669 people, or 28 percent of the city's work force. By 1910 the borough of Manhattan (which before the consolidation of the five boroughs in 1898 had been New York City) had 11,172 clothing establishments, which constituted 47 percent of the city's factories. The industry employed 214,428 people, slightly more than 46 percent of Manhattan's workers. In 1890, 60 percent of the employed immigrant Jews worked in the garment industry and on the eve of the First World War more than half of all Jewish workers, and two thirds of Jewish wage earners, were still to be found in the industry. The Jewish influence was so great that the manufacturing of wearing apparel in the United States came to be regarded as a Jewish endeavor. Hebrews not only labored in the garment factories; they also worked their way up to supervisory positions and the bolder ones opened their own establishments. Before the Second World War it was estimated that Jews controlled 95 percent of the women's dress industry, 85 percent of the manufacturing of men's clothing, and 75 percent of the fur industry.

Initially, the owners were German Jews who at first looked down on their East European coreligionists and exploited their labor. Many of the early twentieth-century factories were nothing more than reconverted lofts and tenements or else small areas of workers' apartments. Many garments were actually finished in home sweatshops. Workdays lasting from 4:00 A M to 10:00 P.M. in these hovels were not uncommon, and wages averaged $6.00 to $10.00 a week for men and $3.00 to $5.00 for women. (Children also worked on these garments and in other industrial areas as well. Naturally, they earned lower wages than adults.) Because of the seasonal nature of the work, few had a steady yearly income. The annual wage of the average garment worker came to $376.23 in 1900, $1,222 in 1921, and $873.85 in 1930.

Low wages, appalling working conditions, and the insecurity of workers' positions prompted many to think about union organization. Among the Jewish immigrants were many socialists and members of the Russian Jewish Bund who had tried to improve social conditions in Europe. Many of these men also provided the backbone for unionization in the garment trades in the United States. The International Ladies' Garment Workers Union (ILGWU) was founded in 1900 but not until the major strikes of clothing workers in 1909 and 1910 were significant victories won and the union firmly established. In Chicago 40,000 garment workers struck in 1910 and in New York 20,000 waist and dressmakers went out from November 1909 through February 1910. In July 1910 as many as 60,000 cloakmakers struck. The strikes attracted wide attention in the press, among social workers, and throughout the Jewish community. The workers won a victory when in July 1910 a "Protocols of Peace" set up a Board of Arbitration, a Board of Grievances, and a Board of Sanitary Control. Four years later the cloakmakers formed the core of the new Amalgamated Clothing Workers of America, a union which had its own origins in Chicago with a less effective group, the United Garment Workers of America.

The ILGWU and the Amalgamated were the two major Jewish unions in the United States. Because of the socialist heritage of so many of their participants, the two unions were concerned not only with improving labor conditions but also with a vast program for improving the living conditions of all their members. The unions were responsible for ending sweatshops, raising wages, and improving working conditions. They also pioneered in the development of a large number of auxiliary services for members. They built housing developments, established educational programs, maintained health centers, provided pensions, set up vacation resorts, developed a system of unemployment insurance benefits long before the state and federal governments assumed this responsibility, and opened banks giving services at significantly lower cost than other financial institutions. The Jewish unions, in sum, initiated social reforms which other labor organizations adopted. Aside from the ILGWU and the Amalgamated, the only other powerful labor union made up primarily of Jewish workers and leaders was the United Federation of Teachers (now the American Federation of Teachers) which galvanized New York City's schoolteachers in the 1960s and propelled its president, Albert Shanker, to the forefront of labor leadership in America.

Education and Social Mobility

Despite the benefits obtained by and from the labor unions, Jews had no desire to remain in the working class. Their ambition to "get ahead" knew no bounds and as soon as possible they, and/or their children, strove to move up to more lucrative and presti-

gious occupations. As early as 1900, American-born sons of Russian Jews constituted six times as many lawyers and seven times
as many accountants as were to be found in their parents' generation but only one third the number of garment workers. As the
years passed, this tendency became even more pronounced. Jewish workers also tried to become manufacturers. Many of those
who started out as peddlers eventually moved into small retail
outlets and some of the latter then expanded into larger empor-
iums. It was the rare community, in fact, that did not have some
Jewish storekeepers. Random samplings in different decades
through the 1940s showed anywhere from 31 to 63 percent of
the Jews engaged in trade. In one study of the South the author
noted, "It is said, 'If there is a Jewish holiday, you cannot buy a
pair of socks in this whole country,' a remark which illustrates
how complete the control of the retail dry-goods trade by Jews is
supposed to be."

The entertainment industry also provided an avenue of
advancement for some immigrant Jews. In 1905 it was estimated
that half of the actors, popular songwriters, and song publishers
in New York City were Jewish. Withing a few years Jews also
pioneered in the motion picture industry.

The Jews made great economic and social advances because educational and business opportunities were available to
the more enterprising and because the masses of East European
Jewish immigrants considered it necessary to "Americanize" their
children and have them learn the language and customs of the
new country as quickly as possible. From their beginnings in this
country, the East European Jews also showed a passion for education and professional advancement unique in American history.
Members of other immigrant groups, before or since, have not
been as zealous in their quest for knowledge. The newcomers
themselves were forced to do manual work, but whenever possible
they encouraged their children to remain in school, attain an
education, and move up in the world. As Samuel Gompers, leader
of the American Federation of Labor, observed, "The Jews were
fairly ravenous for education and eager for personal development.
. . . All industrial work was merely a steppingstone to professional

and managerial positions." Jewish parents wanted their children in high-status positions where they could operate on their own and not be subject to the bigotry of employers. Jewish boys strove to become doctors, lawyers, dentists, accountants, and teachers. They also opened pharmacies and other retail businesses. In these occupations Jewish parents felt their children would be both prosperous and independent at the same time. In 1903 it was estimated that Jews comprised about half of New York City's 5,000 to 6,000 physicians and thirty-four years later 65.7 percent of the city's lawyers and judges, 55.7 percent of its physicians, and 64 percent of its dentists. In the 1960s Jews still made up a majority of these professions in New York City.

Statistics of Jewish occupational categories for other cities are similar. By the 1930s only one third of all Jewish workers were still engaged in manual jobs while two thirds were in white-collar positions. The figures for non-Jews were just the reverse: two thirds in manual occupations, one third in white-collar jobs. Jews also moved into professional positions at a much faster rate and in much higher percentages than non-Jews. In the 1930s eighteen out of every thousand Jews in San Francisco were lawyers and judges, while sixteen were physicians. For every thousand gentiles the figures were five and five, respectively. Similarly, in Pittsburgh fourteen of every thousand Jews were lawyers and judges, thirteen were physicians, while the corresponding figures for non-Jews were five and four, respectively.

The tendency for Jews to seek and obtain the highest status positions in American society has not diminished in recent decades. In 1955, some 55 percent of all gainfully employed Jews, compared with 23 percent of non-Jews, had professional, technical, managerial, executive, or proprietary positions while in 1967, 51 percent of the Jews, compared to 23 percent of the Catholics and 21 percent of the Protestants in the United States were classified as professionals. Among younger Jewish adults the figures for professional occupations were even higher. With higher status occupations came higher incomes. In 1967 the Gallup Poll found that 69 percent of the Jews had incomes over $7,000 a year but only 47 percent of the Catholics and 38 percent of the Protestants claimed earnings of that level or higher. By 1971, 60 percent of the Jewish families where the head of the household was between thirty and fifty-nine years old had annual incomes exceeding $16,000.

But money alone does not tell the whole story. Since the end of World War II not only has there been an almost complete disappearance of Jewish young men in blue-collar jobs, but Jews in increasingly larger numbers have shunned retail businesses— frequently owned by their fathers—to seek careers and greater personal satisfaction as journalists, writers, scientists, architects, engineers, and academics, as well as the traditional favorites of the Jewish immigrants: lawyers and physicians. Discouraged earlier by family preferences and gentile bigotry from seeking careers where they would have to be employed by others, the enormous expansion of opportunities in the 1950s and 1960s made previously unheralded vocations or fields formerly difficult to enter more attractive and more accessible.

Cultural and Religious Life

The East European Jews, despite their poverty, arrived in this country with certain advantages. They had a strong commitment to a religion which rigidly dictated much of their daily behavior and gave their lives a structure and continuity which helped them to overcome problems of displacement in a new society. Moreover, unlike other immigrants to the United States who may have been poor at home but who otherwise "belonged," the Jews had been minorities wherever they had dwelled in Europe. As a result they had acquired a knowledge of how to move deftly among the dominant groups who, at best tolerated them or, at worst, despised them. They had learned how to survive under a variety of hostile conditions and this experience served them well in the United States where they also had to struggle with adversity. Another important advantage that the Jews had brought with them can best be described as a middle-class view of life. They were ambitious, self-disciplined, and intellectually curious. A number of them had been socialists and participants in the revolutionary movement in Russia and Poland. Most had lived in small towns and villages and were attuned to what might now be considered the urban style of life.

The culture that the Jews brought with them to the United States survived in New York City. In recent decades attempts have been made to transplant it, as well, to Miami Beach and Los Angeles. In Boston, Chicago, and other cities where the Jews initially dwelled, they composed too small a percentage of the population to make much impact on the community. They may have had their own food stores and shared an affinity for literature, music, art, and religious observances, and perhaps even were more socialistically inclined than their neighbors, but in time their tastes and views blended with the dominant values of their respective communities, and today outside of the strongholds of the remnants of East European Jewish orthodoxy in New York, Chicago, Cleveland, Pittsburgh, Los Angeles, and Miami Beach, about the only thing left to distinguish Jews from everyone else in the United States is the Reform Temple.

In New York City, however, an East European Jewish culture flowered for decades and still lends a distinctive tone to the life in this vast metropolis. Cafés abounded where Jews would sit around and *shmooze* (talk) for hours over cups of coffee or glasses of hot tea. "For immigrant Jews," one chronicler reminds us, "talk was the breath of life itself." Discussions during these get-togethers ranged over a wide spectrum of topics and no one ever felt the necessity to refrain from participation because of a limited knowledge of the topic under consideration. The cafés gave the Jewish East Side a flavor—"a Yiddish Bohemia, poor and picturesque"—and their patrons included the most intellectual and articulate Jewish actors, poets, playwrights, journalists, and politicians of the day.

Jews also relaxed in the theater. The coming of the East European Jews not only spawned a Yiddish theater in the ghetto but also stimulated vaudeville and the Broadway stage. They also pioneered in the radio industry and virtually founded the motion picture industry.

Jews throughout the United States have been known for their patronage of the arts and their interest in literary endeavors. Between 1885 and 1914, for example, over 150 Yiddish daily, weekly, monthly, quarterly, and festival journals and yearbooks appeared in New York City, including the daily *Forward* which is still published today. Cultural centers were established wherever sufficient numbers of Jews congregated. Typically, the Cleveland Jewish Center had a gym, a roof garden, a library, classes in Hebrew language and literature, a scouting program, art classes, political forums, sewing and baking clubs, etc.

Owners of art galleries and concert halls (about one third of whom in New York City are Jewish) know that the larger a community's Jewish population the more likely it will be that their showings and musicales will be rewarded with large audiences. Jews are also heavily represented in every aspect of radio and television production. They purchase more books and attend more poetry readings than non-Jews and have also been among the major book publishers in New York City.

For the recent arrivals, however, the single most important cultural institution was the synagogue. Unlike the German Jews who came before them and worshiped, for the most part, in Reform temples barely distinguishable from Unitarian churches, the overwhelming proportion of the East Europeans maintained a devout orthodoxy during their first years in the United States. The numbers of synagogues proliferated in a geometric proportion. In 1870 there were 189 Jewish congregations in the United States, the majority peopled by German Jews. By 1906 there were 1,769 and twenty years after that 3,118. In New York City alone the number of synagogues increased from 300 at the turn of the century to 1,200 in 1942. Usually these places of worship were no more than converted store fronts or private homes which came into being because one group of men had an argument with another group and then stormed out to find someplace else to pray. Since the end of World War II Americanized Jews have tended to worship in distinguished and substantial edifices but, aside from New York, Miami, and the four or five other cities in the country with large Jewish populations, it would be rare to find a community with even half a dozen Jewish temples or synagogues.

In the Jewish ghettos early in the twentieth century, shops closed on the Sabbath and the men and women, separated by curtains, prayed in the neighborhood synagogues. On the most holy days of the Jewish year, generally in September, 95 percent of the East European Jewish families went to the synagogue. As the Jewish immigrants and their children assimilated and Americanized, this percentage dwindled considerably. Although no statistics on high holy day attendance are available, it would be a safe guess to say that today the figure is at best 50 percent. All we can assert with accuracy, however, is that "all surveys of religious commitment, belief, and practice in the United States indicate that Jews are much less involved in religious activities than Protestants, who are in turn less active than Catholics." Nevertheless, it is still true today that the New York City public schools are closed for the major Jewish holidays because Jews constitute a majority of the teachers and their absence would create severe administrative headaches. Furthermore, on the Jewish holidays many of the city's businesses are closed, restaurants in commercial areas are nearly empty, and the mass transportation system has no more than half, if that many, of its usual patrons.

German vs. East European Jews

The East European Jews who arrived in the United States in the late nineteenth and early twentieth centuries encountered an unreceptive American Jewry. The American Jews, descended mostly from the German migrations of the middle of the nineteenth century, had achieved a secure middle-class position in the United States. They were doctors, lawyers, bankers, manufacturers, and merchants. They had established or developed some of the leading department stores in the country like Macy's and Sears Roebuck. In addition, they had made every effort to appear indistinguishable from the more prosperous gentile Americans.

The coming of the East European Jews threatened the

security of the German Jews. One of them wrote, in 1893, that the experience of the United Jewish Charities in Rochester, New York, "teaches that organized immigration from Russia, Rumania, and other semibarbarous countries is a mistake and has proved a failure. It is no relief to the Jews of Russia, Poland, etc., and it jeopardizes the well being of American Jews." The Americanized Jews felt little kinship with the newcomers and also feared that their presence would constitute a burden on society and stimulate an outburst of antisemitism. When the *Hebrew Standard* declared, on June 15, 1894, that "the thoroughly acclimated American Jew . . . is closer to the Christian sentiment around him than to the Judaism of these miserable darkened Hebrews," it probably expressed the dominant sentiment of American Jewry at the time.

Despite their antipathy, the Americanized Jews realized that the gentiles in the United States lumped all the Jews together and that the behavior of the Orthodox would reflect on everyone. As Louis D. Brandeis later phrased it,

> a single though inconspicuous instance of dishonorable conduct on the part of the Jew in any trade or profession has far-reaching evil effects extending to many innocent members of the race. Large as this country is, no Jew can behave badly without injuring each of us in the end. . . . Since the act of each becomes thus the concern of all, we are perforce our brothers' keepers.

One should not minimize, however, the fact that the American Jews also had a paternalistic sympathy for their East European brethren and therefore, since they could not contain the stampede from Russia, Galicia, and Rumania, they set about, after an initial display of coldness, to improve the "moral, mental, and physical conditions" of the immigrants.

Once they decided to facilitate assimilation by assisting the newcomers, the American Jews spared no efforts and "few human needs were overlooked." Of all immigrant groups none proved so generous to "their own kind" as did the Jews. Money and organizational talent combined to provide hospitals, orphan asylums, recreational facilities, and homes for unwed mothers as well as for the deaf, the blind, the old, and the crippled. Educational institutions were also established and the "zeal to Americanize underlay all educational endeavor." Part of this Americanizing process also resulted in the building up of the Jewish Theological Seminary in New York City to train Conservative rabbis. The American Jewish establishment could not tolerate orthodoxy but recognized that the East European immigrants would not come around to Reform Judaism. Conservatism provided an acceptable compromise since it preached American values while retaining the most important orthodox traditions.

Another of the projects resulted in an attempt to disperse the immigrants throughout the United States. The Americanized Jews did not want the newcomers to congregate in one massive ghetto. Between 1901 and 1917 the Industrial Removal Office dispatched 72,482 East European Jews to 1,670 communities in forty-eight states. Nevertheless, many of those transplanted eventually returned to New York. In fact, of the 1,334,627 Jews who did arrive in New York City between 1881 and 1911, 73.5 percent remained there.

The most important and lasting agency set up by the Americanized Jews to help—and lead—their brethren was the American Jewish Committee. Ostensibly formed as a result of the outrageous pogroms in Russia between 1903 and 1905 and dedicated to protecting the civil rights of Jews wherever they were threatened, the American Jewish Committee came into being in 1906 primarily because the established Jewish community in the United States wanted "to assert some control over existing Jewish institutions and mass movements." As Louis Marshall, one of the American Jewish Committee's leading members and its president from 1912 to 1929, put it in 1908, the purpose of those who formed the organization was "to devise a simple and efficient instrument which might deal quickly, and at the same time deliberately, and with an understanding based on experience, with the problems that might present themselves from time to time."

The American Jewish Committee, composed of wealthy Jews, exercised great influence politically "through private contacts with men in power." Since Jacob Schiff, Cyrus Adler, Louis Marshall, Felix Warburg, Oscar Strauss, Julius Rosenwald,

Mayer Sulzberger, and others of their stature dealt regularly with the most prominent Americans of their generation, the Committee "on the whole, acted effectively in the interests of American Jewry." The American Jewish Committee, as one scholar has pointed out, "offered American Jewry a vigorous, disciplined and highly paternalistic leadership as well as a program of Americanization," but its members looked down upon the East Europeans and expected them to follow its leadership. This did not occur. Perhaps if the Committee had been more democratically organized it might have served as a bridge to the newcomers and won them over. But as one of the group said,"let us get away from the idea that the American Jewish Committee must be representative and that its members must be chosen in some way by the vote of the Jews in this country. No great moral movement has been undertaken and carried through except in just such a manner in which we are doing our work."

The enormous assistance provided by the Americanized Jews to the immigrants was accepted with reservations. The established Jews showed disdain for East Europeans and their culture and the recipients of their largesse felt like beggars and poor relations. The charity may have been given out of a sense of obligation but it did not come with warmth and kindness. And the leadership provided by the American Jewish committee definitely smacked of elitism which the immigrants would not tolerate. As soon as the East Europeans could provide their own network of charitable and welfare organizations they did so. It would be a long time before they would look upon their "benefactors" without a jaundiced eye.

Antisemitism

The German and East European Jews in the United States recognized the vast gulf that separated them socially, economically, and culturally but gentiles did not. The coming of the new Jews intensified latent antisemitic feelings among gentile Americans and, as the German Jews had originally feared, this hostility erupted in public. The German Jews felt the sting first. In 1877 a prominent banker was barred as a guest from a resort hotel that had previously accepted his patronage. As the nineteenth century came to a close, German Jews also found themselves excluded from private schools, prominent social clubs, and other resorts. In 1890 the editors of *The American Hebrew* sent around a questionnaire to prominent Americans inquiring why gentiles were so hostile to Jews and one university president responded that "All intelligent Christians deplore the fact that the historical evidences for Christianity have so little weight with your people."

The East European Jews were not affected at first by social antisemitism but in early years of the twentieth century the bigotry became acute. In rapid succession crude slurs, journalistic reports, and supposedly learned commentaries lambasted the Jews. A letter to the editor of the *New York Herald* complained that "these United States are becoming rapidly so Jew ridden . . .," while a faculty member at Teacher's College in New York wrote to a colleague and asked him to "please do me the favor of not coming to the banquet tomorrow night, as I have invited a friend who does not like Jews." A magazine writer asked of the Russian Jew, "is he assimilable? Has he in himself the stuff of which Americans are made?" University of Wisconsin sociologist E. A. Ross claimed that "the lower class of Hebrews of eastern Europe reach here moral cripples, their souls warped and dwarfed by iron circumstance . . . many of them have developed a monstrous and repulsive love of gain." Finally, University of Berlin Professor Werner Sombart's prediction "that in another hundred years the United States will be peopled chiefly by Slavs, negroes and Jews," was prominently featured in one of the leading American periodicals of the day.

In view of these prejudices it is no wonder that outside of the garment district and other Jewish-owned establishments Jews had little chance for obtaining decent jobs. Many help-wanted advertisements specified "Christian only," and real estate agents preferred gentile clients. To combat this discrimination one of the older American Jewish fraternal organizations, B'nai B'rith, which had been founded in 1843, established its Anti-Defamation

League in 1913. The League over the years has proved quite successful in combating antisemitism.

Despite the efforts of the Anti-Defamation League, schools and employers continued discriminating against Jews. Quotas in higher education began in the 1920s and became more rigid during the depression years of the 1930s. As late as 1945 the president of Dartmouth College defended regulations which kept Jewish students out of his school, but he was probably the last outspoken advocate of an already waning policy. Beginning with World War II more opportunities opened to practically all skilled white people and the growth of the economy, the passage of state laws forbidding discrimination in employment and entry into universities, and a generally more tolerant spirit in the land led to widened economic and occupational opportunities for Jews. Law firms, scientific organizations, universities, and businesses needing the very best talent available hired goodly numbers of Jews who were among their few qualified applicants.

Bigotry did not disappear completely. The executive suites of America's largest corporations contain relatively few Jews and one still reads of prominent Jews being denied admission to country clubs. On December 14, 1973, *The Wall Street Journal* ran a story on Irving Shapiro, the new chairman and chief executive of Du Pont and Company, the world's largest chemical concern. Well into the article the author noted that being a lawyer, a Jew, and a Democrat were not helpful to Mr. Shapiro in his rise to prominence within the firm (although his talents, of course, overrode these "handicaps") and then tellingly, "Mr. Shapiro's official biography is noticeably lacking in the kind of club affiliations that adorn those of his colleagues."

Legislation and Politics

There were never any specific laws in the United States regarding East European Jews, but their arrival contributed to the movement for immigration restriction. The major American laws keeping out aliens passed Congress in 1921 and 1924 and these set quotas for groups based on a percentage of their population in the United States in 1910 and 1890, respectively. Such laws were designed to drastically curtail southern and eastern European migration to this country. The Jews, being the second largest immigrant group in the early twentieth century, were obviously one of the major targets of this legislation. As early as 1906 an Italian American had been told by a member of President Theodore Roosevelt's immigration commission that the "movement toward restriction in all of its phases is directed against Jewish immigration. . . ." The Irish, the English, and the Germans who constituted the majority of the nineteenth-century immigrants to the United States received the largest quotas. No religious test was allowed by this legislation. Consequently, Jews born in Germany were counted under the German quota and Jews born in England came in under the English quota even though their parents might have come from Russia or Rumania. Subsequent legislation affecting the East European Jews came in 1948 and 1950 when some of the persons displaced by the German policies of the 1930s and the second World War were allowed to come into the United States under special provisions. Current immigration regulations in the United States make no statement about religion and have done away with quotas based on national origins. Present legislation gives preference to immigrants with close relatives in the United States and to those who have occupational skills in demand in this country.

Jews in the United States have never been legally restrained from pursuing any social or economic interests that struck their fancy. Many states originally restricted voting rights to adult males who believed in the divinity of Jesus Christ, but these were abolished in all but a few states by the beginning of the nineteenth century.

The East Europeans, like other whites, voted after becoming citizens (which took only five years after entering the United States), but they registered and voted in much higher proportion to their numbers than did members of other ethnic groups. They took stands on political issues of concern to them and supported candidates for office who appeared to be in harmony with their own views. A number of Jews have been elected to high political office, such as governor of a state or United States senator, but before the Second World War almost all of these people were of German background. In recent years, however, Jews of East European background have achieved similar prominence. The best known of these are former United States Senators Jacob Javits of New York and Abraham Ribicoff of Connecticut, and former Governors Milton J. Schapp and Marvin Mandel of Pennsylvania and Maryland, respectively. Numerous Jews who were born, or whose parents were born, in Russia, Rumania, and Poland have been elected to the United States House of Representatives and the various state legislatures.

Although Jews have supported Republicans, Democrats, and socialists, since the New Deal era the vast majority have been loyal Democrats both with their votes and their financial contributions. In fact, their contributions are so lavish and their votes so important that policies affecting American Jews—and especially Israel—have to be taken into account by the leading Democratic politicos. So devoted to the Democrats are the Jews that in Richard Nixon's overwhelming reelection victory in 1972 they were the only white ethnic group in the nation that gave a majority of its votes to the Democratic nominee for President, George S. McGovern, although not by the overwhelming support usually accorded Democratic candidates. A few Jews, notably Max Fisher of Detroit, also lubricated Republican coffers. As a result, an anti-Israel policy simply would not be politically acceptable to most of the elected officials in Washington.

Summary and Conclusion

The East European Jews have accomplished great things for themselves in the United States. Most of them arrived on the brink of poverty around the turn of the century and their descendants have risen to comfortable and secure middle-class positions in American society. They can live where they like, work almost any place they have the necessary skills, and worship—or not—in any manner that pleases them. This almost total freedom has resulted in a good deal of interfaith marriage and a slackening of religious and ethnic ties. During the past decade one out of every three Jewish marriages has been with a non-Jew.

Overt anti-Semitism, with the exception of the controversy between blacks and Jews arising out of the 1967 and 1968 school-teachers' strikes in New York City, has subsided considerably during the past few decades, and recent laws have forbidden discrimination on the basis of race, creed, or national origins in employment and housing. These laws are not always observed, but they do indicate that the state and federal governments are putting up formal barriers against wanton bigotry. Ironically, diminished discrimination loosens the ties that bind ethnic minorities. The educational system, especially at the college and university levels, inculcates a national culture and a national way of thinking and it is the rare individual who, after being subject to such exposure, can be completely comfortable again in a strictly ethnic setting. With each succeeding generation of educated Jews, therefore, the ties to the traditional culture are weakened. Most American Jews today are products of the American education system and work and live in areas with people of varying backgrounds. Only some of the Jewish immigrants and their children can still be found in ghettos. And with each passing year their numbers fade.

Also on the wane is Orthodox Jewry. The attachment to the traditional faith was strong among the immigrants and their children but later generations found it a burden. Only a tiny fraction of American Jews keep the Sabbath and only a few more observe the dietary restrictions. Outside of New York, Los Angeles, Chicago, and Miami Beach, the Conservative and Reform branches of Judaism hold sway in temple memberships while the way-of-life practiced by practically all American Jews is in the Reform tradition. Thus attendance at religious services is sparse except at the beginning of the Jewish New Year and the Day of Atonement, and a middle-class life style, almost totally devoid of ethnic flavor, is vigorously pursued.

In the early 1960s one American rabbi said, "Today there

is little that marks the Jew as a Jew except Jewish self-conscious-ness and association with fellow Jews." It is difficult to assess the strength and significance of this self-consciousness. If one "feels" Jewish and seeks out other Jews for companionship, the ties are still there. Jewish identity has also been reinforced by the emer-gence and travails of the State of Israel. It is impossible, of course, to predict for how many generations such sentiments will sustain American Jewry.

As the Jews become Americanized, strains and dissimilar-ities between the German and Russian elements have disappeared. When Hitler began persecuting Jews in Germany, and especially in the past score of years, when differences in income and life styles have narrowed considerably, there have been few if any clashes between Jews of German and East European ancestry in the United States. In fact, one might say that with each succeeding generation there is less and less difference among all American Jews regardless of their grandfathers' native lands. Class, geo-graphical location, education, occupation, and income would be more appropriate categories for demarcation than German-Russian or Orthodox-Reform background. The only exception to this generalization would be the American Council for Judaism, whose members are primarily of German-Jewish ancestry. It is supported by only a fraction of 1 percent of the American Jews and it differs considerably from Jewish organizations in its regard of Israel as just another foreign country with which American Jews should have no special relationship.

Still another aspect of the migration and its subsequent impact in the United States is the fantastic influence that East European Jews have had on the academic, intellectual, medical, political, and cultural life in the country, especially since the end of the Second World War. Whereas in the 1930s it was rare to find Jews, let alone those of East European descent, on the faculties of American colleges, in more recent time Jews whose parents or grandparents came from Russia, Poland, and Rumania adorn the most prestigious American universities. It would be difficult to name them all, but even a cursory cataloging would include so-ciologists Daniel Bell, Nathan Glazer, and Seymour Martin Lipset of Harvard University (all, by the way, graduates of New York City's City College in the 1930s); Harvard historian Oscar Handlin; and Columbia University President Michael Sovern. Also on the Harvard faculty is the Russian-born Nobel Prize winner, Simon Kuznets. Herbert Stein, one of President Nixon's chief economic advisers; former United States Supreme Court Justice and Ambassador to the United Nations, Arthur Goldberg; the discoverer of the vaccine to prevent polio, Jonas E. Salk; film-maker Stanley Kubrick; musician Leonard Bernstein; violinist Itzhak Perlman; playwrights Arthur Miller and Neil Simon; and artist Ben Shahn are only a few of the others of East European Jewish descent who have made their mark in the United States. In fact, the East European Jews and their descendants have made a much greater impact, and in a wider range of activities, than people from any of the other contemporary group of immigrants.

And yet, despite their absorption into American society, it is still true, as Jacob Neusner wrote in 1973, that "to be a Jew in America is to be in some measure different, alien, a minority." The dominant culture in the United States is still intolerant of differences among groups of people and of non-Christians loyal to a foreign state or a different faith. This, of course, presents great difficulties to the various ethnic minorities in the United States. On the one hand "cultural pluralism" is celebrated in song and spirit from every official podium while deviation is regarded as a sign of subversion and inferiority. This schizophrenic conflict affects all American minorities and to be a non-WASP is to be somehow marginal and alien. For most Jews who are prosperous, employed, and ensconced in comfortable homes, these feelings are rarely discussed, but the fierce American-Jewish devotion to the State of Israel suggests that even in the United States Jews do not feel absolutely secure. Somehow they feel that loyalty to a Jewish state is necessary. Whether it is because of an attachment to the heritage and traditions of Jewry or because of a sense of being part of the same group, or even because they fear that someday they or their descendants might have to flee the United States and take refuge in Israel is impossible to say. But we do know that the sense of identification with Israel is strong and this, in a very specific way, differentiates Jews from other Americans.

2

Education
and the Advancement
of American Jews

Scholars in various disciplines have frequently commented about the academic and occupational achievements of East European Jews and their descendants in the twentieth-century United States. Some have attributed these accomplishments to their urban experiences in Europe, where they developed skills marketable in the expansive commercial economy of the United States. Others have emphasized respect for learning as a more crucial factor. Many authorities, while acknowledging education as an important aspect of the Jewish heritage, have also pointed out that initial advancement for Jewish immigrants in the United States occurred among those with little education who are engaged in trade and commerce. When one studies what the 2,000,000 or so Jewish immigrants who arrived in this country between 1880 and 1930, and their children, accomplished, however, there can be no doubt that educational endeavors must be regarded as a significant, if not the prime, cause of their social mobility. And the reason that education played this role was the high regard for learning that had for centuries pervaded the Jewish culture.[1]

No other European immigrant group valued learning more than the East European Jews. Historically Jews have always stressed the importance of education[2] and in the East European *shtetl*, or village, no one had more prestige than the talmudic scholar—the man who both studies and interpreted the holy books and the laws of God. Learning in the Jewish tradition was for men and boys, both a duty and a joy. Studying brought prestige, respect, authority, and status. Jews regarded the scholar, in fact, as the ideal man. Rich men vied to support him; parents prayed that their daughter might marry him; individuals regularly sought him out for advice on the numerous dilemmas of daily life. Being educated was regarded not only as a sign of wisdom but of good character as well. "It is assumed," two scholars of the East European Jewish *shtetl* tell us, "that a learned man will be a good husband and father." On the other hand, the community viewed a Jew without learning as incomplete or, as one saying had it, "little better than an animal."[3]

Most of the East European Jews shared those values. The religiously orthodox, the Zionists who aspired to make Palestine the national home, and the radicals who looked upon Marxist teachings with favor, basically agreed upon the importance of education in the development of a full human being. From their earliest days children imbibed this attitude, first unconsciously, later with more awareness. One traditional lullaby had a mother singing,

> Sleep soundly at night and learn Torah by day
> And thou'lt be a Rabbi when I have grown grey.[4]

In the home children learned to venerate books, to remain quiet while father studied, and to treat learned guests with great respect. Once the son started his own formal training, at about the age of four, he too was accorded the respect due to a student. Even before this age, however, children were praised for every clever remark, for every allegedly brilliant saying. They learned that nothing brought greater attention or affection from their parents than precociousness. "Even an impudent question or a naughty remark," one scholar reminds us, "if clever, was received with amused tolerance by parents and proudly relayed to friends and relatives as evidence of . . . wisdom."[5]

   The Jewish immigrants who came to this country in the 1880s and after brought these values and traditions with them. To be sure, in America they were not carried out in the same fashion as in Europe, and the goals here were significantly different than abroad, but the importance of education for a Jewish boy did not decline. "The chief ambition of the new Jewish family in America," one journalist wrote in 1909, "is to educate its sons."[6] An indication of this sentiment is revealed in the letter a distraught immigrant mother in New York's Lower East Side wrote to the most popular Yiddish newspaper, the *Forward*. A widow, with five children, she not only supported the family but maintained a business where she employed a salesman. If she withdrew her fifteen-year-old son from school, the woman wrote, she could dispense with the employee, "but my motherly love and duty . . . do not permit me. . . . So what shall I do when the struggle for existence is so acute? I must have his assistance to keep my business going and take care of the other children; but at the same time I cannot definitely decide to take him out of school; for he has inclinations to study and goes to school dancing. I lay great hopes on my child." The Industrial Commission, which functioned in the first decade of the twentieth century, found this attitude prevalent in the Jewish ghetto: "The poorest among them will make all possible sacrifices to keep his children in school; and one of the most striking phenomena in New York City today is the way in which Jews have taken possession of the public schools, in the highest as well as lowest grades."[7]

   Jewish mothers were modest neither in evaluating their children's performances nor in their limitless ambitions. Only those brought up in the East European Jewish tradition can believe how frequently maternal affection combined with wish fulfillment to blind parents in assessing their children. A boy needed merely to pick up a violin and his mother envisioned another Jascha Heifetz; if he showed some scientific aptitude then he would certainly achieve at least as much as Albert Einstein.[8] When, in 1969, an anthropologist entitled her scholarly article "My Son, the Doctor,"[9] no Jew needed to be told which ethnic mother she was quoting. At the same time Jewish mothers demanded outstanding performances. "What do you mean you only got ninety-eight on that science test? Who got the hundred."[10] many a Jewish child was asked. Mothers especially derived enormous gratification from every honor or accomplishment of their young ones and were extremely competitive with other mothers. As one scholar reminds us, "every distinction that a Jewish child earned, every step that he traversed in his educational career, every career decision, and every advancement was duly reported by his mother to her circle of friends and acquaintances."[11]

Once the East European Jews arrived in the United States, physician ranked first in occupational choice or their sons. Talmudic scholars might be praised in Europe but in America high status positions, which paid well and also allowed the individual freedom from arbitrary and antisemitic employers, were most valued. After medicine, the most approved professions were law, accounting, pharmacy, and teaching. Manual labor, both in Europe and in the United States, was frowned upon as something one did if one were not educated. Only occupations that required brains, not brawn, received any respect in the Jewish household.[12]

A boy also learned that his accomplishments were not only of value for himself but also for the honor, joy, and status of his family. Parents, and again especially mothers, frequently measured their own worth by the achievements of their children, and they never let a son forget that education not only was in his own best interest but was also "a means to fulfill his obligations to his parents, to his people, and to humanity." Mothers would sacrifice a great deal for their sons' education. Jewels would be pawned, food budgets pared, and, some said, parents would even "bend the sky to educate their sons."[13] The fact that parents might not have received much education or had been forced to earn their keep in shops or factories did not in any way reduce the emphasis on learning or achievement. It was expected, as the natural order things, that children would certainly surpass their parents' attainments. As one mother said," "That's a natural Jewish trait, whatever you didn't have, you wanted for your children." The remarks of one New York peddler epitomized the feeling of most Jewish parents: "It is enough I am a merchant. . . . What is such a life? What can I do for my people or myself? My boy shall be a lawyer; learned and respected of men. And it is for that I stand here, sometimes when my feet ache so that I would gladly go and rest. My boy shall have knowledge. He shall go to college,"[14]

Foreign-born Jewish parents almost always stressed the importance of educating their sons but education for girls, especially at college level, was considered less important than for boys. Nevertheless, those few who had sufficient family incomes to maintain themselves without sending their children out to work at an early age allowed, and even encouraged, their daughters to go to school. It was more common, though, for sisters to leave school to support their brothers. One young woman who did this really wanted to continue with her education but acknowledged that for her brother "a college education was 'a matter of life position,' while for her it was not." Although the East European tradition discouraged study for girls, many American Jewish parents ignored this aspect of their heritage when they could afford to do so. They were supported in this decision by the daily *Forward*, which editorialized on the importance of educating females. Children of both sexes attended public schools and, as family income increased, the percentage of daughters continuing their studies increased as well. By the 1920s a disproportionately high percentage of Jewish young women, compared to those of other ethnic backgrounds, attended colleges and universities.[15]

In training their children to achieve, parents continually held up the outstanding accomplishments of other Jews as examples to be emulated. One New Yorker recalled that in his formative years his mother brought to his attention every success of a Jew in the newspapers. She further indoctrinated him with "the idea that Jews were a superior people—more intelligent, more moral, more sober, harder-working, with a destiny to become leaders." Another product of the Lower East Side had a similar experience. "Gentiles," his elders continually reminded him, "were a race of mental inferiors, fit only for the more menial tasks of life. All the world's wisdom was encompassed in the Jewish brain.''[16] As anyone who has grown up in a Jewish neighborhood can testify, these views were not restricted to the sources quoted above.

With ideas such as these implanted from one's earliest childhood, it is no wonder that the Jewish immigrant child devoured books and valued education. In the United States, unlike Russia, public education was free, legal prohibitions against Jews attending public school did not exist, and individual achievement, rather than arbitrary rulings, dictated how much one could accomplish. Opportunities in the United States, many Jews believed, awaited the enterprising. One need merely learn the language, study hard, and success would naturally follow. For a significant minority, this formula worked. Poverty, and the important need to earn a living, however, made these hopes little more than a mirage for the vast majority of the immigrants.[17]

About two-thirds of the 2,000,000 Jewish immigrants who arrived between 1880 and 1930 remained in and around the New York City area. The older, and more established, German Jewish community did not approve of the influx but realized that the more quickly the newcomers Americanized themselves the more beneficial it would be for all of the Jews in the United States. The presence of the East European men and boys, garbed in black with flowing side curls along their faces, practicing orthodox Jewish customs in habit and worship, struck the Americanized Jews as barbaric. Hence, without much affection, but with a considerable amount of financial aid the Americanized or German Jews established numerous institutions like schools, hospitals, orphanages, newspapers, social service centers, etc. to help the newcomers acclimate themselves to the United States.[18]

One of the most important of these, intended to eliminate what the German Jews considered the oriental elements in the life and culture of the East Europeans, was the Educational Alliance on New York City's Lower East Side. The Educational Alliance served as an almost complete welfare center. It provided classes, a gymnasium, a day-care center, a public forum for lectures, and a settlement house. Its English language classes for preschool children and adults, given at all hours of the day and six evenings a week, had a regular attendance of 500 people and a waiting list of another 1,000.[19]

Those who mastered the rudiments of English frequently attended higher grades in the public night school. Others, however, chose the evening schools as the place to begin their studies. In 1906 Jews constituted a majority of the 100,000 or so students enrolled in New York City's evening classes[20] (in 1912, 95 percent of Pittsburgh's night school population was Jewish),[21] and several Yiddish journalists claimed that a majority of all Jewish immigrants who did not attend elementary school as children passed through the night schools at one time or another.[22] About 40 percent of the students were women. The importance of study may have been stressed for males but females, too, had intellectual needs. As one woman wrote to the *Forward*, "I admit that I cannot be satisfied to be just a wife and mother. I am still young and I want to learn and enjoy life. My children and my home are not neglected, but I go to evening high school twice a week."[23]

Another indication of the immigrant Jew's tremendous thirst for knowledge was the huge attendance that public lectures on almost every subject attracted. In addition to the Educational Alliance, New York City's Cooper Union sponsored some of the most popular public forums, and subjects like "The History of Ancient Greece," "Darwin," and "Maxim Gorky" attracted overflowing crowds. Violin concerts, poetry readings, and political rallies drew equally enthusiastic audiences. Anything that might be dubbed educational or intellectually provocative was enough to bring out the ghetto residents. As one recent chronicler pointed out, to the young Jewish adults, "eager to swallow the world's culture at a single gulp, it hardly mattered whether a lecturer spoke on popular science or ancient history, German literature or Indian customs."[24]

The same passion for learning that adults displayed appeared among the children as well. Their diligence, deportment, ambition, precocity, and desire to acquire knowledge, we are told, continually amazed school officials.[25] The Jewish children's intellectual curiosity impressed others as well. One New York City librarian remarked that their "appetite for knowledge is more insatiate than the seminary student in the university."[26] In 1906 the Chatham Branch library, "almost wholly used by Jews," ranked first in the city in the proportion of history and science books taken out.[27] A *New York Evening Post* reporter wrote in 1903: "The Jewish child has more than an eagerness for mental food; it is an intellectual mania. He wants to learn everything in the library and everything the libraries know. He is interested not only in knowledge that will be of practical benefit, but in the knowledge for its own sake."[28] Five years later the city's police commissioner exclaimed, "Think of it! Herbert Spencer preferred to a fairy story by [Jewish] boys and girls."[29]

New York City officials were unprepared for this explosive demand for knowledge. The 60 percent increase in elementary school enrollment, which coincided with the arrival of more than 7,000,000 immigrants to the United States between 1899 and 1914, resulted in overcrowded classes (sixty to eighty children in some rooms), part-time education, and frequent turning away of children for whom the schools had no place. Moreover, before 1898 New York City had no public high schools and by 1914 the boroughs of Manhattan and the Bronx had a combined total of only five. Therefore, much as they might desire an education, only a limited number of children in the city ever had an opportunity to advance with their studies. For most students formal schooling ended with the sixth or eighth grades, which in the Progressive Era at least prepared them sufficiently for entry-level white-collar jobs.[30]

For those students who persevered, however, the city's free but renowned public institutions awaited them—the College of the City of New York (CCNY) for boys, Hunter College for girls. By 1919, 85 percent of the students at CCNY, and 28.7 percent of those at Hunter, were Jewish.[31] As the decades passed, the percentage at Hunter increased. Not until 1969, when selective admission tests ended and open admission guaranteed a place for all of New York City's high school graduates at the City University of New York (which by the 1960s included seven senior, and several more junior, colleges), did the percentage of Jews at these schools decline significantly.

Every decade or so profiles have been taken of the American, as well as the Jewish, college student body. Until the 1960s, they had showed a larger percentage of Jews attending college than members of other ethnic groups. An overwhelming proportion of the Jews were children of immigrants, and most of their fathers had failed to complete high school.[32] Before World War II, fewer than half of all Jews between eighteen and twenty-four attended college[33] during the 1940s, however, with resumed prosperity, more than 60 percent started pursuing advanced studies. According to one 1947 poll, more than two-thirds of all Jewish high school seniors applied for college admission, while one-third of the Protestants and one-fourth of the Catholics did. Avery Corman captured the prevalent sentiment exactly in his novel *The Old Neighborhood*. The hero, a teenager in the Bronx in the 1940s, observed, "In the neighborhood, to be Jewish and not go to college was to commit some unspeakable act for which they would light candles for you, something on the level of going into the navy or getting a tattoo."[34]

By the 1970s, estimates of the number of college-age Jews in school ranged upwards from 80 percent, which may be compared to about 40 percent for non-Jews. The most significant difference among Jewish college students from decade to decade was the increase in the numbers whose parents had been born and/or educated in the United States. Otherwise, as a group, they were more likely to graduate, have high grades, and attend prestigious colleges and universities than students of other ethnic backgrounds. Moreover, despite quota systems, they made up disproportionately large percentages of graduate, law, medical, and dental students at the nation's elite institutions.[35]

Although the Jewish quest for education has been apparent throughout the twentieth century, the increased numbers and percentages of Jews in higher education, especially in the 1920s, proved most alarming to the established WASP community. At the same time the Congress, responding to popular prejudices, drastically curtailed immigration of Jews and others from Europe and Asia. Many WASPs complained about the Jews, who spoke with foreign accents, had "unpleasant personalities," or undermined the "social prestige" of their universities.[36] As one articulate alumnus explained, "so far as the classroom is concerned, Jewish students are one thing; but at the 'prom', or the class-day tea, the presence of the Jews and their relatives ruins the tone which must be maintained if social standing is not to collapse."[37] Another WASP expressed the same sentiment somewhat differently: "The Jew sends his children to college a generation or two sooner than other stocks, and as a result there are in fact more dirty Jews and tactless Jews in college than dirty and tactless Italians or Armenians or Slovaks."[38]

Regardless of the words or phrases used, what most of the elite universities seemed to fear in the 1920s was that the "pushy" Jews, who "had little training in the amenities and delicacies of civilized existence,"[39] might inundate their schools. As a result, throughout the country rigid quotas were established to prevent these institutions from being overrun by people whom they considered undesirable,[40] and this led to a steep decline in the percentage of Jews attending private colleges and universities. While this made less difference, in the long run, at the undergraduate level, it created severe hardships when these restraints were applied to the professional schools: Jews constituted 46.92 percent of the student body at Columbia's College of Physicians and Surgeons in 1920; they totalled only 8 percent in 1940.[41] Other medical and dental schools showed similar declines.[42] The percentage of CCNY graduates who applied, and were admitted, to medical schools throughout the country fell from 58.4 in 1925 to 15 in 1939. In 1930, fewer than 20 percent of CCNY's Jewish graduates who applied, but 75 percent of the gentiles, were accepted into medical school. By 1945, 75 percent of gentile applicants, but only one of thirteen Jewish applicants, were accepted into the United States medical colleges.[43]

The nadir of discrimination was in 1945. When Ernest M. Hopkins, president of Dartmouth College, announced that "Dartmouth is a Christian college founded for the Christianization of its students,"[44] it was the last public pronouncement of its sort by a leading academician. By fall of 1946 the percentage of Jews in New York's medical colleges had increased to 30 and two years later the Empire State became the first to pass a Fair Education Practices Law barring discrimination in college and university admissions on the basis of race, color, religion, creed, or national origin. In 1949, New Jersey and Massachusetts followed suit with similar, but even more stringent, legislation.[45]

Because of this legislation, which both reflected and gave rise to a more tolerant atmosphere in this country, and one other factor, unanticipated earlier, Jews started having fewer problems becoming physicians. The unanticipated factor had to do with an enormous decline in the birthrate as a result of the worldwide depression in the 1930s. Children born in the depression decade therefore had fewer peers to compete with when they applied to medical school in the 1950s. Conversely, medical and dental schools no longer had the luxury of picking and choosing from pools of outstanding applicants. In the words of the director of studies of the Association of American Medical Colleges, the absence of normal supplies of candidates resulted in medical school admissions committees "literally scraping the bottom of the barrel in order to fill their classes."[46]

Discrimination against Jews in employment also began to wane in the 1950s. White-collar and professional positions, from which many Jews had been arbitrarily excluded, especially since the 1920s,[47] started opening up for them. A case in point is the academic world. Before World War II, E. Digby Baltzell tells us, a Jewish Ph.D. had great difficulty in obtaining a tenured position "at any good university in most disciplines."[48] In 1941, Jews constituted fewer than 2 percent of the academic faculty in American colleges.[49] Perhaps in no other field of endeavor has this policy been so dramatically reversed. In the past twenty years the tremendous expansion of colleges and universities, coupled with a greater emphasis on nondiscrimination in American society, has resulted in an avalanche of appointments for Jewish professors. In some disciplines, such as medicine, law, and the social sciences, the percentage of Jews teaching now exceeds 30 percent in the nation's more prestigious universities.[50] The decline in discriminatory practices has also allowed Jews to seek careers as architects, journalists, economists, etc.[51]

The question that must be tackled now is, to what extent did American education promote social mobility? In the immigrant generation, where so many advanced via retail trade, manufacturing, and entertainment, the contribution of education was probably not great. But for the first and second American-born generations, social mobility for most seems to have come primarily because of education.[52] As early as the 1930s two-thirds of all Jews were employed in white-collar positions, one-third in blue-collar; for gentiles the percentage was exactly reversed. In 1937 two-thirds of New York City's lawyers, judges, and dentists, and 55 percent of its physicians, were Jewish. In he same decade a larger percentage of Jews than gentiles were lawyers, judges, and physicians in San Francisco, Pittsburgh, and the state of Ohio.[53] Studies in post-World War II Canton, Ohio; New Orleans; New Haven, Connecticut; Camden and Trenton, New Jersey; Los Angeles; San Francisco; and Rochester, New York, show a disproportionately high percentage of Jewish college graduates.[54] Figures for the 1960s and 1970s, as pointed out earlier, have also shown greater percentages of Jews, compared to gentiles, in colleges and universities. Without universal public education almost all office and professional positions would have been barred to Jews, for in the twentieth century educational and licensing requirements have made it almost impossible for anyone to become a self-taught attorney, physician, or academician.

By looking closely at what happened to members of the February 1948 graduating class of the elite Bronx High School of Science, we can see the importance of education for social mobility. About 90 percent of the 254 male graduates (coeducation had not yet started at the school) were Jewish. Almost all of the boys' parents had been immigrants or first-generation Americans; 80 percent of the students had lived in the Bronx. In those days only one of six applicants, selected by a rigorous competitive examination, earned admittance to what was then considered New York City's finest public high school. Both those who made it and their parents viewed the competition as "the embodiment of the American dream, meritocracy at work." In 1978, about sixty or so of the ninety graduates who could be contacted showed up for a class reunion. The bright boys of yesteryear were now men of achievement. Statistics for the group of sixty showed twenty with M.A. degrees, eight Ph.D.'s, twelve physicians, twelve attorneys, and eight dentists. In addition there were a "handful" of senior executives in advertising, one TV newsman, one TV producer, a few editors, and several of the Ph.D.s taught "at major American universities." "To everyone's astonishment," a fellow alumnus wrote, there was even one rabbi. "In short," this member of the class concluded, "the large majority [of the sixty] had indeed become part of the nation's elite, members of the prosperous professional and upper-middle class. . . . everyone had learned that economic and professional success were possible, provided one were hard-working and diligent and bright . . . and competitive."[55]

In a considerably broader study of more than 1,000 graduates of Columbia University's Dental School from the 1920s through 1975, Philip Yablon, himself a dentist, discovered that the parents of 56 percent of the more than 600 Jewish respondents had failed to finish high school. When their backgrounds are compared with those of Catholic and Protestant respondents, more of whose parents, especially fathers, had better educations and occupied a higher socioeconomic status, it is quite clear how great a leap was made possible by educational opportunities. The works of Stephan Thernstrom, Marshall Sklare, and Seymour Martin Lipset and Everett Carll Ladd, Jr., also show that native-born Jews had the highest mobility rate of any group studied. Finally, Yablon's data on the dentists, Thernstrom's on the Bostonians and Lipset's and Ladd's on the academicians, indicated that Jews are disproportionately represented among the highest income producers in their respective professions.[56]

Have the Jews been more successful than members of other ethnic groups? But here statistics mislead us. For the past four decades information on income and occupation had been broken down according to religious faiths in the United States. In the 1970s, the Gallup Opinion Index Reports informed us that 34 percent of the Jews, compared to 16 percent of the Roman Catholics and 14 percent of the Protestants (when broken down still further, 28 percent of the Episcopalians and 25 percent of the Presbyterians), earned over $20,000 a year. 54 percent of the Jews, compared to 25 percent each for the Catholics and Protestants (37 percent for the Episcopalians, 34 percent for the Presbyterians), were employed in high-level professional and business occupations. In the age category of thirty to forty-nine years old, 75 percent of the Jews, compared to 24 percent of the Catholics and 26 percent of the Protestants (54 percent of the Episcopalians, 41 percent of the Presbyterians), graduated from college.[57]

More meaningful statistics, however, for an ethnic evaluation would be a comparison of Jews with persons of Japanese, Chinese, Greek, Armenian, Lithuanian, and Scandinavian backgrounds. We know that many of those immigrants who adhered to the Roman Catholic faith, such as the Irish, French Canadians, Poles, Mexicans, and Southern Italians, did not value education highly and their children moved more slowly up the socioeconomic scale than did Protestants and Jews.[58] But the few studies that we have of the Rumanians, Japanese, Armenians, Greeks, Basques, Lithuanians, and Swedes indicate a strong cultural appreciation of the importance of education, and high-status positions, for males.[59] Therefore while Jews stand out when measured as a strictly religious group, their successes might not appear as striking when balanced against specific groups that have received less scholarly attention. I would suggest, therefore, that research along these lines would be an enlightening exploration in comparative ethnic studies.

Another area of research that would surely add to our knowledge would be a quantification study of immigrant Jews and their descendants. Certainly this essay is based primarily upon impressionistic history and sociology. A more exacting study of the immigrants and their children would enhance our understanding of their experiences. I believe such an investigation would confirm the impressions that I have stressed, but one does not know that for sure.

Notes

1. Selma C. Berrol, "Education and Economic Mobility: The Jewish Experience in New York City, 1880–1920," *American Jewish Historical Quarterly*, 65 (Mar. 1976), 255–56; Louis Wirth, *The Ghetto* (Chicago: University of Chicago Press, 1928), p. 54; Mark Zborowski and Elizabeth Herzog, *Life Is with People: The Jewish Little-Town of Eastern Europe* (New York: International Universities Press, 1952), pp. 74, 125; Fred L. Strodtbeck, "Family Interaction, Values, and Achievement," in Marshall Sklare, ed., *The Jews* (Glencoe, Ill.: Free Press, 1958), Louis Wirth, "Education for Survival: The Jews," *American Journal of Sociology*, 48 (May 1943), 682; Seymour Leventman, "From Shtetl to Suburb," in Peter I. Rose, ed., *The Ghetto and Beyond* (New York: Random House, 1969), Leonard Dinnerstein, Roger L. Nichols, and David M. Reimers, *Natives and Strangers* (New York: Oxford University Press, 1979), pp. 180–81.

2. Wirth, "Education for Survival," p. 682.

3. Zborowski and Herzog, *Life Is with People*, pp. 73, 80–82, 125; Albert I. Gordon, *Jews in Transition* (Minneapolis: University of Minnesota Press, 1949), p. 22; Marshall Sklare, *America's Jews* (New York: Randon House, 1971), p. 58; see also Leventman, "From Shtetl to Suburb," p. 41; David B. Tyack, *The One Best System: A History of American Urban Education* (Cambridge, Mass.: Harvard University Press, 1974), p. 250; and Sydney Stahl Weinberg, "The World of Our Mothers: Sources of Strength among Jewish Immigrant Women" (unpublished paper presented at the 73rd Annual meeting of the Organization of American Historians, San Francisco, Apr. 10, 1980), p. 3.

4. Zborowski and Herzog, *Life Is with People*, p. 84.

5. *Ibid.*; Leslie Tonner, *Nothing but the Best: The Luck of the Jewish Princess* (New York: Coward, McCann and Georghegan, 1975), p. 27; Zena Smith Blau, "In Defense of the Jewish Mother," in Rose, ed., *The Ghetto and Beyond*, p. 63.

6. Quoted in Charlotte Baum, Paula Hyman, and Sonya Michel, *The Jewish Woman in America* (New York: Dial Press, 1976), p. 123.

7. Both quoted in Thomas Kessner, *The Golden Door: Italian and Jewish Immigrant Mobility in New City, 1880–1915* (New York: Oxford University Press, 1977), pp. 96–97.

8. Blau, "Jewish Mother," p. 61.

9. Marian K. Slater, "My Son, the Doctor: Aspects of Mobility among American Jews, *American Sociological Review*, 34 (June 1969), 359.

10. Tonner, *Nothing but the Best*, pp. 17, 20–21, 23, 26.

11. Blau, "Jewish Mother," p. 62.

12. Zborowski and Herzog, *Life Is with People*, p. 78; Strodtbeck, "Family Interaction, Values, and Achievement," p. 150.

13. Kessner, *Golden Door*, pp. 94–95; Blau, "Jewish Mother," p. 61; Zborowski and Herzog, *Life Is with People*, p. 87.

14. Kessner, *Golden Door*, p. 174; Tonner, *Nothing but the Best*, pp. 149–50; Allon Schoener, *Portal to America—The Lower East Side 1870–1925* (New York: Holt, Rinehart & Winston, 1967), p. 126; see also Pittsburgh Section, National Council of Jewish Women, *By Myself I'm a Book!* (Waltham, Mass.: American Jewish Historical Society, 1972), pp. 67–68.

15. Alan Wiedner, "Immigration, the Public School, and the Twentieth Century American Ethos: The Jewish Immigrant as a Case Study" (unpublished Ph.D. dissertation,

Ohio State University, 1977), pp. 91, 95, 124, 126; Kessner, *Golden Door*, p. 91; Baum, Hyman, and Michel, *Jewish Woman*, pp. 123, 125, 127; Zborowski and Herzog, *Life Is with People*, p. 83.

16. Nathan Hurvitz, "Sources of Motivation and Achievement of American Jews," *Jewish Social Studies*, 23 (Oct. 1961), 230; Morris Freedman, "Education in a Melting Pot," *Chicago Jewish Forum*, 6 (Winter 1947–48), 92; Zalmen Yoffeh, "The Passing of the East Side," *Menorah Journal*, 17 (Oct. 1929), 266–67.

17. Nathan Glazer, "Social Characteristics of American Jews, 1654–1954," in *American Jewish Year Book*, 56 (1955), 15.

18. Samuel Joseph, *Jewish Immigration to the United States from 1881 to 1910* (New York: AMS Press, 1967), p. 195; Leonard Dinnerstein, "The East European Jewish Migration," in Leonard Dinnerstein and Frederic Cople Jaher, eds., *Uncertain Americans* (New York: Oxford University Press, 1977), pp. 225–26; Stanley Feldstein, *The Land That I Show You* (New York: Anchor Press, Doubleday, 1978), pp. 171–72.

19. Henry L. Feingold, *Zion in America: The Jewish Experience from Colonial Times to the Present* (New York: Hippocrene Books, 1974), p. 150; Irving Howe, *World of Our Fathers* (New York: Harcourt Brace Jovanovich, 1976), p. 230; Leonard Dinnerstein and David M. Reimers, *Ethnic Americans* (New York: Harper & Row, 1975), p. 53; Oscar Handlin, *Adventure in Freedom* (New York: McGraw-Hill Book Co., 1954), pp. 153, 158.

20. Berrol, "Education and Economic Mobility," p. 263; Hutchins Hapgod, *The Spirit of the Ghetto*, ed. Harry Golden (New York: Funk and Wagnalls Co., 1965), p. 45.

21. *By Myself I'm a Book!* p. 70.

22. Howe, *World of Our Fathers*, p. 227.

23. Quoted in Baum, Hyman, and Michel, *Jewish Woman*, p. 127.

24. Howe, *World of Our Fathers*, pp. 225, 238–40; see also Feingold, *Zion in America*, p. 136; *By Myself I'm a Book!* p. 76.

25. Charles S. Bernheimer, ed., *The Russian Jew in the United States* (Philadelphia: John C. Winston Co., 1905), p. 187; Berrol, "Education and Economic Mobility," p. 270; Selma C. Berrol, "School Days on the Old East Side: The Italian and Jewish Experience," *New York History*, 57 (Apr. 1976), 205; Schoener, *Portal to America*, p. 126; Stephen Steinberg, "How Jewish Quotas Began," *Commentary*, 52 (Sept. 1971), 69; Moses Rischin, *The Promised City: New York's Jews, 1870–1914* (New York: Harper Torchbook, 1970), pp. 199–200; see also Maxine Seller, "The Education of Immigrant Children in Buffalo, New York, 1890–1916," *New York History*, 57 (Apr. 1976), 198.

26. Quoted in Feldstein, *Land That I Show You*, p. 118.

27. Excerpt from *New York Evening Post*, Oct. 3, 1903, in Schoener, *Portal to America*, p. 137.

28. *Ibid.*

29. Quoted in Rischin, *Promised City*, p. 199.

30. Diane Ravitch, *The Great School Wars: New York City, 1805–1972* (New York: Basic Books, 1974), pp. 113, 244; Tyack, *One Best System*, p. 230; Berrol, "Education and Economic Mobility," pp. 257, 265.

31. Feingold, *Zion in America*, p. 266. Sherry Gorelick's *City College and the Jewish Poor, Education in New York, 1880–1924* (New Brunswick, N.J.: Rutgers University Press, 1981) had not yet come out at the time of this writing. Its title, however, suggests that it might be of interest to those desirous of pursuing the subject further.

32. "May Jews Go to College?" *The Nation*, 114 (June 14, 1922). 708; Ida Cohen Selavan, "Jewish Wage Earners in Pittsburgh, 1890–1930," *American Jewish Historical*

Quarterly, 65 (Mar. 1976), 285; S. Willis Rudy, *The College of the City of New York: A History, 1847–1947* (New York: City College Press, 1949), p. 397; Berrol, "Education and Economic Mobility," p. 261; Judith R. Kramer and Seymour Leventman, *Children of the Gilded Ghetto* (New Haven, Conn.: Yale University Press, 1961), p. 137. The most recent survey that I have seen is Abraham D. Lavender, "Studies of Jewish College Students: A Review and a Replication," *Jewish Social Studies*, 39 (Winter-Spring 1977), 37–52.

33. Stephan Thernstrom, *The Other Bostonians* (Cambridge, Mass.: Harvard University Press, 1973), p. 173; "Jewish Wage Earners," p. 285.

34. Justin Hoffmann, "Toward an Understanding of the Jewish College Student," *Religious Education*, 60 (Nov. 1945), 443; Morton Clurman, "How Discriminatory Are College Admissions?" *Commentary*, 15 (June 1953), 623; Avery Corman, *The Old Neighborhood* (New York: Linden Press, Simon and Schuster, 1980), p. 24.

35. Kramer and Leventman, *Children of the Gilded Ghetto*, p. 137; Seymour Martin Lipset and Everett Carll Ladd, Jr., "Jewish Academics in the United States: Their Achievements, Culture and Politics," *American Jewish Year Book*, 72 (1971), 99; *Time*, Apr. 10, 1972, p. 55; Feingold, *Zion in America*, p. 314; Blau, "Jewish Mother," p. 57; Lipset and Ladd, "Jewish Academics," p. 99; Jerold S. Auerbach, *Unequal Justice: Lawyers and Social Change in Modern America* (New York: Oxford University Press, 1976), p. 184; Albert I. Goldberg, "Jews in the Legal Profession: A Case of Adjustment to Discrimination," *Jewish Social Studies*, 32 (1970), 150; Steinberg, "How Jewish Quotas Began," p. 67; raw data gathered for, but not used in, Philip Yablon, "Career Satisfaction of Dentists: A Study of the Practice of Dentistry" (unpublished Ph.D. dissertation, Columbia University, 1979).

36. "May Jews Go to College?" p. 708; Ralph Philip Boas, "Who Shall Go to College?" *Atlantic Monthly*, 130 (1922), 446; Steinberg, "How Jewish Quotas Began," p. 74.

37. Boas, "Who Shall Go to College?" p. 446.

38. Quoted in Feingold, *Zion in America*, p. 266; see also Morton Rosenstock, "Are There Too Many Jews at Harvard?" in Leonard Dinnerstein, ed., *Antisemitism in the United States* (New York: Holt, Rinehart & Winston, 1971), pp. 102–9.

39. Steinberg, "How Jewish Quotas Began," p. 74.

40. *Ibid.*, pp. 72–73; "Anti-Semitism at Dartmouth," *New Republic*, 113 (Aug. 20, 1945), 208. For historical analysis of discrimination against Jews, and others, at the nation's elite universities, see Marcia G. Synnot, *The Half Opened Door* (Westport, Conn.: Greenwood Press, 1979); and Harold S. Wechsler, *The Qualified Student* (New York: Wiley, 1977).

41. Frank Kingdom, "Discrimination in Medical Colleges," *American Mercury*, 61 (Oct. 1945), 395.

42. *Ibid.*, p. 392; Feldstein, *Land That I Show You*, p. 249; Morris Freedman, "The Jewish College Student: 1951 Model," *Commentary*, 12 (Oct. 1951), 311; Dan W. Dodson, "College Quotas and American Democracy," *American Scholar*, 15 (July 1946), 269; M. F. Ashley Montagu, "Anti-Semitism in the Academic World," *Chicago Jewish Forum*, 4 (Summer 1946), 221–22; Alfred L. Shapiro, "Racial Discrimination in Medicine," *Jewish Social Studies*, 10 (Apr. 1948), 134.

43. Kingdom, "Discrimination in Medical Colleges," pp. 392, 394; Lawrence Bloomgarden, "Medical School Quotas and National Health," *Commentary*, 15 (Jan. 1953), 31.

44. Dodson, "College Quotas and American Democracy," p. 270.

45. Arnold Forster, *A Measure of Freedom* (New York: Doubleday & Co., 1950) pp. 138–39.

46. Quoted in N. C. Belth, ed., *Barriers: Patterns of American Discrimination against Jews* (New York: Anti-defamation League of B'nai B'rith, 1958), p. 77.

47. Feingold, *Zion in America,* p. 266; Lipset and Ladd, "Jewish Academics," p. 90; Felix Morrow, "Higher Learning on Washington Square," *Menorah Journal,* 18 (June 1930), 351.

48. E. Digby Baltzell, *The Protestant Establishment: Aristocracy and Caste in America* (New York: Random House, 1964), p. 212 .

49. Montagu, "Anti-Semitism in the Academic World," p. 221.

50. Steinberg, "How Jewish Quotas Began," p. 67; Feingold, *Zion in America,* p. 314; Lipset and Ladd, "Jewish Academics," pp. 99–100.

51. Leventman, "From Shtetl to Suburb," p. 50; see also Kramer and Leventman, *Children of the Gilded Ghetto,* p. 134.

52. Steinberg, "How Jewish Quotas Began," p. 67.

53. Dinnerstein, "East European Jewish Migration," p. 223; Glazer, "Social Characteristics of American Jews," p. 24; Lee J. Levinger, "Jews in the Liberal Professions in Ohio," *Jewish Social Studies,* 2 (1940), 430.

54. Ronald M. Goldstein, "American Jewish Population Studies since World War II," *American Jewish Archives,* 22 (Apr. 1970), 29; C. Bezalel Sherman, *The Jew within American Society* (Detroit: Wayne State University Press, 1961), p. 110; Aaron Antonovsky, "Aspects of New Haven Jewry," *YIVO Annual of Jewish Social Science,* 10 (1955), 138.

55. Gene Lichtenstein, "The Great Bronx Science Dream Machine," *New York Times Magazine,* June 25, 1978, pp. 33, 34, 36.

56. Yablon, Career Satisfaction of Dentists"; Thernstom, *Other Bostonians,* pp. 173–74; Lipset and Ladd, "Jewish Academics," pp. 99–100; Sklare, *America's Jews,* p. 56.

57. *Gallup Opinion Index Report, Religion in America,* Report 130 (Princeton, N.J.: American Institute of Public Opinion, 1976), pp. 39, 40, 41, 46, 47.

58. Ed Falkowski, "Polonia to America," *Common Ground,* 2 (Autumn 1941), 35; Nathan Glazer and Patrick Moynihan, *Beyond the Melting Pot,* 2nd ed. (Cambridge, Mass.: MIT Press, 1970), p. 199; Wellington G. Fordyc, "Attempts to Preserve National Cultures in Cleveland," *Ohio Archaeological and Historical Quarterly,* 39 (1940), 136; Judith R. Kramer, *The American Minority Community* (New York: Thomas Y. Crowell, 1970), pp. 97, 102, 118–19, 173–74: Lois Rankin, "Detroit Nationality Groups," *Michigan History Magazine,* 23 (1939) 177; Thernstrom *Other Bostonians,* pp. 53, 168, 174; Dinnerstein, Nichols, and Reimers, *Natives and Strangers,* p. 171.

59. In his book, *Greek Americans* (Englewood Cliffs, N.J.: Prentice-Hall, 1980), Charles C. Moskos, Jr., wrote: "A well known study by Bernard C. Rosen in 1959 found that Greek Americans had the highest achievement motivation compared to white Protestant Americans and a sample of other ethnic groups in America. The utility of such a cultural predisposition toward success, a cardinal tenet of Greek immigrant folk wisdom, is supported by U. S. census data. A careful analysis of the 1960 census revealed that second-generation Greek Americans possessed the highest educational levels of all, and were exceeded only by Jews in average income. The same pattern was confirmed in the 1970 census, which showed that among twenty-four second-generation nationality groups, Greeks trailed only Jews in income levels and continued to rank first in educational attainment," p. 111; see also Bernard C. Rosen, "Race, Ethnicity and the Achievement Syndrome," *American Sociological Review,* 24 (Feb. 1959), 47–60; Leonard Broom, *et al.,* "Status Profiles of Racial and Ethnic Populations," *Social Science Quarterly* 12 (Sept. 1971), 379–88; Theodore Saloutos, "The Greeks of Milwaukee," *Wisconsin Magazine of History,*

53 (Spring 1070), 183: Helen Zeese Papanikolas, "Toil and Rage in a New Land: The Greek Immigrants in Utah," *Utah Historical Quarterly,* 38 (1970), 203; Grant Edwin McCall, *Basque Americans and a Sequential Theory of Adaptation* (San Francisco: R & E Research Associates, 1973), p. 37; Fordyce, "Attempts to Preserve National Cultures in Cleveland," p. 137; Rankin, "Detroit Nationality Groups," pp. 130, 174; Thernstrom, *Other Bostonians,* pp. 173–74; Josef J. Barton, *Peasants and Strangers: Italians, Rumanians, and Slovaks in an American City, 1890–1950* (Cambridge, Mass.: Harvard University Press, 1975), p. 125; Kramer, *American Minority Community,* p. 102; Robert Mirak, "The Armenians in the United States, 1890–1915" (unpublished Ph.D. dissertation, Harvard University, 1965), p. 311; Tyack, *One Best System,* p. 244.

3

Franklin D. Roosevelt, American Jewry, and the New Deal

When Franklin D. Roosevelt died in April 1945, no group praised him more lavishly than did the American Jews. "The Jewish people lost its best friend," a California rabbi eulogized. "He gave, for the first time in American history, America's common man a sense of real security; he inspired the common man of the world with tremendous hope in the future. The big man was friend; the little man, his sole concern. His every word and deed vibrated with concern." As if this tribute were not quite sufficient, the rabbi went on, "His garments were justice and humanity; his weapons were words that came from the heart; orphaned America has lost a second Lincoln." Another Jew observed that the active support Roosevelt gave "the cause of liberalism, the preservation of the rights of minorities, and the dignity of the human personality rebounded to the welfare and security of the Jew in this and other lands." And a third proclaimed, "He gave meaning to the words—Liberty and Justice."[1]

Those encomiums were expressed in 1945. Now, with the passage of time and the publication of several major books questioning the depth of Roosevelt's commitment to the Jews and their concerns,[2] I am glad to be able to address the subject of Jews and the New Deal and to put the relationship of Roosevelt and the Jews in a somewhat—but not a radically—different perspective.

Roosevelt and the domestic New Deal undoubtedly did a great deal for American Jewry. The legislation and newly established agencies that the President recommended and/or approved not only laid the groundwork for a more secure and socially just capitalistic system, but also provided thousands of new jobs. Sticking to the three Rs—relief, recovery, and reform—the New Deal helped reverse a downward spiraling economy that appeared to be destroying the nation. The New Deal did not end the Depression, but it did deal directly with the dire consequences that befell people during its most severe downturn.

More specifically, the programs enunciated and developed during the New Deal years—such as protection for bank deposits, social insurance, regulation of banks and the stock market, control of the excesses of big business, bills to provide jobs and housing, and aid to students trying to finish school—coincided with Jewish teaching and values. "For just as the New Deal advocated concern for the poor and jobless," one scholar wrote, "so did Judaism." The tradition of *Tsedekah*, emphasizing aid to the less fortunate, goes back to biblical times and has been transmitted from generation to generation, from country to country, wherever Jews have lived. As Lawrence Fuchs of Brandeis has written, "Within the framework of the Jewish cultural tradition, wealth, learning, and other tangible possessions are channeled from the strong to the weak and from the rich to the poor, as a matter of right."[3]

There were other reasons for Jews backing the President. During his twelve years in office, Roosevelt, a master of ethnic politics, appointed more Jews to office—and in especially prominent places—than had any of his predecessors. The same may also be said about Roosevelt and Irish Catholics, Roosevelt and blacks, and Roosevelt and women. Groups that had formerly been ignored were starting to receive recognition.

Although many of these appointments were symbolic, and of slight numerical or political consequence, this was not true about those given to Jews. Because Roosevelt needed, wanted, and felt stimulated by competent, imaginative, and intellectual individuals, he took them wherever he found them. A person's religious or philosophical background seemed irrelevant to the President. "I don't think a man's Jewishness entered his stream of consciousness much more than whether a man had red hair or black hair," his longtime aide, Samuel I. Rosenman, reminisced in the 1970s. And although his own social circle included no Jews aside from Henry and Elinor Morgenthau, Hyde Park neighbors, Roosevelt valued the advice and opinions of Jewish labor leaders like Sidney Hillman and Rose Schneiderman; his "favorite economist," Isador Lubin[4] and Supreme Court Justices Louis D. Brandeis and Felix Frankfurter.[5] For political and other reasons, at various times he kept Sam Rosenman, Ben Cohen, and David Niles near him in the White House.

But more important than these very visible symbols of Roosevelt's respect for Jews, the establishment of a wide variety of New Deal agencies and the expansion of government employment created opportunities for hundreds, if not thousands, of Jews who would never have been hired by the federal government. To be sure, outside of the White House Roosevelt did not bother with appointments beneath those at the highest levels of policymaking. But by bringing Jews into the White House, and by letting it be known that Professor Felix Frankfurter of the Harvard Law School could supply untold numbers of bright young law school graduates, he signaled his approval to subordinates that they should hire people on the basis of talent and not religious, social, or class background.

Two of his Cabinet members, Frances Perkins at Labor and Harold Ickes in the Interior Department, not only shared the President's openness in this area but also had a high regard for the views of Frankfurter and therefore solicited his advice about policies and personnel. Perkins had worked with Jewish immigrants and labor leaders in New York during most of her adult life and respected them. She told one subordinate, in fact, that she preferred working "with young, alert people of a kind of urban Jewish background." Much of what the Secretary of Labor believed necessary for federal policies to improve labor's lot had already been called for by New York's lower east side Yiddish newspaper, the *Forward*. She favored legislation which would provide "these natural, effective protections, like reasonable hours, subsistence wages, protection against damage to life and limb, protection against bad sanitation and all that kind of thing," and she hired bright young men and women to help her obtain these goals.[6]

In the Interior Department, Ickes, upon the advice of Frankfurter, took on Nathan Margold as Department Solicitor. Margold, in turn, looked to Frankfurt and Brandeis for suggestions on staff appointments and "procedures for exercising authority."[7] Perhaps no other Cabinet department, aside from Labor, included so many Jews in high-level positions during Roosevelt's lifetime. In addition to Margold, Abe Fortas served as Director of the Division of Manpower and later Undersecretary, Saul K. Padover worked as Ickes's assistant, Michael W. Straus became Director of the War Resources Council, and Ernest Gruening was appointed Governor of Alaska.[8]

Jews in the Department of the Interior, in fact, absolutely dominated American Indian policy. Although John Collier, the Commissioner of Indian Affairs, framed the philosophical issues, that is, cultural pluralism and tribal sovereignty, the real architect of the Indian New Deal was Felix Cohen, a militant New York attorney, and son of Morris Raphael Cohen, the great guru of City College students. Felix Cohen wrote the Indian legislation with Nathan Margold; later Fortas figured prominently as a defender of Indian rights. It is interesting to observe that although Jews in the New Deal did little to promote civil rights for Jews, they were instrumental in contributing to reforms in Indian affairs.[9]

By the end of the 1930s, Jewish attorneys appeared disproportionately concentrated in the Department of Labor, parts of the Justice Department, the Securities and Exchange Commission, the National Labor Relations Board (NLRB), and the Social Security Administration. During the early period of the New Deal they had also appeared prominently in the Agricultural Adjustment Administration (AAA), and their presence made them a target for bigoted attacks. Adlai Stevenson of the AAA complained, "There is a little feeling that the Jews are getting too prominent." Southern and Western farmers also made it clear that they did not like dealing with large numbers of Jewish lawyers at the AAA. Moreover, in December 1938, the chairman of the Institute of

Human Relations Conference meeting in Houston charged that there were too many Jews in the NLRB and the Department of Labor, and a year or two later one person told a journalist, "You can't find an official in the whole [government] who hasn't got a damned Jew lawyer sitting by him at his desk."[10]

Many of the people who did not like Jews did not like the President either. The businessmen and upper classes of society who denounced the Administration and its policies—the so-called Jew Deal—also frowned upon the numbers of Jews they saw about Roosevelt. Rumors passed about Roosevelt's alleged Jewish heritage and the influence of the left-leaning Jewish "radicals" who were responsible for the New Deal policies. "The anti-Semitic and racial overtones which marked so many of the anti-Roosevelt stories and which soon became an obsession among the members of the country-club establishment were not accidental," E. Digby Baltzell later wrote.[11]

Jews represented the new breed in Washington and the new directions marked out by the government. Although many members of the WASP elite feared the erosion of their positions, New Deal policies should have reinforced their feelings of security rather than threatening them. The reverse seems to have been true. Moreover, with Roosevelt so popular, it was much easier to attack the Jews than the President and make them the culprits for the unwelcome changes. "Thus," one scholar tells us, "the onslaught began, the slurs, the snide comments, the whispering campaign that Jews were running the New Deal, that Roosevelt was a tool of the Jews, that Jews were responsible for the administration's allegedly leftist policies."[12]

Roosevelt weathered the attacks both on his Administration's policies and on the number of Jews that he brought into government. At the very time that most of society was excluding Jews, he drew them closer to his side. In 1936, for example, he wanted Judge Samuel Rosenman, who had been his chief aide when he was Governor of New York, to be with him during the election campaign. Rosenman questioned whether it would be politically wise for a Jew to accompany the President on a tour through the Bible Belt in the Midwest, but Roosevelt dismissed the objection. "That's no way to handle anti-Semitism," the President supposedly replied in anger. "The way to handle it is to meet it head-on."[13] The prime opposition again came from other Jews who feared an increase in American anti-Semitism when Roosevelt indicated he would go ahead with his desire to appoint Felix Frankfurter to the Supreme Court. But again the President knew what he wanted to do and he did it.[14] For support of this kind, therefore, most American Jews warmly embraced Roosevelt as their champion.

However, in areas where the President had to rely on the initiative and approval of both Houses of the Congress, Roosevelt acted more cautiously and responded more politically. And it is in these areas—immigration policy and aid to Jews victimized by Hitler in Europe—that more recent historical analyses have questioned whether American Jews should have so revered Franklin Roosevelt.

When Roosevelt took office in 1933, immigration policy had been settled; it created no divisions in the country. No recent immigration group, and that included the Jews, indicated any desire to change the established quota policy.[15] As the 1930s went on, however, and as Hitler's treatment of the Jews in Germany became more restrictive and brutal, individual Jews made some informal attempts to have the President liberalize the State Department's interpretation of immigration policy. This Roosevelt refused to do. Keenly attuned to the isolationist and restrictive sentiments that pervaded the United States (in 1939, 85 percent of the Protestants and 84 percent of the Catholics opposed less restrictive immigration laws to aid refugees),[16] Roosevelt did almost nothing to prevent the extermination of six million European Jews between 1939 and 1945.[17]

Not until 1944, in fact, did the President establish the War Refugee Board to help rescue those Jews who still might be saved. But he did that (1) after the Senate Foreign Relations Committee passed a resolution recommending that the President establish a commission "to assist rescue of Jewish victims of Nazi persecution" (2) after Supreme Court Justice Frank Murphy, Vice-President Henry Wallace, and former Republican presidential nominee Wendell Willkie headed up a group called the National Committee Against Nazi Persecution, calling for a "sustained and vigorous action by our government and United Nations to rescue those who may yet be saved"; and (3) after Secretary of the Treasury Henry Morgenthau presented the President with a report entitled "Acquiescence of This Government in the Murder of the Jews" in January 1944. In other words, not until sufficient political pressure had been put upon him did Roosevelt attempt anything of consequence to rescue European Jews from Hitler's ovens.[18]

But American Jews, for a variety of reasons, never put the kind of pressure on Roosevelt to do something to save their European brethren that many American Jews in subsequent generations think they should have. There were several reasons for this. The increase and pervasiveness of anti-Semitism, along with a cultural pressure in the United States calling for the assimilation of Jews into the dominant society,[19] made American Jews reluctant to speak out as members of a minority group. Furthermore, American Jews did not look kindly upon an influx of European Jews because they assumed that the presence of the newcomers would exacerbate American anti-Semitism. Third, the fragmented nature of the American Jewish community and its lack of adequate leadership precluded any concerted political efforts. And finally, not until 1942 or 1943 did a large number of American Jews understand the enormity of the Holocaust then underway.[20]

The ambiguity of American Jewish attitudes during the New Deal years must also be explored to understand American Jewish reservations about boldly calling for assistance for their European coreligionists. The middle- and upper-class Jews, whether succumbing to pressures against parochialism, or out of a real desire to assimilate the values of the dominant society, were not quite sure how to behave. To speak up for increased Jewish immigration smacked of parochialism; to acquiesce in allowing existing immigration policies to stand meant a rejection of their heritage and ignoring the plight of their European brethren.[21]

The most famous American Jewish spokesman of the era, Rabbi Stephen S. Wise (who represented only a small segment of American Jewry at that time) perhaps best captured the American Jewish dilemma when he testified at a 1938 congressional hearing in support of a proposed bill to bring twenty thousand German children to the United States. While favoring the measure, he also stated quite clearly: "I want to make it plain that, so far as I am concerned, there is no intention whatsoever to depart from the immigration laws which at present obtain. I have heard no sane person propose any departure or deviation from the existing law now in force." He then added that if there were any conflict between the needs of the children and those of the United States, "I should say, of course, that our country comes first."[22]

Although Wise did not hesitate to speak out as a Jew, many Jews were so eager to be accepted as full-fledged Americans, indistinguishable from others except for nominal religious affiliation, that they prostituted themselves in the most embarrassing fashion. Perhaps the worst example of this occurred when the *Saturday Evening Post* published Judge Jerome Frank's essay "Red, White, and Blue Herring" the day before the Japanese attack on Pearl Harbor in 1941. Frank tried to assure readers of that archetypical American magazine that most American Jews had rejected "all or most of the old Jewish customs," that they thought "as Americans . . . not as Jews," and that they voiced the same opinions, saw the same movies, and rooted for the same ball teams as their Christian neighbors. He went even further by asserting that the religion practiced by most American Jews "is clearly closer to liberal Protestantism than to Jewish orthodoxy." Frank elaborated: "For those American Jews who broke the hold of the old Jewish code, what remains of the historic Jewish religion consists principally of some noble ethical principles and special values. . . . To call them 'Jewish' is to be a pedantic antiquarian." Frank dismissed the fervent Zionists as "a small group of fanatic Jewish nationalists," and told readers that all shades of American Zionist opinion at that time constituted "only a small percentage of the American Jewish population." The judge even acknowledged that in the past he had been upset that "because I was a Jew, I was barred from fraternities in college, [and] when I found I was not wanted in a hotel or club, I didn't like it, of course. But . . . I accepted such social disabilities with a sense of humor." Nonetheless, he identified himself completely as an American and said that "however much I might be anguished at the plight of the oppressed peoples in other countries, Jews or Gentiles, I [do] not believe that America should sacrifice its welfare to rescue them." He assumed that most American Jews shared his sentiments.[23]

With such self-effacement, which probably represented the thoughts and actions of many Jews who aspired to be accepted as Americans and not Jewish Americans, Roosevelt did not have to concern himself too much about changing American immigration policies or spending any of his political capital trying to rescue Jews desperate to escape from Germany. In fact, it would probably be most accurate to state that the intensified antisemitism in the United States during the New Deal era, and the fearful responses of the Jews to it, contributed more toward Roosevelt's attitudes on increased immigration than any callousness or calculation on his part.

Roosevelt was a realistic politician who rarely bucked the tide of public and congressional opinion. He helped Jews indirectly with his New Deal programs and directly with his appointments. But he never tried to do more than he knew he could accomplish for them, and he was unwilling to expend his political capital on an issue that he probably saw as politically destructive for other policies that he wished to pursue. An all-out attempt to rescue Jews would have resulted in a direct confrontation with the Congress and an aroused and hostile American public, and a threat to the harmonious pursuit of wartime and planned postwar policies.

How, therefore, should we evaluate Franklin Roosevelt and his relationship to American Jews? Was he saint or sinner? Should he be revered or excoriated? Well, if Roosevelt is praised for what he did, he should also be censured for what he did not do, namely for not moving vigorously and imaginatively to give refuge to the threatened Jews of Europe.

Notes

1. *Emanu-El* (San Francisco), April 20, 1945, pp. 2, 3; William B. Furie, "Jewish Education," *Jewish Advocate* (Boston), April 19, 1945, p. 12; *Buffalo Jewish Review*, April 20, 1945, p. 73.

2. See, for example, Henry L. Feingold, *The Politics of Rescue* (New Brunswick: Rutgers University Press, 1970); Saul S. Friedman, *No Haven for the Oppressed* (Detroit: Wayne State University Press, 1973); Bernard Wasserstein, *Britain and the Jews of Europe* (New York: Oxford University Press, 1979); and David S. Wyman, *Paper Walls* (Amherst: Uiversity of Massachusetts Press, 1968).

3. Myron I. Scholnick, "The New Deal and Anti-Semitism in America" (Ph.D. dissertation, University of Maryland, 1971), p. 22; Lawrence H. Fuchs, "American Jews and the Presidential Vote," *American Political Science Review* (June 1955) 49:400.

4. Rosenman quotation is from Samuel I. Rosenman Oral History Memoir, William E. Wiener Oral History Library, American Jewish Committee, New York City, Tape 2, p. 18. Forrest Davis, "Minister to Moscow," *Saturday Evening Post* (June 16, 1945) 217:17.

5. On the influence of Brandeis and Frankfurter, see Bruce Allen Murphy, *The Brandeis/Frankfurter Connection* (New York: Oxford University Press, 1982).

6. Frances Perkins Oral History Memoirs, Columbia University Oral History Collection, 1:57, 61; 3:522, 590; 7:16. See also *Brandeis/Frankfurter Connection*, p. 114; Michael E. Parrish, *Felix Frankfurter and His Times* (New York: Free Press, 1982), p. 225; Benjamin Stolberg, "Madam Secretary," *Saturday Evening Post*, July 27, 1940, p. 9. Quotations are from Charles E. Wyzanski, Jr., Oral History Memoir, Columbia University Oral History Collection, p. 185; and Perkins Memoirs, vol. 1, p. 57.

7. Murphy, *Brandis/Frankfurter Connection*, p. 114.

8. Milton Persitz, "Jews in Government Service," *Jewish Chronicle* (Indianapolis), March 27, 1942, in folder, "U.S.—Politics and Government—Jews," in Blaustein Library, American Jewish Committee, New York City.

9. Interview with Allison Bernstein, who is compiling a dissertation on New Deal Indian policy at Columbia University.

10. W. M. Kiplinger, "The Facts About Jews in Washington," *Reader Digest* (September 1942) 41:3; *The New Dealers*, by an unofficial observer (New York: Literary Guild, 1934), p. 322; Albert Jay Nock, "The Jewish Problem in America, II," *Atlantic Monthly* (July 1941) 168:74. Quotations are from Jerold S. Auerbach, *Unequal Justice* (New York: Oxford University Press), p. 188; and "Too Many Jews in Government?," *Christian Century* (December 28, 1938) 55:1614.

11. "Anti-Semitism Is Here," *Nation* (August 20, 1938)147:167; George Wolfskill and John A. Hudson, *All But the People* (New York: Macmillan Co., 1969), p. 86; *The New Dealers*, p. 322; Marquis W. Childs, "They Still Hate Roosevelt," *New Republic* (September 14, 1938) 96:148; E. Digby Baltzell, *The Protestant Establishment* (New York: Random House, 1964), p. 248.

12. Scholnick, "The New Deal and Anti-Semitism," pp. 76–77.

13. Samuel I. Rosenman Oral History Memoir, William E. Wiener Oral History Library, American Jewish Committee, Tape 2–19, 20.

14. Stephen S. Wise to Milton Krensky, September 23, 1938, in Carl Hermann Voss, *Stephen S. Wise: Servant of the People* (Philadelphia: Jewish Publication Society of America,

1970), pp. 229–30; Rabbi Ferdinand M. Isserman, "FDR and Felix Frankfurter," *National Jewish Monthly* (November 1965) 80:16; Joseph P. Lash, *From the Diaries of Felix Frankfurter* (New York: W.W. Norton & Co., 1975), p. 64; Parrish, *Felix Frankfurter and His Times*, p. 276.

15. David Brody, "American Jewry: The Refugees and Immigration Restriction (1932–1942)," in Abraham J. Karp, ed., *The Jewish Experience in America*, 5 vols. (Waltham, Mass.: American Jewish Historical Society, 1969), 5:340.

16. "The Fortune Survey: XX," *Fortune* (April 1939) 19:102.

17. Henry L. Feingold, *Zion in America* (New York: Twayne, 1974), p. 276; Melvin I. Urofsky, *A Voice That Spoke for Justice* (Albany, N.Y.: State University of New York Press, 1982), p. 136; Robert Dallek, *Franklin D. Roosevelt and American Foreign Policy* (New York: Oxford University Press, 1979), p. 446.

18. Isaiah Berlin, *Washington Despatches, 1941–1945*, H. G. Nicholas, ed. (Chicago: University of Chicago Press, 1981), p. 295; Leonard Dinnerstein, *America and the Survivors of the Holocaust* (New York: Columbia University Press, 1982), pp. 4, 5; Urofsky, *A Voice That Spoke for Justice*, p. 330. See also, Naomi W. Cohen, *Not Free To Desist* (Philadelphia: Jewish Publication Society of America, 1972), p. 170.

19. For articles typical of the type that put pressure on the Jews to assimilate, see the following in *Christian Century:* Alfred William Anthony, "Explaining the Jew" (August 16, 1933) 50:1034–36; Joseph Ernest McAfee, "Jewish Solidarity in America" (January 10, 1934) 51:52–53; "The Jewish Problem" (February 28, 1934) 51:279–81; Albert Levitan, "Leave the Jewish Problem Alone!" (April 25, 1934) 51:555–57; "Jewry and Democracy" (June 9, 1937) 54:734–36. In the last, the author wrote, "The situation in which the Jewish problem arises is in large measure Jewry's own creation" (p. 736).

20. Cohen, *Not Free to Desist*, pp. 194, 204.

21. Brody, "American Jewry," pp. 324, 326, 332, 334, 338.

22. Wise's comments are quoted in ibid., p. 331.

23. Jerome Frank, "Red, White, and Blue Herring," *Saturday Evening Post* (December 6, 1941) 214:9, 10, 83, 84, 85.

Part II.
Jews in the South

4

A Note
on Southern
Attitudes

Toward Jews

Contemporary American historiography has largely neglected the story of the Jews in the South, and insofar as the subject has been treated, antisemitism is generally dismissed as a non-event. Much of the evidence available, however, gives one cause to wonder and raises suspicions to the contrary. The study of southern attitudes toward the Jews therefore merits scholarly consideration.

In the 1950's three of the most prominent American historians—Oscar Handlin, Richard Hofstadter, and John Higham—discussed the causes of antisemitism in this country. Each of them attributed its development to late-nineteenth-century phenomena. Handlin, for example, has noted that "philo-Semitism was far more characteristic of the national attitude before 1900 than anti-Semitism,"[1] and that the hostile sentiments expressed toward Jews at the beginning of the twentieth century "were quite new to American society."[2] Hofstadter has set forth the thesis that "the Greenback-Populist tradition activated most of what we have of modern popular anti-Semitism in the United States."[3] And Higham, who carried out the most extensive research on antisemitism in America, has found that during the Gilded Age, three groups—the agrarian radicals of the Populist movement, certain eastern patricians, and "many of the poorest classes in urban centers"—harbored very strong anti-Jewish feelings.[4]

Neither Handlin, Hofstadter, nor Higham has supported his remarks with significant data from the South. What is even more striking, however, is that practically all of the southern sources cited by these historians show evidence of hostility toward Jews. Therefore they should have either qualified their generalizations or else indicated that the nature of the material available precluded any definitive conclusions about the South.

Professor Handlin uses five southern sources: John M. Mecklin's *Ku Klux Klan;* C. Vann Woodward's *Tom Watson;* Zebulon Vance's *The Scattered Nation;* A. W. Miller's *The Restoration of the Jews,* and the *Letter of Henry R. Jackson of Georgia to Ex-Senator Allen G. Thurman.*[5] The Ku Klux Klan, of course, did not like Jews. Woodward includes a chapter of Tom Watson's ferocious anti-semitism in connection with the Leo Frank case in 1914–15. Vance, it is true, did make a plea for the tolerance of Jews in his "Scattered Nation" speech which was delivered in more than one hundred American cities over a period of twenty years beginning in 1874. His talk, however, was motivated more by the hostility he observed toward Jews in North Carolina and elsewhere than by the warm feelings of southern Christians. In fact, the central point that Vance made was that there was a great deal of anti-semitism despite the reverence for much of the Jewish religious heritage. "Never before," Vance said, "was there an instance of such a general rejection of the person and character, and acceptance of the doctrines and dogmas of a people. We affect to despise the Jew," he continued, "but accept and adore the pure conception of a God which he taught us."[6] Handlin's other two references to the South also detract from his generalizations about philo-semitism. Miller is cited as evidence for the point that the Jew was "everywhere alien," while Jackson is the source of the statement that "to the city, and particularly New York, whole regions of the South and West felt themselves in bondage."[7] There are no other references to the South in Handlin's article.

Professor Hofstadter has only two references concerning the attitudes of southerners toward Jews in his book, *The Age of Reform*. The first is a statement made by Governor Alexander G. McNutt of Mississippi in 1837 defending the practice of baiting Baron Rothschild: "The blood of Judas and Shylock flows in his veins, and he unites the qualities of both his countrymen." The second is a comment on Tom Watson's conduct in the Leo Frank case.[8] It is noteworthy that in his entire discussion of Populist antisemitism there are no other references to southerners.

Professor Higham, who has written about antisemitism in four articles,[9] displays the most insight of the historians under discussion. "In the case of the Jew," Higham writes, "especially diverse and conflicting attitudes have always existed side by side in American minds. The Jewish stereotype took two entirely different forms, one religious and the other economic; and in either case attractive elements mingled with unlovely ones."[10] Nevertheless, of the seventeen sources referring to the South in Higham's articles, thirteen show some degree of animosity to Jews. They include Vance's "Scattered Nation" speech and Henry Hanaw's *Jew Hating and Jew Baiting,* an essay that I have been unable to obtain but whose title suggests less than fond feelings. In addition, Professor Higham has used Jacob Marcus' *Early American Jewry;* Harry Golden's article, "Jew and Gentile in the New South: Segregation at Sundown" and his *Jewish Roots in the Carolinas;* Reginald McGrane's *Foreign Bondholders and American State Debts;* Oscar Cohen's unpublished essay, "Public Opinion and Anti-Jewish Prejudice in the South"; *Niles' Weekly Register;* Bertram Korn's *American Jewry and the Civil War;* Charles and Louise Samuels' *Night Fell on Georgia;* Isidor Blum's *The Jews of Baltimore;* the Bernsteins' article on Richmond, Virginia; Selig Adler's essay on Vance, and "The Jew's Daughter," a folk ballad.[11] Marcus includes both positive and negative references to colonial Jews. Harry Golden claims that there is a tradition of philosemitism in the South, but in the same essay states that "Southern Jew of the city lives in constant fear of someone's passing an anti-Semitic remark 'to his face.' "[12] McGrane is cited as the source for the remark that the Governor of Mississippi sounded "a rare sour note" about Jews in 1841.

(Since Hofstadter also cites an antisemitic comment by a Mississippi Governor in 1837, I wonder how "rare" such remarks were.) Oscar Cohen's unpublished paper does discuss the existence of antisemitism in the South, but also states that it is on the wane—which, of course, means it was worse earlier.[13] *Niles' Register* reported the failure of the "Jew bill" (extending the franchise to Jews) to pass the Maryland legislature in 1820. It finally passed in 1826. Korn is cited to show that antisemitism did exist during the Civil War and the Samuels' book is on the Leo Frank case. The Bernsteins retell the experience of Richmond's Jews and they point out that the Jewish community of that city did not feel completely secure in its position after World War II. Adler's article on Vance indicates that antisemitism must have been prevalent, otherwise the North Carolinian would not have spent so much time delivering "The Scattered Nation." Finally, "The Jew's Daughter," a folk ballad of "sacred legend" in the South, has undergone numerous versions in different states—in West Virginia alone there are fourteen variants.[14] Arthur Palmer Hudson has speculated that the ballad "may have started out as a vessel of anti-semitic propaganda."[15] The verse, which originated in the Middle Ages but has been passed on from generation to generation, details how a Jew's daughter "carried off Christians, especially children, to torture and murder [them] in the most atrocious ways."[16] One stanza tells what happened to a boy who, after chasing his ball into a Jew's garden, was then enticed into the house by the young mistress:

> She pinned a napkin round his neck,
> She pinned it with a pin,
> And then she called for a tin basin
> To catch his life-blood in.[17]

Other than Professors Handlin, Hofstadter, and Higham, American historians have shown little interest in the subject of antisemitism in the United States before the end of the nineteenth century.[18] Jewish historians have either passed over the subject quickly—like Jacob R. Marcus who remarks that "there never was a period of American Jewish history in which anti-Jewish prejudice was absent"[19]—or have referred to it obliquely—like Bertram Korn who observes that "the columns of the daily press in almost any [antebellum] community and the pages of the diaries and private letters of non-Jews demonstrated that age-old myths and fears were not totally absent."[20] Others have maintained a "discreet silence" about the manifestations of antipathy.[21] Yet southern aversion toward Jews has been affirmed by the more perceptive regional commentators. Wilbur J. Cash declares that the Jew "is everywhere the eternal alien; and in the South, where any difference has always stood out with great vividness he was especially so."[22] Benjamin Kendrick asserted that southern small farmers regarded Jews "as alien and outside their kin" despite "revering and worshiping the Jew God."[23]

Because there were no pogroms, no tax-supported churches (after colonial times), and no state-wide legal restrictions on most economic and social activities, possibly erroneous conclusions have been reached about the position of Jews in southern society. It seems that a number of writers have equated equal opportunity with social approval. Or else, after comparing the status of Jews in the United States with their counterparts in Europe, American historians have waxed eloquently. Just as we now know that equal legal rights and economic opportunities have not wrought significant changes in popular feelings between ethnic groups, so too must we acknowledge the possibility that a similar situation might have existed between Jews and gentiles in the South. Although it has been acknowledged that by 1920 "a full-fledged racial ideology colored the thinking of many Americans,"[24] the roots of these feelings have not been adequately explored. It seems certain that racial prejudice predated the 1890s in the South.[25]

The major difficulty in understanding the nature of southern attitudes is the lack of significant scholarly analysis of southern Jewry. In 1948 the editors of *Commentary* called a conference "to consider the problems of interpreting and recording the Jewish experience in America." The participants agreed "upon the central point, that we live in abysmal ignorance of the real past of American Jewry."[26] The works published since then have, with few exceptions, added little to our knowledge. In 1965 Alfred Hero wrote:

> Extremely little of the rather voluminous social research on American Jewry, primarily by Jewish social scientists, has devoted any attention to Southern Jews. . . . Published knowledge about Jews in the South consists of a handful of biographies, autobiographies, and historical works (mostly of dubious quality), and the results of interviews in several Southern Jewish communities.[27]

Furthermore, a good deal of the writing by Jews about themselves has been steeped in filiopietism and provincial pride.[28] Jewish historians, for the most part, have felt it necessary to vindicate the Jew's position in the United States and to establish his loyalty and attachment to American ideals. Oscar Handlin offered an explanation for this when he pointed out that Jews, "most sensitive to the opinions of others," accepted the premises of their antagonists in the 1890's, that a "group's place in the United States was to be judged by the achievements of its ancestors." Hence some earnest Jews embarked upon "the endless task of apologia," founded the American Jewish Historical Society in 1892, and "labored thereafter to reveal the antiquity of the Jews on the continent, their services in the colonies and in the Revolution, and their loyalty in successive national crises."[29]

Unfortunately that trend has continued almost unabated into our time. One can read Handlin's own observation that the American Revolution "summoned forth the best energies of American Jews. They expanded devotion and effort far beyond their duty, and far more than their numbers required; and they contributed substantially to the winning of American independence."[30] Jacob Rader Marcus speculates that "Jewish Americans must have been thrilled when they read the Declaration of Independence [because] they had more to gain than the average Gentile American who already possessed all rights." Marcus also concludes that "the Jews were elated" after the adoption of the new Constitution in 1788.[31] Little attempt has been made to portray Jews as a group composed of various individuals with different attitudes, opinions, positions, desires, and goals. The continual self-reassurance appears to mask an insecurity that Jews have about their place in American society. In the Jewish chronicles of their southern experiences there are no villains, no traitors, no dissenters, no abolitionists, and no scalawags. This, of course, may have been true; Jews might have been too frightened to consider engaging in deviant activities. We know from our own day that they are profoundly dependent upon their neighbors' good will. Hence they have adapted themselves to the dominant cultural standards.[32] The same might have been true in earlier times.

Contemporary regional commentators have written that the fear of antisemitism is pervasive. Jews are afraid to speak out because they are fearful of how their gentile neighbors will react. Harry Golden, for example, notes:

> The mildest New Deal expression in a "letter to the editor" signed with a Jewish name sends a shiver through the entire Jewish community—("Now we've got *someone else* to worry about.") But the greatest fear of all is that the next Jewish newcomer to town may be an "agitator," a "pink," an organizer for the CIO, or even a worker for some Negro cause.[33]

In city after city Jews have refused to endorse publicly the Supreme Court ruling calling for school integration. As one Mississippian put it:

> We have to work quietly, secretly. We have to play ball. Anti-Semitism is always right around the corner.
> ....
> We don't want to have our Temple bombed. If we said out loud in Temple what most of us really think and believe, there just wouldn't be a Temple here anymore. They [the gentile neighbors] let it alone because it seems to them like just another Mississippi church. And if it ever stops seeming like that, we won't have a Temple. We have to at least pretend to go along with things as they are.[34]

The above quotations indicate how uneasy some Jews are about their position in mid-twentieth century southern society. The roots of this discomfort have never been adequately explored.

A better understanding of eighteenth- and nineteenth-century Jewish experiences in the South will come only after scholars critically examine contemporary manuscripts and periodicals and make some attempt to generalize on the basis of well-documented fact. Such an undertaking would enhance our understanding of the Jew's role and position in southern society in the past as well as suggest the basis for southern Jewish attitudes in contemporary society. Until further information is adduced, however, one must weigh conclusions carefully and hold opinions tentatively.

Notes

1. Oscar Handlin, "How U.S. Anti-Semitism Really Began: Its Grass-Roots Source in the '90s," *Commentary* (September 1951)11:541.

2. Oscar Handlin, "American Views of the Jew at the Opening of the Twentieth Century," *Publications of the American Jewish Historical Society* (June 1951) 40:523. Cited hereafter as *PAJHS*.

3. Richard Hofstadter, *The Age of Reform* (New York: Knopf, 1955), p. 80.

4. John Higham, "Anti-Semitism in the Gilded Age: A Reinterpretation," *Mississippi Valley Historical Review* (March 1957) 43:572. Higham's other essays on the subject are "Social Discrimination Against Jews in America, 1830–1930," *PAJHS* (1957–1958) 47:1–33; "Another Look at Nativism," *The Catholic Historical Review* (July 1958) 44:147–58; and "American Anti-Semitism Historically Reconsidered," in Charles Herbert Stember, ed. *Jews in the Mind of America* (New York: Basic Books, 1966).

5. C. Van Woodward, *Tom Watson, Agrarian Rebel* (New York, 1938); J. M. Mecklin, *The Ku Klux Klan* (New York 1924); Zebulon Vance, *The Scattered Nation* (New York, 1904); A. W. Miller, *The Restoration of the Jews* (Atlanta 1887); and *Letter of Henry R. Jackson of Georgia to Ex-Senator Allen G. Thurman . . .* (Atlanta 1887).

6. Vance, *Scattered Nation*, p. 16.

7. Miller, *Restoration of the Jews*, p. 335 n. 47; *Letter . . .* , p. 341, n. 68.

8. Hofstadter, *Age of Reform*, pp. 7–81. Hofstadter gives the date as 1837. Actually McNutt was elected governor in 1837 but took office in 1838.

9. See note 4.

10. Higham, "Anti-Semitism in the Gilded Age," p. 563.

11. Henry Hanaw, *Jew Hating and Jew Baiting* (Nashville 1894); Jacob Rader Marcus, *Early America Jewry: The Jews of Pennsylvania and the South* (Philadelphia, 1953); Harry Golden, "Jew and Gentile in the New South: Segregation at Sundown," *Commentary* (November 1955) 20:403–12; Golden, *Jewish Roots in the Carolinas: A Pattern of American Philo-Semitism* (Greensboro, 1955); Reginald McGrane, *Foreign Bondholders and American*

State Debts (New York, 1935); Oscar Cohen, "Public Opinion and Anti-Jewish Prejudice in the South" (unpublished paper delivered at the National Executive Committee Meeting, Anti-Defamation League, September 25, 1959); *Niles' Weekly Register* (October 21, 1820) 7:114; Bertram W. Korn, *American Jews and the Civil War* (Philadelphia, 1951), p. 177–88; Charles and Louise Samuels, *Night Fell on Georgia* (New York, 1956); Isidor Blum, *The Jews of Baltimore* (Baltimore, 1910); David and Adele Bernstein, "Slow Revolution in Richmond, Va.," *Commentary* (December 1949) 8:539–46; Selig Adler, "Zebulon B. Vance and the 'Scattered Nation,' " *Journal of Southern History* (August 1941) 7:357–77; and "The Jew's Daughter," *Journal of American Folklore* (October–December 1906) 19:293–94. The other southern materials used by Higham are C. B. Sherman, "Charlestown, South Carolina, 1750–1950," *Jewish Frontier* (April 1964) 31:19–22; Julian B. Feibelman, *A Social and Economic Study of the New Orleans Jewish Community* (Philadelphia, 1941); Charles Reznikoff and Uriah Z. Engelman, *The Jews of Charleston* (Philadelphia, 1950); and *De Bow's Review* (1868) n.s. 5:694–700.

12. Golden, "Jew and Gentile in the New South," p. 410.

13. Cohen, "Public Opinion and Anti-Jewish Prejudice in the South."

14. Reed Smith, ed., *South Carolina Folk Ballads* (Cambridge, 1928), p. 148.

15. Arthur Palmer Hudson, "Folk-Songs of the Southern Whites," in W. T. Couch, ed., *Culture of the South* (Chapel Hill: University of North Carolina Press, 1934), p. 544.

16. "A Discovery in Ballad Literature," *The University of Virginia Magazine* (December 1912), p. 114.

17. "Old Country Ballads in Missouri," *Journal of American Folklore* (October–December 1906) 19:293–94; for other versions see ibid. (October–December 1922) 35:344–45, and ibid. (April–June 1926) 39:108–9.

18. Higham, "American Anti-Semitism Historically Reconsidered," in Stember, ed., *Jews in the Mind of America*, p. 273.

19. Jacob R. Marcus, "The Periodization of American Jewish History," PAJHS (1958–59) 47:130.

20. Bertram W. Korn, "Factors Bearing Upon the Survival of Judaism in the Ante-Bellum Period," *American Jewish Historical Quarterly* (June 1964) 53:346.

21. Leonard A. Greenberg, "Some American Anti-Semitic Publications of the Late 19th Century," PAJHS (1947) 37:421.

22. Wilbur J. Cash, *The Mind of the South* (New York, 1941), p. 342.

23. Benjamin Kendrick, "The Study of the New South," *The North Carolina Historical Review* (January 1926) 3:10. In his analysis of the southern mystique, *The South and the Nation* (New York: Pantheon, 1969), Pat Watters reaffirms previous observations by Cash and Kendrick. Watters notes that in the 1960's, "Jews and *foreigners* were, of course, suspect on race and the like; one of the sadder phenomena across the South," he adds, "was the figure of the lonely, fearful Jew who sought to outbigot his white neighbors, not merely as a member but a leader often, in the Citizens' Councils, when they were going strong, with their own anti-Semitism" (p. 299).

24. Oscar and May F. Handlin, *Danger in Discord: Origins of Anti-Semitism in the United States* (New York: Anti-Defamation League of B'nai B'rith, 1948), p. 24.

25. For example, Jews were unable to vote in the colonies, north and south, until after the American Revolution. Maryland and North Carolina refused to grant Jews the franchise until 1826 and 1868, respectively. Many Jewish politicians who reached high political office (for example, Judah P. Benjamin and David Yulee, United States Senators from Louisiana and Florida, respectively) married gentiles and raised their children as

Christians. During the Civil War, Benjamin was scorned and epithets were hurled at him because of his Jewish ancestry. An Alabama Senator in 1878 referred to a political opponent as a "Jew Dog," and the President of the University of Virginia explained in 1890 that "the mere fact of different is a persistent cause" of hostility toward Jews in the South. For a fuller discussion of southern hostility to Jews before the twentieth century, see Leonard Dinnerstein, *The Leo Frank Case* (New York: Columbia University Press, 1968), pp. 65–68.

26. Oscar Handlin, "New Paths in American History," *Commentary* (November 1949) 7:388–89.

27. Alfred A. Hero, Jr., *The Southerner and World Affairs* (Baton Rouge: University of Louisiana Press, 1965), p. 636.

28. Handlin, "New Paths," p. 388; see also Benjamin Kaplan, *The Eternal Stranger* (New York: Bookman Associates, 1957), p. 13.

29. Oscar and Mary F. Handlin, "The Acquisition of Political and Social Rights by the Jews in the United States," *American Jewish Yearbook* (1955) 56:77.

30. Oscar Handlin, *Adventure in Freedom: Three Hundred Years of Jewish Life in America* (New York: McGraw-Hill, 1954), p. 23.

31. Marcus, *Early American Jewry*, pp. 531, 533.

32. Hero, *The Southerner and World Affairs*, p. 482.

33. Harry L. Golden, "The Jews of the South," *Congress Weekly* (December 31, 1951) 18:10; see also Hero, *The Southerner and World Affairs*, pp. 498–99.

34. Quoted in Marvin Braiterman, "Mississippi Marranos," *Midstream* (September 1964) 10:33. See also Murray Friedman, "Virginia Jewry in the School Crisis: Anti-Semitism and Desegregation," *Commentary* (January 1959) 27:17–22; Joshua A. Fishman, "Southern City," *Midstream* (September 1961) 7:39–56; and Morton J. Gaba, "Segregation and a Southern Jewish Community," *Jewish Frontier* (October 1954) 21:12–15.

5

A Neglected Aspect
of Southern Jewish History

Jewish experiences in the United States history have been, for the most part, happy ones. Since colonial times Jews have enjoyed opportunities for self-development the equal of which they had not known in other Christian countries. Jews have thrived in the American climate, but it is important to note that strong religious prejudices are also a part of the American background. To what extent these prejudices have affected Jews has never been studied fully.

Jews in the South have received less attention from historians than their coreligionists in other parts of the nation. Aside from the works of Jacob Marcus, Bertram Korn, and two or three others,[1] historians have neglected Jewish experiences in the region. As a result we do not have a thorough knowledge of Southern Jewish life.

During the course of previous research in the history of Southern Jewry we have been struck by the frequency of discriminatory laws and derogatory rhetoric against them. This does not mean to imply that the chronicle of Southern Jewry is one of unrelieved intimidation, prejudice, and protective coloration. Southern Jews, however, have been affected more by regional attitudes than Jews in other sections of the United States.

Jews arrived in the American colonies in 1654 when a group
landed in the Dutch colony of New Amsterdam. By the time of
the American Revolution Jewish settlements existed in New York,
Philadelphia, Savannah, Charleston, and Newport, Rhode Island.
Colonial reactions to them varied little from one region to another.
Although America allowed greater self-expression and more expansive opportunities, it did not mean that colonists, North or
South, had discarded European prejudices toward the Jew. Antisemitic attitudes subsided on this side of the Atlantic but they did
not disappear.[2] A good many colonists resented Jews who refused
to accept Christianity as the only true faith; and at least one
minister accused Jewish merchants of exploiting Christian
craftsmen.[3]

The first group of Jews to arrive in the Southern colonies—
forty-two people of German, Spanish and Portugese descent—
landed in Georgia in 1733. They met immediate opposition. Although Governor James Oglethorpe permitted them to remain,
the trustees of the colony, residing in London, feared that the Jews
would damage the colony's reputation, and ordered the proprietor
to get rid of them as soon as possible.[4] Oglethorpe refused to obey
instructions and took responsibility for allowing the new settlers
to stay. At first they participated in community activities without
serious discrimination, but as the colony matured and became
more secure, Jews encountered political barriers.[5] By the 1740s
many Jews and non-Jews became disillusioned with the severe
restrictions placed upon them by the trustees—prohibition of slavery being the most important—and they sought greater economic
freedom in South Carolina. Some Jews settled in Charleston; in
1750 they erected the city's first synagogue—*Beth Elohim.*[6] Aside
from Savannah and Charleston, there were no other Jewish settlements in the colonial South. Individual Jews lived in other parts
of the region but no other towns established congregations. In
fact, it is unlikely that the entire Jewish population in the South
numbered even 500 people by the time of the Revolution.[7]

Despite the limited number of Jews, many colonial legislatures—North and South—denied them the franchise and cir-cumscribed their liberties. The same, of course, was true for other minorities, such as the Quakers, Baptists, Roman Catholics, and Huguenots. Not only were these groups barred in many places from voting, but they were harassed in numerous ways, and often restricted economically and socially to a much greater degree than Jews. Most colonial communities demanded conformity and the Jews were only one of the deviant sects. Nevertheless, state con-stitutions which barred those from voting who did not accept the divinity of the Christian faith applied almost exclusively to Jews. After the war of independence, New York led the states in revising its law codes and granting suffrage more liberally. By the early nineteenth century only New Hampshire, Maryland, and North Carolina still proscribed Jews from voting.[8]

In addition to voting restrictions, a host of other examples can be cited noting Southern antagonism toward Jews. The list, though, may only be partially reflective of the temper of Southern Jewish experiences. The sketchiness of our historical knowledge about the life of Southern Jews makes almost all generalizations rash. One does not know, for example, whether the following were merely isolated events or whether they constituted a pro-gression of intensity of hostile feelings. Nevertheless one might say that collectively they suggest that Jews in the South may not have been made to feel welcome there: a Georgia pamphlet of 1784 condemned Jews for "eternally obtruding themselves . . . upon every public occasion"; a Jew elected to the North Carolina legislature had his right to be seated challenged in 1809 because he did not accept the divinity of Jesus; Thomas Jefferson, in 1826, acknowledged existing prejudices toward Jews; Henry Timrod, a South Carolina poet, claimed that his affection for the Jewess, Rachel Lyons, conquered his "old prejudices against the Hebrew"; the state of Arkansas worded its marriage law of 1838 in such a way as to prohibit Jewish rabbis from conducting legal ceremo-nies; during the next decade stories circulated to the effect that Florida's David Levy (elected to the United States Senate in 1845), to win the hand of Nancy Wickliffe, promised to change his name to "Yulee"—which he did—and raise his children as Christians;

and in the 1850s one Mississippi newspaper charged Jews with "swindling whites and Negroes alike"; across the border in Alabama the Tuskegee *Republican* had the reputation of being an "anti-Jewish paper."[9]

Despite these instances of Judaeophobia, Jews found that life in the South afforded many pleasures. The reasons for this are manifold. Although religious prejudice existed, countervailing American ideas stressed the essential equality of all white men and the abundance of opportunities for those who worked hard. In addition, as John Higham has pointed out, "behavior and belief do not necessarily coincide in any area of life."[10] There is a significant difference between prejudice and discrimination. On the one hand, a group of people might not be cherished in any given society yet no legal action is taken to circumscribe its rights. If a community is concerned with a more important issue, aggressive thrusts are aimed, if possible, at the major grievance while lesser ones recede temporarily. Conflicting attitudes and feelings frequently exist side by side and for opportunistic or other practical concerns deep prejudices are not always acted upon.

In the South—as well as other regions—non-Jews who resented Jews and desired to restrict their political influence accepted the usefulness of Jewish merchants and artisans. In Charleston, South Carolina, Jews established a line of steamships connecting the city with Havana, Cuba, reestablished the chamber of Commerce, introduced illuminating gas to the city and pioneered in other industrial enterprises. At one period, in the 1820s, Jews edited two of Charleston's four newspapers. In Charleston and elsewhere in the South Jews also wrote, painted, taught, and served as physicians and lawyers. They were slave traders in major cities like New Orleans, Mobile, and Richmond.[11] But the fact that Jews could succeed in American society did not mean that prejudices had disappeared. As Korn has pointed out, "the columns of the daily press in almost any community and the pages of the diaries and private letters of non-Jews demonstrate that age-old myths and fears were not totally absent."[12]

Nevertheless, as enslavement of Negroes became the chief

distinguishing characteristic of the South, the test of the true Southerner was his acceptance of the institution. Southern Jews appear to have had little ambivalence on this score. Rabbi David Einhorn of Baltimore is the only prominent southern Jew who is known to have spoken out against slavery. Others either kept silent or gave wholehearted support to the Southern ideology. In contrast, northern Jews could be found on both sides.[13]

In times of crisis, such as the Civil War, latent prejudices surfaced. The conflagration aroused strong feelings of in-group solidarity, exacerbating demands for unity, and heightened southern nationalism. Similar emotions came to the fore in the North. Korn has noted that "anti-Jewish prejudice was a characteristic expression of the age, part and parcel of the economic and social upheaval effectuated by the war."[14] Northern Judaeophobes, like a writer in *Harper's Weekly*, denounced all Jews as "secessionists, copperheads, and rebels,"[15] while southerners accused them of being "merciless speculators, army slackers, and blockade-runners across the land frontiers to the North."[16] South Carolina's Governor Orr believed that the Jews in the confederacy were loyal to the Union and "generally averse to rendering military service . . . or upholding the rebel cause. . . ."[17] Judah P. Benjamin, Confederate Secretary of State, aroused the ire of numerous southerners. One observer believed it "blasphemous" for a Jew to hold such an important position while another was certain that the "prayers of the confederacy would have more effect if Benjamin were dismissed."[18] Denunciation of Jewish merchants was a common practice in many towns in Georgia, and the *Southern Illustrated News* observed "all that the Jew possesses is a plentiful lot of money, together with the scorn of the world."[19]

When the war ended in 1865, the attitudes toward Jews took on a more positive cast among those who wished for commercial growth. Many southerners wanted to emulate northern industrial accomplishments and therefore Jews appeared desirable members of society. The Sandersonsville *Central Georgian* hailed their presence "as an auspicious sign." "Where there are no Jews," the newspaper observed, "there is no money to be made."

Virginia's Richmond *Whig* noted that "a sober, steadier, and more industrious and law abiding class of population . . . [does] not exist."[20]

But economic interests of some Jews, which allegedly attracted southerners, made them vulnerable, especially in times of strife. Numerous southerners, humiliated by defeat in the Civil War and military occupation thereafter, plagued by low incomes and crop failures, and aroused by Reconstruction governments which included Negroes, chafed under the bit and could barely contain their anger and resentment. Furthermore, while the North continued to prosper and grow industrially, the South wallowed for decades in subservience to northern bankers and manufacturers who dictated what crops should be planted and monopolized the production of key agricultural implements. Southern attempts to imitate the successful industrial growth of the North succeeded only fitfully.

Scholars who have studied American history of the late nineteenth century have paid so little attention to the activities of southern Jews in the context of national and regional affairs that we have only scattered bits and pieces of information which suggest certain types of attitudes and behavior but which, by themselves, cannot possibly give us an understanding of the whole picture. We know, though, from the shreds of material that we do have, that some Jews were looked upon with disfavor in the South and that many of them served as scapegoats for a society unable to cope with—or recognize—the major sources of its grievances.

Rural folk who felt that they were being kept in bondage by the merchant or peddler with whom they traded blamed Jews for economic reverses. Hence angry mobs forced Jewish merchants out of Somerville, Tennessee in 1876, Avoyelles Parish, Louisiana in 1887, and various small towns in Georgia in 1893. Robert Louis Stevenson perhaps expressed the prevailing view when he wrote that "Jew storekeepers . . . lead on the farmer into irretrievable indebtedness, and keep him ever after as their bond-slave hopelessly grinding in the mill."[21]

Numerous incidents lend credence to the view that the derisive image of the Jew received support from the leading members of southern communities. An Alabama minister railed in 1875 that no matter where Jews locate "they are a *curse* to the country." Three years later John T. Morgan, United States Senator from Alabama, referred to a political opponent as a "Jew dog"; and a judge in Rome, Georgia, disallowed a Jew's testimony because he refused to acknowledge the divinity of Jesus.[22]

Even Jews who moved easily in southern society were cognizant of their neighbors' animosity. "We are even now suffering from intolerance," Bernard Baruch's father told him while they were still living in South Carolina in the 1880s and Baruch's biographer, Margaret Coit, acknowledged that "as few Jewish children can be, the Baruch boys were accepted for themselves. . . ." Joseph Proskauer, who spent his childhood in Mobile, Alabama, in the late nineteenth century believed and felt as a child that he "lived in a wonderful world where I could love and be loved and all was 'right as right could be.' " Yet in high school other boys beat him up for being a "Christ killer." Ludwig Lewisohn had similar experiences in Charleston, South Carolina, at about the same time.[23]

Anti-Jewish feeling was more an American reaction than a southern one and Jews in other parts of the country had similar experiences. John Higham, whose studies were based primarily upon information gathered in the North and the West, found "a pattern of discrimination" beginning to take root in the 1870s.[24] Nevertheless it must be pointed out that the South had fewer immigrants than other regions, contained a more homogeneous population than existed elsewhere in the United States, and regarded conformity as a more important trait than the polyglot cities of the North or the continually changing frontiers in the West where differences were commonplace.

The southern attitude about conformity received perhaps its most eloquent expression in 1890 when the editors of *The American Hebrew* conducted a survey to discover why Americans were so hostile to Jews. The comments of the two Southerners responding, W. W. Thornton, President of the University of Virginia, and Zebulon Vance, United States Senator from North Carolina, reveal the deep-seatedness of Southern prejudice.

"The mere fact of difference," the University of Virginia President emphasized, "is a persistent cause."[25] In elaborating upon the reasons for the hostility, President Thornton noted that "Jews certainly care less for what is embraced in the term culture than Christians who are equally well off." "Never," in his career, the university President added, had he ever seen "a really scholarly" Jewish student. Thornton thought that the prejudices might subside if Jews married Christians and accepted the true faith. "All intelligent Christians," he concluded in his answer to questions asked by the editors of *The American Hebrew*, "deplore the fact that the historical evidences for Christianity have so little weight with your people."[26]

Senator Vance, an outspoken critic of antisemitism, had attested to its presence by delivering a plea for tolerance of Jews in a speech, "The Scattered Nation," in over one hundred towns and cities of the country between 1874 and his death twenty years later. In responding to the queries put to him by *The American Hebrew*, Vance wrote that although the various Southern churches may not have preached antisemitism:

> Sufficient care is not taken to point out, with reference to the crucifixion, the injustice of holding responsible a whole people, generation after generation, for the acts of a few. No doubt this unconsciously lays a foundation of prejudice, which is largely added to by the jealousy of Gentile rivals in business. Nothing is so satisfactory to a man as to be able to excuse an unworthy motive by referring to it a love of God and his religion. This prejudice is also increased by the unreasonable propensity to consider the Jew under all circumstances as a foreigner, in which case we veneer our motive with a love of country.[27]

The 1890s witnessed a marked increase in virulent remarks about Jews. The Populist crusade[28] aroused southern and midwestern farmers to the outrageous behavior and colossal indifference of the nation's industrialists. Trying circumstances resulted in prejudicial outbursts. Throughout the nation the specter of the Jewish Shylock haunted those who felt oppressed by the maintenance of the gold standard and the ogreish "Wall Street Bankers." Jews, Jewish Shylocks, Jewish money and Jewish mortgage holders were blamed for all the troubles besetting the nation. And in North Carolina the Governor proclaimed, "Our Negro brethren, too, are being held in bondage by Rothschild."[29]

The prevalent fear of "racial pollution" added to the woes created by the economic crises. The idea of Anglo-Saxon superiority pervaded the United States at this time and prominent individuals warned of mongrelization of the race. In the South, where many people had nothing more to be proud of than the color of their skin and their Protestant, Anglo-Saxon heritage, the fear of being subdued by an allegedly inferior breed like the Jews, who by the 1890s were considered racially as well as religiously different, intensified the burdens of an already depressed people. One of the more offensive incidents occurred when advertising solicitors for *The Jewish Sentiment*, "The only Jewish Paper South of Richmond and East of the Mississippi River," were "told pointedly" by merchants in 1897 that the Jewish trade was not wanted.[30]

Negative attitudes toward Jews carried into the twentieth century. The new technology had quickened the pace of life; families moved from their farms and villages to urban areas; Italian and Jewish immigrants led a parade of southern and eastern Europeans into the United States; and the frustrated and frightened lower classes found it more difficult to cope with the tribulations of a changing society. Under these circumstances long held suspicions largely restricted to verbal attacks now became activated through violence. The first decade of the new century marked an increased number of lynchings in the South as well as the notorious Atlanta race riot of 1906. The riot ostensibly began as a result of newspaper headlines reporting alleged Negro assaults upon white women. The underlying reasons, however, were more basic: a discontented urban working class forced to endure meager wages, crowded and uncomfortable tenements, and little hope for eventual improvement.[31]

It is not surprising, therefore, that Horace Kallen should write, also in 1906, "there is already a very pretty Jewish problem in our South." The same conditions which heightened antagonisms toward Negroes worsened relations between Jews and non-Jews. Jews, the eternal strangers and killers of the Savior, had been the traditional scapegoat for many Christians and could always be used as a whipping boy to help alleviate the frustrations and pressures of deprived and confused lives. In times of economic crises, or when the poor felt particularly victimized, the predatory Jew reappeared in public discussions. A year after the Atlanta race riot, Georgia's patrician historian, Lucian Lamar Knight, wrote: "It is quite the fashion to characterize the Jew as exacting his interest down to the last drachma."[32]

The major example of southern resentment of Jews before the First World War occurred in Atlanta between 1913 and 1915. Until that time animosity in the city had manifested itself primarily in social restrictions. Then, in April 1913, Leo Frank, a Jewish industrialist, was accused of murdering one of his employees, a thirteen year old girl. After that episode, overt hostility toward Jews became apparent. A correspondent of *The Atlanta Georgian* pointed out that it was the first time that a Jew had ever been in serious trouble in the city and complained because she saw "how ready is every one to believe the worst of him."[33]

Antisemitic epithets punctuated many a conversation. Just before the Frank trial opened *The Atlanta Journal* attempted to stem the attacks and published an article entitled, "The Jews—Our Benefactors." The author praised the Jews as "great people" and condemned "the irrational feeling of opposition so many ignorant people cherish against [them]."[34] But the bigoted did not yield their beliefs. The South's largest circulating periodical at that time, the *Southern Ruralist,* pinpointed the problem:

> The incontestable fact is that Jew and Gentile, white man and black man, Caucasian and Mongolian, live here side by side in perfect harmony, under normal conditions, the same as in most American communities. Let these relations be subjected to some sudden strain and the dormant prejudice flares up with explosive force. Such a strain resulted in the kindling of smoldering prejudice against the Jew who was accused of murdering a child of the dominant race.

> Let anyone who doubts the significance of this fact—or that prejudice has played an important part in this case—board an Atlanta street car filled with home-going working people, of the class to which the murdered girl belonged. Not a week ago we personally heard this remark under such circumstances: "If the Court don't hang that *damned Jew,* we will."[35]

Eventually the Frank case emerged as a national cause célèbre and Tom Watson, the champion of Georgia's antisemites, began attacking the Jew. His columns won superlative praise from followers, one of whom supplicated, "May God give you the power to keep the good work going on, until all the Protestants of this Nation can and will see what is coming upon us."[36]

II

There is yet another aspect of Jewish life in the South which is revealing. Jews are particularly concerned about their image in the Christian community. In city after city there are indications that Jews are especially interested in presenting themselves in the proper light. Many a southern rabbi is judged by the esteem that he possesses in the gentile community. Two examples may be used to illustrate this point.

In the 1930s Rabbi Benjamin Goldstein of Montgomery, Alabama's Temple Beth Or protested against the injustices heaped upon the Scottsboro boys (nine Negro youths accused of raping two white women). The boys had been tried and found guilty despite medical testimony which made the charge of rape absurd. The members of Goldstein's congregation demanded that he cease his public protestations of the court verdict or else resign from his position as the Temple's spiritual leader. He resigned. Subsequently members of the Temple freely admitted to newspaper reporters that they agreed with Rabbi Goldstein's remarks but viewed their airing as an "open threat to the welfare of the congregation."[37]

In Richmond, Dr. Edward N. Calisch, the most prominent Jew in the city during the first half of the twentieth century, devoted his life to creating an image of the assimilated Jew. He served on both community and Jewish councils and frequently exchanged pulpits with Protestant ministers. "In his relations with Christian neighbors," two observers have written, "the rabbi created in himself the most ingratiating of Jewish stereotypes—the man completely unaware of any personal problem as a Jew, at ease and unselfconscious, articulate but not argumentative, intelligent but not arrogant, worldly but not cynical." Dr. Calisch also helped found the American Council for Judaism, an anti-Zionist organization. Because southern gentiles showed no objection to the new group, members of his congregation, who may have been sympathetic to the Zionist cause, saw no reason to thwart his activities or ask for his resignation.[38]

In other southern communities Jews have employed different ways of winning their Christian neighbors' approval. In an essay on a pseudonymous "Southern City" in 1950, Joshua Fishbein pointed out that the leading Jews in the community never refused an invitation from a gentile. "When the Diehls get an invitation from a Christian friend," he wrote *they make sure to go* whether or not they have a headache or a previous engagement."[39] In another Deep South community the President of a Reform congregation told a reporter who had questioned the fact that the Jewish spiritual leader was being muzzled by his congregation: "I don't know where you get the idea our rabbi doesn't have freedom of the pulpit. We give him freedom of the pulpit— we just don't let him exercise it."[40]

The fear of antisemitism is pervasive among Jews in the twentieth century South. This sets the tone for a good deal of Jewish behavior in the region. Jews are very anxious not to stand out from everyone else. As Alfred Hero, Jr., author of *The Southerner and World Affairs,* has written:

> It was one thing for Judge X, descendant of several esteemed families of the region, leader in the Episcopal Church, and relative of the socially prominent in the Deep South, to write critical letters to the arch-conservative papers in the state, chair the discussion groups in the library on public issues, and inform all and sundry of his views on world affairs—people merely said he was getting old and was just another genteel eccentric. A Jew who did likewise

needed considerably more courage or less sensitivity to probable public reactions. The whole Jewish community might become a target for antagonism—other Jews would fear that one was risking the status of the entire ethnic group, and many local Jews felt that no one had any right to upset the delicate balance whereby Jews had been treated well and accepted generally as fellow Southerners.[41]

Jewish tradition dictates that Jews should speak up on issues about which they feel strongly. In the North this continues to be the case and many Jews have been outspoken advocates of controversial programs like integration, civil rights legislation, and firm adherence to constitutionally guaranteed civil liberties, not to mention opposition to the war in Vietnam. In the South it is rare for a Jew to support publicly controversial issues. The best example of this is the position taken by most Southern Jews on civil rights and integration. While many privately believe the Negro should have equal rights, few come out and say so.[42]

There are exceptions, of course. Rabbis Jacob Rothschild of Atlanta, Charles Mantinband of Alabama, Mississippi, and Texas, William Silverman of Nashville, Emmet Frank and Malcolm Stern when they were in Virginia, Perry Nussbaum of Jackson, Mississippi, and perhaps a few others, did not remain silent but, to varying degrees, spoke out against segregation. But each of them recognized that significant numbers of their congregants strongly opposed any remarks which might disturb members of the Christian community. Rabbi Frank labeled segregation a "sin," condemned Senator Harry Byrd and his followers for supporting "massive resistance" to federal integration orders, and even wrote, perhaps facetiously, that he expected "to have burning crosses on my lawn any night." Oldtimers in Rabbi Nussbaum's congregation called him "all kinds of names, 'Communist' being the least complimentary," while Rabbi Mantinband, whose own activities in behalf of integration surpassed, perhaps, those of every other southern Jew, noted that "Lillian Smith of Georgia speaks of a conspiracy of silence. This practically characterizes our [Southern] Rabbis and other Jewish leaders." And although Clarksdale, Mississippi's Rabbi Benjamin Schultz's 1962 statement that "What

America needs is more Mississippi, not less," may not represent Southern Jewish opinion, it is noteworthy that his congregation found him perfectly satisfactory and retained him as spiritual leader. Probably Rabbi Julian B. Feibelman's words, that on the segregation issue leadership for change "must come from the Christian group, where the problem centers," are most characteristic of the dominant Jewish attitude below the Mason-Dixon line.[43]

Desegregation has stirred many latent antagonisms in the south. Since 1954 Jewish temples have been bombed in Nashville, Atlanta, Birmingham, Miami, Jacksonville, and Jackson. In January 1967, Jewish gravestones in New Orleans were desecrated and marked "They Shall Die" and "Six Million—Was It Enough?"[44] In October 1968, an Orthodox rabbi in New York publicly stated that the civil rights issue "may well threaten the survival of the Jewish community in America":

> The reality is that Jews simply cannot speak their minds, openly and honestly, on such burning issues without jeopardizing Jewish lives. Every statement by the Northern liberal Jew for the civil rights of the Negro causes some Jew to suffer at the hands of White racists in the South.[45]

The fears about being different extend to other areas besides civil rights. Alfred Hero, Jr., discusses the reluctance of Jews to speak openly on issues which divide the community. He found strong pressures for conformity affecting almost every area of thought and behavior. Southern Jews, on the whole, although better versed on international affairs than their gentile neighbors, spoke out much less frequently on these issues than the Christians. In addition, because Jews accepted regional mores and feared social and economic repercussions, they were less well read, less intellectually alert, less cosmopolitan and more conservative than Jews of the same socioeconomic position in the North.[46]

Jewish suspicions of antisemitic attitudes in the South have been confirmed by a number of investigators. In 1966 Charles Y. Glock and Rodney Stark found Southern Baptists to be the single most antisemitic religious group in the nation. Only 8 percent of these Baptists were found free of antisemitic traits while 80 percent sincerely believed that "the Jews can never be forgiven for what they did to Jesus until they accept Him as the True Savior." Nationally only 33 percent of the Protestants and 14 percent of the Catholics surveyed shared this opinion.[47] At the Jewish-Southern Baptist Scholars Conference, held in Louisville, Kentucky, in August 1969, Baptist minister Bob Adams acknowledged, "It is probably and tragically only too true that many Southern Baptists are as anti-Semitic as their portrayal in the Glock and Stark report."[48]

Additional conformation for Southern prejudices comes from other sources. In a Gallup Poll, released in June 1967, respondents were asked whether they would vote for a Jew for President of the United States if he were a member of their political party and was in all other ways qualified. In the Midwest, West and North the respondents answered favorably over 87 percent of the time; in the south 33 percent of those queried said "no." That same year a survey of 2,000 people in North Carolina disclosed that between 25 percent and 50 percent of the people interviewed held "hostile religious images of modern Jews, regarding them as Christ-killers, beyond salvation, and in need of conversion to Christianity."[49] In a 1963 analysis of discrimination against Jews at resorts the nationwide figures averaged 9.8 percent while 20 percent of the establishments in North Carolina and Virginia barred Jews. At that time the only state with a higher rate of discrimination was Arizona. In 1971 *Newsweek* published a lengthy essay on "The American Jew." Most of the Jews quoted found life in this country quite comfortable. The only Southerner to give an opinion, a college senior in Houston, Texas, differed from the majority: "We're not accepted; we're tolerated."[50]

Although prejudice exists, discrimination toward Jews has diminished considerably since the end of the Second World War. There are a number of reasons for this. Perhaps the most important is the focus on black-white relations. With so much time and effort devoted to preventing integration there has been less concern with keeping Jews away also. Another factor is the growth of employment opportunities in the universities, in the government, and in science and technology. Expanding firms have tried to obtain employees with the necessary skills. For many jobs the demand has exceeded the supply, thus lessening discrimination against qualified applicants. The federal government, by law, does not discriminate and therefore new jobs provide opportunities for many minority group members. Government financed research projects also carry the stipulation that contractors must obey federal laws. As a result, Jews are as fully represented in Southern universities and scientific establishments as their talents and skills warrant. Genteel anti-Semitism still exists (Agnes Scott College in Atlanta did not hire a Jew to teach in the school until 1968)[51] but its impact is minimal.

It is difficult to say whether past experiences will continue to set the tone for the future. At present Jews are a dying breed in the rural and conservative South but are increasing in the cosmopolitan and growing urban areas. Altogether they constitute less than 1 percent of the entire southern population. Outside of Florida the ratio of Jews to the rest of the population has declined in every southern state since 1937. In six—Alabama, Arkansas, Kentucky, Louisiana, Mississippi and Tennessee—the total number of Jews is lower than it had been in 1927. In 1968, the total Jewish population in the South was 395,280, a figure only slightly higher than the Jewish population of New Jersey. Of these, slightly over 300,000 were concentrated in Florida, Georgia, Texas and Virginia. Many of these are migrants from the North attracted to the sunny climes of Florida, the regional centers of Dallas, Houston, and Atlanta, and in the case of federal government employees, the suburbs of Washington, D. C. in northern Virginia.[52]

Historically intermarriage between Jews and non-Jews has occurred frequently in the South. Rates of intermarriage vary according to time and place but have averaged somewhere between 10 and 40 percent.[53] Children of these unions are usually raised as Christians. With a high rate of intermarriage, a lower than average birth rate, and an older and more mobile population, the number of southern Jews is likely to continue declining in the future. Only a major wave of antisemitism or some other spectacular occurrence on the order of complete acceptance of Jews as Jews can prevent the dwindling of the southern Jewish population. Such contingencies do not appear imminent.

Notes

1. Among these are Bertram W. Korn, *The Early Jews of New Orleans* (Waltham: American Jewish Historical Society, 1969) and *American Jewry and the Civil War* (Philadelphia: The Jewish Publication Society of America, 1951); Jacob R. Marcus, *Early American Jewry: The Jews of Pennsylvania and the South* (Philadelphia: The Jewish Publication Society of America, 1953), and Charles Reznikoff and Uriah L. Engelman, *The Jews of Charleston* (Philadelphia: The Jewish Publication Society of America, 1950). Other studies include Isidor Blum, *The Jews of Baltimore* (Baltimore: Historical Review Publishing Company, 1910), and three books on the Leo Frank case: Charles and Louise Samuels, *Night Fell on Georgia* (New York: Dell, 1956), Harry Golden, *A Little Girl Is Dead* (Cleveland: World, 1965), and Leonard Dinnerstein, *The Leo Frank Case* (New York: Columbia University Press, 1968).

2. Merle Curti, *The Growth of American Thought* (New York: Harper, 1943), p. 51.

3. Marcus, *Early American Jewry*, p. 525.

4. Ibid., p. 523; Malcolm H. Stern, "New Light on the Jewish Settlement of Savannah," *American Jewish Historical Quarterly* (hereafter *AJHQ*) (March 1963) 52(3):169–99.

5. Marcus, *Early American Jewry*, p. 522.

6. Reznikoff and Engelman, *Jews of Charleston*, p. 17.

7. Ira Rosenswaike, "An Estimate and Analysis of the Jewish Population of the United States in 1790," *Publications of the American Jewish Historical Society* (hereafter *PAJHS*) (September 1960) 50(1):34.

8. Marcus, *Early American Jewry*, pp. 166–67, 180, 228, 231, 332–33, 521; Blum, *The Jews of Baltimore*, p. 5; Paul Masserman and Max Baker, *The Jews Come to America* (New York: Bloch, 1932), pp. 151–52; Anita Libman Lebeson, *Jewish Pioneers in America* (New York: Brentano's, 1931), p. 246.

9. Ibid., pp. 187, 245; Clement Eaton, *Freedom of Thought in the Old South* (New York: Peter Smith, 1951), p. 27; Harry Simonhoff, "Jews in Confederate Society," *The Chicago Jewish Forum* (Spring 1963) 21:209; *The Jewish Encyclopedia*, 2:113; Arthur W. Thompson, "David Yulee: A Study of Nineteenth-Century American Thought and Enterprise" (Ph.D. diss., Dept. of History, Columbia University, 1954), p. 9; Leon Hühner, "David L. Yulee, Florida's First Senator," *PAJHS* (1917) 25:18–19; and W. Darrell Overdyke, *The Know-Nothing Party in the South* (Baton Rouge: Louisiana State University Press, 1950), pp. 238, 278.

10. John Higham, "Social Discrimination Against Jews in America, 1830–1930," *PAJHS* (Sept., 1957) 47(1):3.

11. Bertram W. Korn, "Jews and Negro Slavery in the Old South, 1789–1865: An Address of the President," *PAJHS* (September 1957) 47(1):3.

12. Korn, "Factors Bearing Upon the Survival of Judaism in the Ante-Bellum Period.

13. Korn, *American Jewry and the Civil War*, p. 20. Robin Tanzman, "American Rabbis and the Slavery Question," unpublished essay, History Department, Columbia University, 1969.

14. Korn, *American Jewry and the Civil War*, p. 156.

15. Ibid., p. 157.

16. E. Merton Coulter, *The Confederate States of America* (Baton Rouge: Louisiana State University Press, 1950), p. 233.

17. *The New York Times*, June 7, 1871, p. 1.

18. Korn, *American Jewry and the Civil War*, p. 177; Hudson Strode, *Jefferson Davis: Confederate President* (New York: Harcourt, Brace, 1959), p. 150.

19. Quoted in Rudolph Glanz, *The Jew in the Old American Folklore* (New York, 1961), p. 54.

20. E. M. Coulter, *The South During Reconstruction* (Baton Rouge: Louisiana State University Press), p. 203.

21. *The American Israelite*, April 21, 1876, p. 5; *Menorah* (1887) 2:210–11; John Higham, *Strangers in the Land* (New Brunswick: Rutgers University Press, 1955), p. 92.

22. *The American Israelite*, December 5, 1873, p. 6; in *Donkle v. Kohn*, 44 *Georgia Reports* 266, 271. The Georgia Supreme Court overturned the courtroom decision, stating, "A belief in God and in a future state of rewards and punishments, has, by some Courts, been held necessary to render a witness competent. But a Jew is competent at common law." Dinnerstein, *Leo Frank Case*, p. 68.

23. Margaret L. Coit, *Mr. Baruch* (Boston: Houghton Mifflin, 1957), pp. 24, 26; Harold U. Ribalow, ed., *Autobiographies of American Jews* (Philadelphia: The Jewish Publication Society of America, 1965), p. 133; Stanley F. Chyet, "Ludwig Lewisohn in Charleston (1802–1903," *AJHQ* (March 1965) 54(3):302.

24. Selig Adler, "Zebulon B. Vance and the 'Scattered Nation,' " *Journal of Southern History* (1941) 7:357–77; John Higham, "Social Discrimination Against Jews," *PAJHS* (September 1957) 47(1):7.

25. *The American Hebrew* (April 4, 1890) 42:191.

26. Ibid.

27. Ibid., pp. 196–97.

28. No attempt will be made here to isolate the Populists for special treatment. I do not believe that antisemitism in the South was a Populist phenomenon. The most extensive discussions, and refutations, of alleged Populist antisemitism have been based solely upon the expressions of northern and western Populists. See, for example, Richard Hofstadter, *The Age of Reform* (New York: Alfred A. Knopf, 1955); Norman Pollack, "Hofstadter on Populism: A Critique of 'the Age of Reform,' " *Journal of Southern History* (1960), vol 21; Pollack, *The Populist Response to Industrial America* (Cambridge: Harvard University Press, 1962); W. T. K. Nugent, *The Tolerant Populists* (Chicago: University of Chicago Press, 1963); Frederic Cople Jaher, *Doubters and Dissenters* (New York: Free Press, 1964); V. C. Ferkiss, "Populist Influences on American Fascism," *Western Political Quarterly* (1957). C. Vann Woodward has written the most insightful analyses of southern Populists, but an examination of his works fails to disclose any pronounced antisemitism among members of this group in the 1890s, C. Vann Woodward, *Origins of the New South* (Baton Rouge: Louisiana State University Press, 1951), ch. 9; and "The Populist Heritage and the Intellectual," *The American Scholar* (1959–60) 21:55–72.

29. Edward Flower, "Anti-Semitism in the Free Silver and Populist movements and the Election of 1896" (M.A. thesis, History Department, Columbia University, 1952), p. 36; Golden, *A Little Girl Is Dead* p. 226.

30. Leonard Dinnerstein and Frederic Cople Jaher, eds., *The Aliens: A History of Ethnic Minorities in America* (New York: Appleton-Century-Crofts, 1970), pp. 8–9; *Jewish Sentiment*, November 26, 1897, p. 3.

31. Dinnerstein, *The Leo Frank Case*, pp. 7–9.

32. Horace M. Kallen, "The Ethics of Zionism," *The Maccabean* (August 1906) 11:69;

Lucian Lamar Knight, *Reminiscences of Famous Georgians* (Atlanta: Franklin Turner, 1907) 1:512.

33. *The Atlanta Georgian*, May 28, 1913, p. 3.

34. *The Atlanta Journal*, July 20, 1913, magazine section p. 10.

35. *Southern Ruralist*, March 15, 1914, clipping located among the Leo Frank papers (American Jewish Archives, Cincinnati).

36. *The Jeffersonian*, May 7, 1914, p. 4.

37. Dan T. Carter, *Scottsboro* (Baton Rouge: Louisiana State University Press, 1969), pp. 258–599.

38. David and Adele Bernstein, "Slow Revolution in Richmond, VA.," *Commentary* (1949) 8:539–46.

39. Joshua A. Fishman, "Southern City," *Midstream* (Summer 1961) 7:41.

40. Albert Vorspan, "The Dilemma of the Southern Jew," *The Reconstructionist* (January 9, 1959) 24:7.

41. Alfred O. Hero Jr., *The Southerner and World Affairs* (Baton Rouge: Louisiana State University Press, 1965), p. 499.

42. Hero writes, "Growing insecurity has tended to silence many thoughtful Jews, particularly on the race issue and national and international questions with racial overtones, but also indirectly in other controversial fields as well," ibid., p. 494. In Waycross, Georgia, James Lebeau has noted, "those who hold liberal views [on integration] do not discuss them freely." "Profile of a Southern Jewish Community: Waycross, Georgia," *AJHQ* (June 1969) 58(4):442.

43. Ruth Silberstein, "A Southern Rabbi Takes a Stand," *Congress Weekly*, January 20, 1958, p. 7; Perry E. Nussbaum, "And Then There Was One—In the Capital City of Mississippi," *CCAR Journal* (October 1963):15–19; "Jacob Rothschild's Sermons," microfilm no. 1032, American Jewish Archives, Cincinnati (hereafter AJA), and the following letters in AJA: Malcolm Stern to Albert Vorspan, October 2, 1958; Malcolm H. Stern to Gabriel Cohen, December 26, 1958; Charles Mantinband to J. L. Marcus, December 9, 1960. Also, boxes 2335 and 2143 of Rabbi Emmet Frank's papers at AJA; newspaper clippings in box 2800; Rabbi Julian B. Feibelman to J. L. Marcus, January 17, 1956, Nearprint File, AJA; and Perry Nussbaum to J. L. Marcus, October 23, 1961, misc. folder of correspondence relating to Freedom Riders, AJA. In addition, Bill Kovach, reporter for *The New York Times* and formerly of the *Nashville Tennessean* wrote to the author: "Following the trail of civil rights workers through Tennessee, Georgia, the Carolinas and Alabama, I was personally impressed with the number of Jews who acted as individuals in support of the Negroes' pursuit of equal rights." Kovach to L.D., October 28, 1968.

44. Benjamin Kaplan, "Jews and Social Equality," in Belden Menkus, ed., *Meet the American Jew* (Nashville: Broadman Press, 1963), p. 141; *New York Post*, December 6, 1967, p. 52. *American Jewish Yearbook* (1968) 69:237.

45. "American Jewry Divided on Strategy," *The Reconstructionist* (November 22, 1968) 34:4.

46. Hero, *Southerner and World Affairs*, pp. 475–77 and 502–3.

47. Charles Y. Glock and Rodney Stark, *Christian Beliefs and Anti-Semitism* (New York: Harper and Row, 1966), pp. 63, 202; Arthur Gilbert, "Prejudice and Social Justice" (paper presented at Jewish-Southern Baptist Scholars Conference held in Louisville, August 20, 1969), p. 3.

48. Bob Adams, "Christians, Racism and Anti-Semitism" (paper delivered at conference cited above), p. 5.

49. *American Jewish Yearbook* (1968) 59:234; (1967)58:67.

50. C. Bezalel Sherman "In the American Jewish Community," *Jewish Frontier* (April 1964) 31:19; "The American Jews Today," *Newsweek,* March 1, 1971, p. 63.

51. Pat Watters, *The South and the Nation* (New York: Pantheon Books, 1969), p. 158.

52. *American Jewish Yearbook* (1930–31) 32:220; (1940–41) 220:227–8; (1968) 59:282–83.

53. Arnold Schwartz, "Intermarriage in the United States," *American Jewish Yearbook* (1970) 71:104–5; and Erich Rosenthal, "Studies of Jewish Intermarriage in the United States," ibid. (1963) 54:3–53. For other comments and statistics on intermarriage in the South, see Marcus, *Early American Jewry,* p. 504; John Higham, "American Anti-Semitism Historically Reconsidered," in Charles Herbert Stember, ed., *Jews in the Mind of America* (New York: Basic Books, 1966), p. 243; Benjamin Kaplan, *The Eternal Stranger* (New York: Bookman Associates, 1957), p. 85; Harry L. Golden, "The Jews of the South," *Congress Weekly* (December 31, 1951) 18:9; Lebeson, *Jewish Pioneers in America,* p. 310; Harry Simonhoff, "Jews in Confederate Society," *The Chicago Jewish Forum* (Spring 1963) 21:208–12; Reznikoff and Engelman, *Jews of Charleston,* p. 239; and Leonard J. Fein, "Some Consequences of Jewish Intermarriage," *Jewish Social Studies* (January 1971) 33:44–58.

6

Atlanta
in the Progressive Era:
A Dreyfus Affair
in Georgia

Frustration and disillusionment with the rapid social changes caused by the industrial transformation at the end of the nineteenth century set off racial attacks in the United States and Europe. Alfred Dreyfus, Mendel Beiliss, the Haymarket anarchists, and Sacco and Vanzetti were all aliens victimized by societies undergoing rapid conversion. Jews, Italians, Germans, immigrants, anyone, in fact who deviated from the ethnic norm easily served as a scapegoat for the turmoil accompanying industrialism. Barbara Tuchman attributed antisemitism in France to "building tensions between classes and among nations. Industrialization, imperialism, the growth of cities, the decline of the countryside, the power of money and the power of machines . . . churning like the bowels of a volcano about to erupt." To a considerable extent, many of these same forces—in greater or lesser degree—also applied in Kiev, Chicago, and Boston. In Russia, Maurice Samuel tells us, "the Beiliss case was mounted by men who hoped by means of it to strengthen the autocracy and to crush the liberal spirit that was reviving after the defeat of the 1905 revolution." In Chicago, fear of foreigners, social revolution, and labor ascen-

dency triggered the vigilante response to eight immigrant anarchists charged with the bomb-throwing incident in Haymarket
Square. "A biased jury, a prejudiced judge, perjured evidence,
extraordinary and indefensible theory of conspiracy, and the temper of Chicago led to the conviction. The evidence never proved
the guilt." Sacco and Vanzetti, atheists, labor agitators, and "Reds"
of Italian birth, were convicted of robbery and murder in Dedham,
Massachusetts in 1920. The case made by the prosecution led
many observers to believe in the innocence of the defendants, but
the jury foreman allegedly concluded, "Damn them, they ought
to hang anyway."[1]

Social bias played a crucial role in obtaining the convictions
described above. The industrial transformation of society uprooted
too many too quickly, and made those caught up in the whirlpool
of change cling all the more tightly to their old ways. Situations
that might have been tolerated or handled differently in more
stable societies seemed like conspiratorial attempts to undermine
civilization. Dreyfus, Beiliss, the Haymarket anarchists, and Sacco
and Vanzetti symbolized unwelcome innovations. So, too, did Leo
Frank, a Jew upon whom Atlantans would vent their unveiled,
nervous tensions in 1913.

I

Atlanta was not spared the problems that industrialism brought
to other cities. Indeed the traditions of southern culture intensified
the burden of social change. Typical of most American cities during
the Progressive era, Atlanta's population practically doubled between 1900 and 1913 (89,870 to 173,713). The population in
other urban areas in the United States also increased at an impressive rate during the first decade of the twentieth century. In
the South, though, of cities with populations over 100,000, only
Birmingham outpaced Atlanta's population spurt between 1900
and 1910.[2] Newly established industrial enterprises offered jobs
to all comers. Although urban conditions were better than rural
squalor, the city fell far short of the industrialists' promise of the

good life. Large groups of recently displaced Georgia crackers mingled uneasily with each other and with the foreign immigrants who wore strange costumes and spoke unintelligible tongues. In the concrete jungle, the newcomers worked together in the most menial jobs and congregated in the least desirable housing. Although foreigners comprised less than 3 percent of the city's residents,[3] the few Europeans loomed as a great menace to those many southerners who retained strong feelings about racial purity and community homogeneity.

Working conditions in Atlanta compared unfavorably with those in other parts of the country.[4] Despite a periodic shortage of workers, factory wages were low and hours long. The normal work week lasted sixty-six hours, and, except for Saturday, the working day generally extended from 6 A.M. to 6 P.M. with only a half hour for lunch.[5] In 1902, the average wage-earner took home less than $300 a year. Atlanta's Commissioner of Public Works commented that the prevailing wages did not enable the men in his department to provide even the minimum necessities for their families.[6] By 1912, when average earnings rose to $464[7] living costs had increased correspondingly and Atlanta's relief warden reported a record number of public assistance applications. "Even where women and children worked," he observed, "the money they receive is not enough for their support." There are too many people on the ragged edge of poverty and suffering," the warden concluded.[8] A year later, some children still earned 22 cents a week for their labor in the city.[9]

Atlanta's unplanned growth plagued officials and created problems similar to those in other cities at the time. Health hazards abounded, educational facilities were found wanting, and recreational outlets could not increase fast enough to service the burgeoning population. As late as 1912, for example, Atlanta provided no public swimming pools or parks for its Negro citizens. An overabundance of gambling dens, dope dives, and brothels, on the other hand, beckoned both whites and Negroes who sought to escape from factory drudgery and dingy tenements. On a number of occasions, in fact, the Mayor of Atlanta, James G. Woodward, "disgraced the city . . . by public drunkenness." His private conduct, however, proved no political liability. Woodward received a third renomination after being "found in a state of intoxication in the red light district of the city."[10]

Living conditions were no better than public facilities. In 1910, there were only 30,308 dwelling units for 35,813 families. Eighty-two miles, or more than half of the city's residential streets, existed without water mains and more than 50,000 people—over a third of the population—were forced to live in areas of the city not served by sewers. A continuous fog of soot and smoke irritated people's lungs and eyes, and an appalling number of urban dwellers suffered from ill health. Ninety percent of the city's prisoners in 1902 were syphilitic.[11] Wherever records were kept, the statistics indicated that the problems grew worse during the next decade, rather than better. A comparison of the number of residents afflicted by disease in 1904 and 1911, when the city's population had increased by only 64 percent, showed that cases of diphtheria had increased by 347 percent, typhoid by 307 percent, and tuberculosis by 602 percent.[12]

Atlanta also suffered an above average death rate. A United States census report for 1905 noted that of 388 cities in this country, only 12 had more deaths per thousand persons than Georgia's capital. In 1911, Atlanta's figures still exceeded the national average by almost 40 percent (13.9 to 18.75 per thousand). A year earlier, sixty-nine people had died from pellagra, a vitamin deficiency prevalent among the poor. This was more than triple the figure for any other city in the country. Birmingham and Charleston, S.C., the two cities that ranked second to the Georgian metropolis, reported only seventeen deaths from the illness in 1910. The situation did not improve much in succeeding years. In 1914 the United Textile Workers complained that far too many Atlanta children still fell victim to the disease. Although exact statistics for all ailments are difficult to obtain, industrialism provided its share of fatal illness. One Georgian official reported in 1912, "occupational diseases are much more common than is believed true. Lead, arsenic and phosphorous poisoning have caused much suffering and many deaths."[13]

The crime rate in Atlanta highlighted the stresses of the

new urbanites. In 1905, Atlanta policemen arrested more children for disturbing the peace than did those in any other municipality in the United States. Two years later, only New York, Chicago, and Baltimore, cities with considerably larger populations, exceeded Atlanta's figure for children arrested. That very year, the police booked 17,000 persons out of a total population of 102,702. The Mayor found the statistic "appalling." "It places Atlanta," he said, "at or near the top of the list of cities of this country in criminal statistics."[14]

The police force, another city institution overwhelmed by the population spurt, proved unable to grapple with the new problems thrust upon it. The major reasons for its incapacity were inadequate staffing and facilities. In 1912, the Mayor acknowledged that two hundred men were unable to protect the city, "and, as a result, the residential sections cannot be effectively policed." Atlanta, alone among American cities whose area exceeded twenty-five square miles, existed with only one police station and no substations.[15]

Besides the pathological conditions that menaced the growing city, the southern heritage also conditioned the crackers'[16] reaction to the enormous differences in urban living. Of all the sections in the country, none has been so tied to the past as has the South. W. J. Cash characterized this southern revulsion to change as "the savage ideal—the patriotic will to hold rigidly to the ancient pattern, to repudiate innovation, in thought and behavior, whatever came from outside and was felt as belonging to Yankeedom or alien parts."[17]

The race riot that erupted in Atlanta in 1906 was an example of the periodic explosions of violence that occurred when transplanted rural dwellers rebelled against the drudgery and disruptiveness of their new urban existence. Rampaging white mobs attacked Negroes with abandon. Before the National Guard successfully quelled the rioters several days later, twelve people had been killed (two white and ten black) and seventy had been injured (ten white and sixty black). The riot had been incited by sensational newspaper reports exaggerating black assaults upon white women. These incendiary statements were published a few weeks after Hoke Smith had whipped up popular passions in his racist campaign for the gubernatorial nomination. Subsequent explanations blamed the newspapers for the outburst, but the press could not be held responsible for the poverty and squalor of the new urban masses. One "educated negro" shrewdly noted that recently arrived rural whites resented the relative prosperity of black business people in the city. A national reporter spoke more bluntly in calling Atlanta "one of the very worst of American cities" filled with the "riff-raff that the mining towns of the West used to relieve us of."[18] In either case, the exacerbated race relations in Atlanta focused national attention upon the city. The upheaval was obviously an admission that discontent with city life had become unbearable for the erstwhile rural folk.[19]

The conservative nature of the dominant religious groups in the South compounded the difficulties of adjustment to urban life. No secular influence of any kind, C. Vann Woodward has attested, had the power to sway men's thoughts with as much vigor as did those who allegedly spoke with the authority of God.[20] Baptists and Methodists, the two largest denominations in the South since colonial times, have, for the most part, preached a Fundamentalist creed that opposed change, glorified the past, and uttered invectives against aliens of any stripe. During the nineteenth century, these sects "became centers of conservative political sentiment and of resistance both to the invasion of northern culture and to the doctrine of the New South." Their allegiance to the past and fundamental theological beliefs continued well into the twentieth century.[21]

The great bedrock of Fundamentalist support came from the rural population. When these people moved into the towns and cities, they brought their ministers along with them. Many of the Fundamentalist preachers, who had earlier railed against urban wickedness, "continued to regard the great city centers as 'jungle areas' no less pagan than the Congo, and looked upon themselves as life-saving missionaries."[22] Southern ministers also eyed the new industrialists with great suspicion. Among Methodists, both "pulpit and press inveighed against corporate wealth for denying labor a living wage,"[23] while Baptist objections "to industrialization arose from the fear that industry would lead to rapid urbanization which in turn would corrupt the morals of the people and hinder the spread of Christianity."[24]

The Fundamentalists stressed the godliness of maintaining the homely virtues and living a simple, agricultural life. They also believed in a literal obedience of God's word. In fact, they considered adherence to scriptural instruction as man's most sacred duty. Their preachers continually railed against modern innovations and warned parishioners that dancing, card-playing and theater-going undermined Christian teaching. The Fundamentalists also abhorred the alteration of woman's traditional role. She belonged in the home, they believed, and any changes in her position must invariably lead to a loosening of Christian morality.

The Fundamentalists hoped to stem the floodtide of progress by condemning social change as blasphemy against God's revealed word. This resistance, although unsuccessful, complicated and delayed adjustments to modern times. Anyone and anything that violated their own literal interpretation of the Bible became subject to assault. Violence frequently accompanied accusations. The self-righteous crusade to restore the simple, godly life often justified the use of weapons against those who dissented.

Southern Baptists also considered the influx of immigrants one of the great dangers of modern times. During the 1880s, southern Baptist periodicals expressed concern with the foreigners whom they regarded as "a threat to American customs and traditions." Many Baptist editors attributed the moral corruption of the nation to the newcomers and felt that national good demanded a cessation of our traditional open-door policy. One spokesman enunciated his anxieties at the Southern Baptist Convention in 1895: "Foreigners are accumulating in our cities, and hence our cities are the storm centers of the nation. But the great misfortune of all of this is that these foreigners bring along with them their anarchy, their Romanism, and their want of morals."[25]

In his analysis of southern mores, W. J. Cash perceptively summarized the Fundamentalists' demands. They wanted "absolute conformity to the ancient pattern under the pains and penalties of the most rigid intolerance; the maintenance of the savage ideal, to the end of vindicating the old Southern will to cling fast to its historical way."[26]

Despite the pervasive influence of the Fundamentalist creeds and the inherent southern hostility toward innovation, the leaders of the new South—the railroad magnates and the owners of cotton mills and factories—endeavored to build an industrial community patterned after the North. To a considerable extent they succeeded and "by 1900 the industrialization of the South had become largely a case of capital seeking labor supply." Atlanta's *Journal* succinctly expressed the prevailing need: "The Southern States have reached a point in their industrial progress where the work necessary . . . can not be done by the present force of workers. . . . The South needs more folks—folks for the farm, folks for the factory." In Georgia, for example, it was said that without immigrant labor, the development of the iron and cotton mills and the building of the railroads would have to be halted.[27]

The desperate plight of industry forced southern state governments to establish immigration bureaus in the hope of attracting suitable laborers. But most southerners were quite specific as to whom they would welcome. Senator Ben Tillman of South Carolina announced "We do not want European paupers to come to the South." Tennessee's Governor Ben Hooper expressed his opposition to receiving the "motley mass of humanity that is being dumped upon our shores. . . ." And Georgia's Federation of Labor "objected to 'flooding' the South and Georgia with a population composed of the scum of Europe. . . ." Atlanta's two major newspapers stated their preferences clearly. The *Journal* desired persons of Teutonic, Celtic, and Scandinavian origins, "peoples near akin to [our] own by blood, and capable of full assimilation. . . ." And *The Constitution* editorialized, "The German makes a splendid citizen."[28]

Unfortunately for both the South and the arriving immigrants, most of the newcomers were from eastern and southern Europe. They were treated, for the most part, with conspicuous inhospitality. In some sections, Italians, or " 'dagoes' were regarded as about on a par with 'niggers,' and the treatment of them corresponded."[29] In 1891, eleven Italians were lynched in New

Orleans after three of them had been acquitted of murdering the police chief. Five years later, three Italians suspected of homicide were strung up in Hahnville, Louisiana. In 1899, five Italians were lynched in Tallulah, Louisiana, after injuring a doctor in a quarrel over a goat. The twentieth century had hardly begun when three more Italians were mysteriously shot in Erwin, Mississippi. Czechs and Slovaks established a colony south of Petersburg, Virginia, in the nineteenth century, yet forty years after their arrival, the "natives" still resented their presence.[30]

In Atlanta, the single largest influx of immigrants was 1,342 Russian Jews who constituted 25 percent of the city's foreign-born in 1910.[31] Although this group made up less than 1 per cent of the population, it was well-known that they ran a large percentage of the saloons, pawnshops, and restaurants catering to black trade. The Jews were viewed contemptuously by other whites. One reporter wrote, "as to the white foreigners who cater to negro [sic] trade and negro [sic] vice . . . it is left to the judgement of the reader which is of the higher grade in the social scale, the proprietors or their customers." Sensual pictures of nude white women allegedly decorated the walls of the saloons, and some people even thought that the liquor bottle labels aroused the Negroes' worst passions. Many Atlantans thought that the beer parlors "served as the gathering and hatching place of criminal negroes." When the patrons got drunk and caused social disturbances, the nearby whites blamed the saloon owners for the mischief. One analyst of the 1906 riot, for example, observed, "It was the low dives where mean whiskey was sold to Negroes by whites that bred the criminality which furnished an excuse for the outbreak of the mob; and it was from the doors of the saloon that the ruffians of the mob poured forth to do their deadly work on the innocent."[32]

Although Jews had been in the South since colonial times, they had never been accepted by the dominant Protestant community. To be sure, opportunities to assimilate existed, but those who desired to retain their faith suffered restrictions upon their political and religious liberties. Denial of the trinity, for example, had subjected Jews to imprisonment in Virginia and Maryland in the colonial era. Therefore, Jews did not settle in Maryland until after the American Revolution. Virginia, on the other hand, did not permit Jews to enter the colony without express permission. Georgia granted Jews political and religious equality in 1798, but not until 1826 were Jews allowed to vote in Maryland. Although John Locke's original Constitution for the Carolinas provided for toleration, both North and South Carolina deprived Jews of their political rights. A South Carolina law of 1759 barred non-Protestants from holding office and the North Carolina Constitution of 1776 forbade them to vote. A Jew elected to the North Carolina Legislature in 1809 was challenged, upon taking his seat, but defended himself successfully. A Constitutional Convention, however, banned all Jews from holding office in the Tar Heel State in 1835, and the restriction remained in effect until 1868. In 1818, in a letter to the Jewish editor of a New York City newspaper, Thomas Jefferson acknowledged "the prejudice still scowling on your sect of our religion. . . ."[33]

Despite restrictions on office holding, concerted anti-Jewish prejudice did not occur in the South until the Civil War era. During this period, however, Jews did become scapegoats for Confederate frustrations. They were accused of being "merciless speculators, army slackers, and blockade-runners across the land frontiers to the North." One southern newspaper observed, "all that the Jew possesses is a plentiful lot of money together with the scorn of the world."[34]

Some Georgia towns singled out the Jews as the cause of their woes. In 1862, 103 citizens of Thomasville resolved to banish all Jewish residents and a grand jury in Talbotton found the Jews guilty of " 'evil and unpatriotic conduct.' " Talbotton prejudices, in fact, forced the Lazarus Straus family—later to become famous for its development of Macy's department store in New York City—to leave Georgia during the Civil War.[35]

The next major antisemitic eruption occurred in the 1890s. The Populist crusade, the severe economic depression of 1893, and the squalid living conditions in urban slums all helped to intensify hostility toward those who loomed, on the one hand, as the seeming monopolizers of material possessions, and on the other, as the manipulators who unfeelingly deprived the people of their purchasing power. In Georgia, for example, it was "quite the fashion to characterize the Jew as exacting his interest down to the last drachma."[36]

Accusations of financial manipulation gave rise to suspicion of a vast Jewish international conspiracy. One writer, in fact, concluded that the "Rothschild combination has proceeded in the last twenty years with marvellous rapidity to enslave the human race." In North Carolina, Elias Carr, Governor from 1893 to 1897, frequently reiterated his point that "Our Negro brethren, too, are being held in bondage by Rothschild."[37]

When rural southerners flocked to the cities at the end of the nineteenth century, their impressions of the Jew combined traditional stereotypes of financial wiliness with the time-worn southern prejudices. In 1906, Horace M. Kallen, the Jewish philosopher, observed that "there is already a very pretty Jewish problem in our South. . . ." William Robertson, author of *The Changing South*, later noted, "It was enough for Jews to prosper right under [southern] noses, without affording the added insult of being the descendants of the murderers of Christ."[38]

A lack of scholarly studies makes it risky to generalize about antisemitism in the South or to suggest regional differences. The two most prominent historians who have investigated American attitudes toward Jews in the nineteenth and twentieth centuries—Oscar Handlin and John Higham—have found evidence supporting positive and negative judgments.[39] Both historians, however, dealt primarily with northern experiences and provided relatively few examples from southern states. Studies about alleged Populist antisemitism, moreover, have concentrated almost entirely on the expressions of northern and western agrarians.[40] There are no indications, for example, that Tom Watson, the Georgia leader, engaged in any antisemitic diatribes in his Populist heyday.

A significant clue to southern attitudes may be garnered, however, from Higham's findings. He noted that American antisemitism was deeply ingrained in the agrarian tradition—which was suspect of urban prosperity based upon the toil of others—and cropped up most frequently in times of crisis. "The prophets of anti-Semitism," Higham continued, "were alienated and often despairing critics of the power of money in American society," and frequently attributed their own woes to the "lords of finance and trade": banks, moneylenders, and bond-holders. He discovered, moreover, that hostility toward Jews in this country was strongest in those sectors of the population where there were relatively few Jews and where "a particularly explosive combination of social discontent and nationalistic aggression prevailed."[41] Finally, he found nationalistic fervor "most widespread and in many ways most intense in the small town culture of the South and West."[42] The South was the least urbanized and most discontented region in the United States. Consequently, if Higham's conclusions are accurate, the South must figure as the most antisemitic area in the country.

Certain aspects of southern culture—aside from the squalor that existed in Atlanta and other fledgling urban areas—tended to make the natives react more violently to Jews than did residents of the North and West. Southerners were more inbred than were northerners and were therefore more concerned with the purity of their Anglo-Saxon heritage.[43] Religious fundamentalism, another force that encouraged antisemitism, was more widespread in the South than the North. According to William J. Robertson, most southern Methodists and Baptists were advised by their spiritual leaders that Jews were "Christkillers."[44] Social instability accompanied by personal anxiety was the final factor that intensified regional hostility toward Jews. Throughout history, the position of the Jews has reflected the degree of security prevailing in a given society. They have frequently been blamed for defeats, depressions, and other disruptive crises.[45] Southerners, notoriously insecure and continually on the defensive, seized upon hatred for Jews as one outlet for the frustrations of their existence.

The above mentioned factors existed, to some extent, in different parts of the North as well, and antisemitism appeared among different northern groups. But despite temporary interludes of cataclysm and depression, most northerners expected progress to improve the conditions of life. Many southerners, however, clung to fantasies of past heroics to compensate for a

forbidding contemporary life, and looked upon change as sub-
verting cherished values.

It is against this complex background of social change and
the resistance it engendered that the murder of a thirteen-year-
old girl, in 1913, triggered a violent reaction of mass aggression,
hysteria, and prejudice.

II

Mary Phagan had been found dead and disfigured in the basement
of the National Pencil Factory by a black nightwatchman at 3 A.M.
on April 27, 1913.[46] Near her body lay two notes, purportedly
written by the girl while being slain. They read:

> Mam that negro hire down here did this i went to make water and
> he push me down that hole a long tall negro black that hoo it wase
> long tall negro i wright while play with me.

> he said he wood love me land down play like the night witch did
> it but that long tall black negro did but his slef.[47]

Georgia, and particularly Atlanta, newspapers milked every
ounce of sensationalism that they could from the tragedy. One
daily indicated that the "horrible mutilation of the body of Mary
Phagan proves that the child was in the hands of a beast unspeakable,"[48] while the editors of another added: "Homicide is bad
enough. Criminal assault upon a woman is worse. When a mere
child, a little girl in knee dresses, is the victim of both, there are
added elements of horror and degeneracy that defy the written
word."[49]

An aroused public demanded vengeance. One of the victim's neighbors remarked to a reporter, "I wouldn't have liked to
be held responsible for the fate of the murderer of little Mary
Phagan if the men in this neighborhood got hold of him last night."
The minister of Atlanta's Second Baptist Church thundered, "The
very existence of God seems to demand that for the honor of the
universe the murderer must be exposed."[50]

Atlanta's inadequate police force was under intense pressure to find the culprit. Aside from being understaffed, the force left much to be desired in terms of intelligent action. They had been accustomed to a slower pace and simpler life and their inability to handle the problems of an industrial metropolis made them rely increasingly on an irrational use of power. On one occasion, for example, when Atlanta had experienced a labor shortage, the police attempted to rectify the condition by arresting all able-bodied men found on one of the main streets. Employed and unemployed, black and white, were hauled into court, fined, and sentenced to the stockade without being given a chance to defend themselves. One man so punished had been in the city for only three days. Neither relatives nor employers were notified of the round-up or the sentencing.[51]

The police also had a poor record for solving crimes. A few years before Mary Phagan's death, a national periodical had revealed that only one murder in one hundred was ever punished in Georgia.[52] Atlanta policemen allegedly used brutality with those people who were picked up. In 1909, they were accused of beating one Negro to death and chaining a white girl to the wall until she frothed at the mouth. In 1910 a commission investigating prison conditions in the city uncovered "stories too horrible to be told in print."[53] During 1912–13, more than a dozen unsolved murders tried the public's patience.[54] Because these victims had been black, there had been no great protestations over the constables' inefficiency. But Mary Phagan was, as a Georgian so characteristically put it, "our folks."[55] Failure this time would not be tolerated.

A great deal of action seemed to be taking place at the police station. Seven people were arrested, and although four were quickly released, three were still held on suspicion, including the black nightwatchman who had discovered the corpse. Of the trio, the one upon whom suspicion quickly fell was Leo Frank, the superintendent of the National Pencil Factory where Mary Phagan had been employed and where her body had been found.

When the police had first questioned Frank, he appeared quite nervous and overwrought. From him, they discovered that Mary Phagan had come to pick up her pay shortly after noon on April 26—Confederate Memorial Day. The superintendent admitted having been alone in his office, and having paid the girl her $1.20 in wages for the ten hours that she had worked that week. Mary had then left his office, and no one else ever admitted to having seen her alive again.[56]

The day after the corpse had been discovered, strands of hair "identified positively"[57] as Mary Phagan's, and blood stains, were found in a metal workroom opposite Frank's office. The night watchman had also told the police that Frank had asked him to come in early on the day of the girl's death, but dismissed him when he arrived and ordered him to return at the normal time. Frank's uneasy behavior before the police and the pressure from an hysterical public led to his arrest.[58]

Leo Max Frank, although born in Texas, in 1884, had been reared in Brooklyn and educated at Cornell University. His first position had been with a firm in a Boston suburb, and he did not settle in the South until 1907. Once in Atlanta, however, he planned to stay. He married Lucille Selig, daughter of one of the more prominent Jewish families in the city, and was popular enough to be elected president of the local chapter of the B'nai B'rith in 1912.[59]

The arrest of the northern, Jewish industrialist won the approval of Atlanta's citizenry. Rumors spread that the prison might be stormed and the prisoners, Frank and the nightwatchman, Newt Lee, lynched.[60] Street talk had it that one of the two must be guilty and killing both would avenge the murder. The *Atlanta Constitution* cautioned its readers to "Keep An Open Mind." "Nothing can be more unjust nor more repugnant to the popular sense of justice," its editorial read, "than to convict even by hearsay an innocent man."[61] The advice went unheeded.

The furor that erupted after the murder can largely be attributed to the deed having rekindled the residents' awareness of the harshness of their lives; having reawakened traditional southern resentment toward outsiders who violated southern mores; and having, once again, dramatized the inherent iniquities of industrial life. "What was uppermost in the minds of those who were indignant," the *Outlook* reflected in 1915, "was the fact that the accused represented the employing class, while the victim was an employee."[62] And the Jew, more than the Negro, provided a symbol for the grievances against industrial capitalism and its byproduct, urbanism. The Baptist Minister of Mary Phagan's church made the conventional southern identification of Jewishness, evil, the stranger, and hated northern industrialism when he recalled: "[My] own feelings upon the arrest of the old Negro nightwatchman, were to the effect that this one old Negro would be poor atonement for the life of this innocent girl. But, when on the next day, the police arrested a Jew, and a Yankee Jew at that, all of the inborn prejudice against Jews rose up in a feeling of satisfaction, that here would be a victim worthy to pay for the crime."[63]

The employment of minors in factories particularly aroused the ire of Atlanta's residents. A spokesman for those crusading to restrict child labor viewed Mary Phagan's death as the inevitable consequence of industrial perfidy: "If social conditions, if factory conditions in Atlanta, were what they should be here, if children of tender years were not forced to work in shops, this frightful tragedy could not have been enacted." The antagonism and venom harbored toward the entrepreneurs and their characteristically inhumane attitudes found expression in Atlanta's *Journal of Labor:* "Mary Phagan is a martyr to the greed for gain which has grown up in our complex civilization, and which sees in the girls and children merely a source of exploitation in the shape of cheap labor. . . ." The *Southern Ruralist,* Atlanta's largest circulating periodical, also interpreted the slaying as the product of a heartless and cruel society. It branded "every Southern legislator" who thereafter refused to vote for laws prohibiting the employment of children in factories, "as a potential murderer."[64]

There were other reasons for resenting the factories. White females had always been placed on a pedestal, to be worshipped, exalted, and protected. To southerners they embodied the purity and nobility of the South itself. Considered a "queen worthy of honor [and] deserving protection from the contamination of a man's world," the white woman had to be zealously guarded from the evils of society.[65]

Industrialism, however, had inaugurated factory work for

women. Since tradition dictated that women belonged in the
home, southern society regarded the change as subversive of regional honor and family ties. Few white men accepted the alteration without qualms. They may have felt unmanned because
they could not maintain their families without an additional income—a feeling particularly disturbing in a society that had always emphasized virility. Guilt was also aroused in the
traditionalist southern conscience because the factory system
forced wives and daughters to come in contact with strange men.
The Southern Baptists, it is said, had an "abnormal fear of the
intimate association of the sexes."[66] An Atlanta judge later elaborating upon this argument claimed: "No girl ever leaves home
to go to work in a factory, but that the parents feel an inward fear
that one of her bosses will take advantage of his position to mis-
treat her, especially if she repels his advances."[67] A factory owner
expressed similar southern sentiments: "It was considered belit-
tling—oh! very bad! It was considered that for a girl to go into a
cotton factory was just a step toward the most vulgar things. They
used to talk about the girls working in mills upcountry as if they
were in places of grossest immorality. It was said to be the same
as a bawdy house; to let a girl go into a cotton factory was to
make a prostitute of her."[68]

Given the nature of southern prejudices, Atlantans were
particularly receptive to the devastating indictments the authorities apparently unearthed against Leo Frank. One newspaper reported that pictures of Salome dancers "in scanty raiment"
adorned the walls of the National Pencil Factory.[69] At the coroner's
inquest, a thirteen-year-old friend of Mary Phagan's told his audience that the girl had confessed her fears of the superintendent's
improper advances. Former factory employees recalled that Frank
had flirted with the girls, that he had made indecent proposals,
and that he had even put his hands on them.[70]

Regardless of the veracity of the accusations, other witnesses at the inquest corroborated Frank's statements as to his
whereabouts on the day of the murder which, if true, made it
almost impossible for him to have been the culprit.[71] Nevertheless
the coroner's jury ordered Frank held on suspicion of murder.

Subsequent police disclosures incriminated the factory manager even more in the eyes of many Georgians. A park policeman swore that he had seen Frank and a young girl behaving improperly in a secluded section of the woods a year earlier, while the proprietress of a bordello confessed that the superintendent had phoned her repeatedly on the day of the murder in an effort to obtain a room for himself and a young girl. Both statements were eventually repudiated but not before an impact had been made upon the public. At the time of the madam's affidavit, newspaper readers were informed that her remarks constituted "one of the most important bits of evidence" that the state had against the factory superintendent.[72]

The numerous suggestions dropped by newspapers and police gave rise to the wildest rumors, most of them concerned with the "lasciviousness" of the "notorious" Leo Frank. The Jewish faith, it was widely asserted, forbade violations of Jewesses but condoned similar actions with Gentiles. Frank had allegedly killed another wife in Brooklyn, had illegitimate offspring too numerous to count, drank heavily, was about to be divorced by his wife, and finally, was a pervert. One man said he knew that Frank was a "moral pervert" because he looked like one.[73] These tales, lacking any foundation in fact, suggest how concerned Atlantans were with the religious and social background of Mary Phagan's suspected slayer. Gossip magnified fears. The people, it seemed, wanted Frank to have the characteristics attributed to him.

III

The trial of Leo Frank for the murder of Mary Phagan opened on July 28, 1913, amidst great hullabaloo. It lasted until August 26. During the entire period, the temper of the crowd indicated the antipathy Atlantans felt toward the defendant. "The fact that Frank is under indictment today," one reporter explained the day before the trial began, "means to many minds that he is therefore guilty. . . ."[74]

The state's case rested primarily upon the testimony of Jim

Conley, a black sweeper who had been employed in the National Pencil Factory. He charged Frank with having committed the murder and acknowledged that he had helped his employer remove the body to the factory basement.[75] There were no witnesses to corroborate any of the sweeper's statements.

The defense based its case primarily upon proving that Frank did not have the time to commit the murder. Witnesses were presented who corroborated the superintendent's account of his whereabouts on the fatal day. Frank maintained his innocence and characterized Conley's tale as "the vilest and most amazing pack of lies ever conceived in the perverted brain of a wicked human being."[76]

The jury needed less than four hours of deliberation before finding the defendant guilty. The judge sentenced Frank to hang. Atlantans were jubilant with the verdict. A crowd outside of the courthouse, estimated at between two and four thousand, screamed itself hoarse. As he stepped out of the courthouse, the prosecuting attorney was lifted to the shoulders of two husky men and carried to his office amidst huzzahs and cheers. After what was perhaps one of the wildest celebrations in Atlanta's history The *Marietta Journal and Courier* observed, "It seems to be the universal opinion that Frank was guilty and that he was the cause of the demonstration when the verdict was announced."[77]

Frank's lawyers appealed his case through the Georgia courts and ultimately to the United States Supreme Court. None of the tribunals ordered another trial. The Governor of Georgia re-evaluated the evidence in June, 1915, and commuted the death penalty to life imprisonment. Two months later, in August 1915, a band of men stormed the prison, kidnapped Frank, and lynched him.[78]

IV

The joyousness with which Frank's conviction was received revealed the people's desire for a scapegoat for their deeper resentments.[79] Georgia's Governor, John M. Slaton, explained the hostility toward Frank as "the prejudice of the employe *[sic]* against the employer. The fact that the head of a large factory is accused of attacking a girl, one of his employes, [sic] has been sufficient to give rise to this kind of prejudice."[80]

The antisemitism that erupted in Atlanta also suggested the need for a particular type of a villain. Manifestations of this sentiment are evident in the widespread acceptance of Negro Jim Conley's testimony; the numerous rumors that Frank's Jewish friends had collected a "fund of hundreds of thousands of dollars" to buy the jury; and tales to the effect that some defense witnesses had been bought with "jew money." In addition, Frank's lawyers had received anonymous phone calls with the cryptic message, "If they don't hang that Jew, we'll hang you." Crowds outside of the courtroom frequently hurled epithets like, "Lynch him!" and "Crack that Jew's neck!" The jury was also threatened with lynching if it did not "hang that 'damned sheeny'!"[81] This passionate hatred disclosed the Atlantans' intense yearning for some culprit upon whom they could fix blame for the frustrations of their barren lives. "People haunted by the purposelessness of their lives," Eric Hoffer has written, "try to find a new content not only by dedicating themselves to a holy cause but also by nursing a fanatical grievance."[82] This was especially true of the newly urbanized working classes in the South.[83]

Ignorant, frustrated, and frightened, the workers sought a devil to exorcise. Moreover, their severe tribulations and limited education made necessary a dogmatic oversimplification. In such a situation, Leo Frank could easily be visualized as the diabolical perpetrator of savage crimes against society.

Reinforcing these cultural and emotional sources of prejudice is the herd tendency in human nature. Widely shared personal opinions are difficult to sway. People tend to absorb the knowledge to which they are exposed through the refraction of their own emotional needs and experiences and through the evaluations prevalent among the groups with which they identify. Facts and opinions that differ from one's own or that are disturbing to convention are frequently not perceived. Psychologists have found a high correlation between belief and desire ($+.88$) but a negative one in regard to belief and evidence ($-.03$). In other words, factual information is insufficient to disturb established opinions.[84] Ellen Glasgow, the Virginia novelist, has noted that in the South for people "to think differently meant to be ostracized."[85]

Enthusiastic acceptance of Frank's conviction was further enhanced because people are conditioned to defer to those whom they have been trained to respect. Statements made by public officials are accepted as accurate unless there is some reason to suspect obfuscation. This was especially true in the South where the ruling classes "had extraordinary powers over the whole social body."[86] Hugh Dorsey, the Georgia-born prosecutor, had announced before the trial: "the possibility of a mistake having been made is very remote."[87] Southern Pinkerton and Burns detectives, who had conducted separate investigations, had also expressed their firm belief in the factory manager's guilt.[88] Why, then, should the masses have assumed that the alien Jew was telling the truth while their own leaders were not?

The members of the jury, a representative cross-section of Atlantans,[89] pleased their peers with the verdict. A spokesman for the jurors stated that they had all accepted the prosecution's arguments and conclusions.[90] To be sure, they may have been convinced of Frank's guilt on the basis of the evidence presented in court. But even if the material had been less persuasive, the opinion of the Atlanta crowds would certainly have influenced those who had to decide Frank's fate. What would have happened to their jobs, their social relationships, and the position of their families, for example, if the jurors had voted to acquit the man who most of Atlanta assumed had ravished the little girl? More than a year after the trial had ended, one juror confessed to a northern reporter that he was not sure of anything except that unless Frank was found guilty the jurors would never get home alive.[91]

V

A Boston newspaperman wrote in 1916 that had Frank been a native Georgian he would never have been convicted of Mary Phagan's death.[92] More likely, had he been a respected member of the gentile community, no southern prosecutor would have staked his case on a black's accusations. Moreover, had the people of Atlanta not found the cares of life so great a burden, there would have been less demand for a scapegoat to pay for their accumulated frustrations. The coming of industrialism was not solely responsible for Frank's fate. But the technological changes in society, which uprooted people and set them down in strange, urban areas, aggravated whatever intolerance and anxiety the southern culture had already nurtured.

The murder of Mary Phagan stood out as a symbol of industrial iniquity. She was continually referred to as "the little factory girl" long after the focus of the case had shifted to Leo Frank. A newspaperman observed during the trial: "The little factory girl will be remembered as long as law exists in Atlanta." A Confederate War veteran contributed "a dollar for the erection of a monument to Mary Phagan, the little factory girl who recently laid down her life for her honor." And Georgia's patrician historian, L. L. Knight, narrating the events of the murder and the solution arrived upon, years later wrote, "Espousing the cause of the little factory girl, [Tom] Watson in a most dramatic vein of appeal, summoned the true manhood of the South to assert its chivalry in vindicating the child's honor."[93] The "little factory girl's" death, and the factory owner's responsibility for it, had at last provided an acceptable outlet for the discontented. Employment of minors, unconventional association of the sexes, and the evils of the factory system deeply disturbed a conservative society uneasily confronting the beginnings of industrialism. Most Atlantans, having uprooted themselves from rural origins, were alienated by their work in the factory and by life in the city. The murder of an innocent southern girl by a northern, Jewish factory superintendent evoked the hostility latent in their unsettled existence and directed this hostility to the symbol of their fears and grievances.

Postscript

In 1982 an elderly gentleman came forth with an affidavit indicating that as a 13-year-old office boy employed by the National Pencil Factory in 1913 he had come into the building the Saturday of Mary Phagan's death and had seen Jim Conley carrying the girl's body across the first floor. Conley had allegedly warned him that if he told anyone what he had seen, he would kill the boy. The youth did tell his mother and she advised him not to tell anyone what he had seen. It was not until 69 years later that he finally got two reporters to listen to what he had witnessed.

The two reporters used the man's affidavit as a basis for a major news story about the Frank case and the Anti-Defamation League and other Jewish organizations in Atlanta thought the new information would serve as a basis for a posthumous pardon for Leo Frank. The combined efforts of these Atlanta based Jewish organizations ultimately did lead to such a pardon for Frank by the Georgia Board of Pardons in 1985.[94]

Notes

1. Barbara Tuchman, *The Proud Tower* (New York: Macmillan, 1966, p. 182; Maurice Samuel, *Blood Accusation* (New York: Alfred A. Knopf, 1966), p. 7; Henry David, *The History of the Haymarket Affair* (New York: Russell & Russell, 1936), p. 528, 535, 541; Louis Joughin and Edmund M. Morgan, *The Legacy of Sacco and Vanzetti* (Chicago, Quadrangle Books, 1964), p. 201–203.
2. A partial listing of growing American cities, and their population figures for 1900 and 1910, follows:

		Population	
State	*City*	*1900*	*1910*
Alabama	Birmingham	38,415	132,685
California	Los Angeles	102,479	319,198
	San Francisco	342,782	416,912
Colorado	Denver	133,859	213,381
Florida	Tampa	15,839	37,782
	Miami	1,681	5,471
Georgia	Atlanta	89,872	154,839
Illinois	Chicago	1,689,575	2,185,283
Indiana	Indianapolis	169,164	233,650
Kansas	Kansas City	51,418	82,331
Louisiana	New Orleans	287,104	339,075
Massachusetts	Boston	560,892	670,585
Michigan	Detroit	285,704	465,766
Minnesota	Minneapolis	202,718	301,408

Mississippi	Jackson	7,816	21,262
Missouri	Kansas City	163,752	248,381
Nevada	Reno	4,500	10,867
New Jersey	Newark	246,070	347,469
New Mexico	Albuquerque	6,238	11,020
New York	Buffalo	352,387	423,715
	New York	3,437,202	4,766,883
North Carolina	Charlotte	18,091	34,014
Ohio	Cleveland	381,768	560,663
	Youngstown	44,885	79,066
Oklahoma	Oklahoma City	32,452	64,205
	Tulsa	7,298	18,182
Oregon	Portland	90,426	207,214
South Dakota	Aberdeen	4,087	10,753
Tennessee	Memphis	102,320	131,105
	Nashville	80,865	110,364
Texas	Dallas	42,638	92,104
	Fort Worth	26,688	73,312
	San Antonio	53,321	96,614
Utah	Salt Lake City	53,531	92,777
Virginia	Norfolk	46,624	67,452
	Richmond	85,050	127,628
Washington	Seattle	80,671	237,195
	Tacoma	37,714	83,743
West Virginia	Charleston	11,099	22,966

SOURCE: *Abstract of the Thirteenth Census of the United States, 1910, pp. 65–75, passim.*

3. *Atlanta Constitution,* Jan. 18, 1915, pp. 1, 2, cited hereinafter as *AC.*

4. The cost of living in 1913 was the second highest in the nation. (Boston was first), and wages lagged behind those paid in northern cities. *Atlanta Journal,* Sept. 17, 1913, p. 1, hereinafter cited as *AJ.* See also W. J. Cash, *The Mind of the South* (New York: Alfred A. Knopf, 1941), p. 247. C. Vann Woodward reported that in 1912 and 1913 hourly earnings in New England averaged 37 percent above those in the South, *Origins of the New South* (Baton Rouge: Louisiana State University Press, 1951), p. 420–21.

5. United States, *Report of the Industrial commission,* 1901, 7:56, 57. A few years later the U.S. Senate's *Report on Condiditons of Woman and Child Wage-Earners in the United Staes,* 61st Cong., 2nd Sess., 1910, *Senate Document,* no. 645, serial no. 5685, l, 261, noted that the average work week in Georgia cotton mills in 1908, was 64 hours, which was linger than that in Virginia, North Carolina, South Carolina, Alabama, and Mississippi. Of the 31 establishments the Commission investigated, sixteeen had a 66 hour week; forty minutes was the average lunch time.

6. *Annual Reports of the Committees of Council, Officers and Departments of the City of Atlanta,* 1902–1903, pp. 96, 192. During the period 1900–1914, the average hourly wage in the United States was 20–21 cents an hour. For a 60 hour week this would be about $12. The average annual earnings in manufacturing for the following years indicated: 1907, $522; 1908, $475; and two different estimates for 1909, $518 and $557. John R. Commons and Associates, *History of Labor in the United States,* 1896–1932 (New York: The Macmillan Co., 1935), p. 59–61.

7. Atlanta, *Comptroller's Report for 1913*, p. 57.

8. Quoted in *Journal of Labor*, November 7, 1913, p. 4.

9. "Dixie Conditions Stir Unionists—Description of Actual State of Atlanta Textile Workers Make Delegates Weep," *Textile Worker* (December, 1914), 3:21.

10. *AC*, March 4, 1907, p. 3; June 4, 1913, p. 2. Franklin M. Garrett, *Atlanta and Environs*, (3 vols.; New York, 1954) 2:574; "Decency As An Issue," *Outlook* (December 19, 1908) 90:848; "An Advertising Campaign Against Segregated Vice," *The American City*, (July, 1913), 9:3, 4; *Annual Report of the Park Commissioner of the City of Atlanta for the Year Ending December 31, 1910*, p. 20. *Report . . . for the Year Ending December 31, 1913*, p. 32.

11. Atlanta Chamber of Commerce, *Annual Report for 1909*, p. 5; U.S. Bureau of the Census, *General Statistics of Cities: 1909*, pp. 88, 148; Atlanta, *Comptroller's Report for 1911*, p. 41; Atlanta, *Annual Reports 1902–1903*, pp. 100–101; Herbert R. Sands, *Organization and Administration of the City Government of Atlanta, Georgia* (New York: New York Bureau of Municipal Research, November, 1912), 62.

12. *AC*, January 18, 1915, p. 1; U.S. Bureau of the Census, *Statistics of Cities Having a Population of Over 30,000: 1905*, p. 111. There were 114 diphtheria cases in 1904 and 396 in 1911; for typhoid fever the figures were 85 and 315, respectively, and for tuberculosis, 37 and 223, Atlanta's population in 1904 was 98,776; in 1911 it was 161, 515; Atlanta, *Comptroller's Reprot*, 911, p. 19.

13. *Ibid.*, 20; *Annual Reprot of the Atlanta Chamber of Commerce*, 1909, p. 5; U.S. Bureau of the Census, *Historical Statistics of the United States: Colonial Times to 1957*, p. 27; U.S. Bureau of the Census, Bulletin, no. 109, *Mortaility Statistics*, 1910, p. 31; "Dixie Conditions Stir Unionists . . . ," *The Textile Worker* 3:21; *Preliminary Report of the Commissioner of Commerce and Labor, State of Georgia, for the Term Ending June 11, 1912*, p. 7.

14. U.S. Bureau of the Census, *Statistics of Cities Having a Population of Over 30,000: 1905*, p. 111; U.S. Bureau of the Census, *Statistics of Cities Having a Population of Over 30,000: 1907*, pp. 102, 107, 410; Inaugural Address of Mayor James G. Woodward, *Annual Report of Atlanta for 1905*, p. 27.

15. *Comptroller's Report*, 1911, p. 43; *Annual Report*, 1902–1903, p. 302; Sands, *Organization and Administration*, p. 36.

16. The term "cracker" connoted isolated, ignorant, backward frontiersman. Bevode C. McCall, "Georgia Town and Cracker Culture" (Ph.D. dissertation, University of Chicago, 1954), 105–106.

17. Cash, *Mind of the South*, p. 327. See also Stewart G. Cole, *The History of Fundamentalism* (New York: R. R. Smith, Inc. 1931), p. 26; Josephine Pinckney, "Bulwarks Against Change," in *Culture in the South*, ed. W. T. Couch (Chapel Hill: University of North Carolina Press, 1935), p. 41.

18. "Facts About the Atlanta Murders," *World's Work*, (November, 1906) 13:8147.

19. Glen Weddington Rainey, "The Race Riot of 1906 in Atlanta" (M.A. thesis, Emory University, 1929), no pagination; Ray Stannard Baker, "Following the Color Line," *American Magazine* (April 1907) 63:569; Anon., "The Atlanta Massacre," *Independent* (October 4, 1906) 91:799–800.

20. Woodward, *Origins*, 448.

21. Joseph H. Fichter and George L. Maddox, "Religion in the South, Old and New," in *The South in Continuity and Change*, ed. John M. McKinney and Edgar T. Thompson (Durham: Duke University Press, 1965), pp. 360, 364.

22. Carroll Edwin Harrington, "The Fundamentalist Movement in America, 1870–1920" (Ph.D. dissertation, University of California at Berkeley, 1959), p. 102.

23. Hunter Dickinson Farish, *The Circuit Rider Dismounts* (Richmond: The Dietz Press, 1938), pp. 333–34.

24. Rufus B. Spain, "Attitudes and Reactions of Southern Baptists to Certain Problems of Society, 1865–1900" (Ph.D. dissertation, Vanderbilt University, 1961), p. 229.

25. *Ibid.*, 230; Carl Dean English, "The Ethical Emphases of the Editors of Baptist Journals Published in the Southeastern Region of the United States, 1865–1915" (Th.D. dissertation, Southern Baptist Theological Seminary, 1948), p. 187.

26. Cash, *Mind of the South*, p. 347. The major sources of my commentaries on fundamentalism have been Norman F. Furniss, *The Fundamentalist Controversy, 1918–1931* (New Haven: Yale University Press, 1954), pp. 35–44; Harrington, *Fundamentalist Movement*, vi–vii; Cash, *Mind of the South*, p. 341; Cole, *Fundamentalism*, pp. 53, 322; and H. Richard Niebuhr, "Fundamentalism" in the *Encyclopaedia of the Social Sciences*, ed. Edwin R. A. Seligman (15 vols.; New York: The Macmillan Co., 1931) 6:526–27.

27. Rupert B. Vance, *Human Geography of the South* (Chapel Hill: University of North Carolina Press, 1932), 279; *AJ*, December 23, 1906, as cited in *Congressional Record*, 59th Cong., 2nd Sess., 3018; Rowland T. Berthoff, "Southern Attitudes Toward Immigration," *Journal of Southern History* (August 1951) 17:329.

28. *Congressional Record*, December 15, 1907, p. 3031; Berthoff, "Attitudes," p. 329; "Amendment of Immigration Laws," *Senate Document*, no. 251, 62nd Cong., 2nd Sess., 1912, Serial no. 6174, p. 5; *AJ*, December 23, 1906, December 30, 1906, as cited in *Congressional Record*, 59th Cong., 2nd Sess., 3018–19; *AC*, March 13, 1914, p. 4.

29. "Southern Peonage and Immigration," *Nation* (December 19, 1907) 85:557.

30. Berthoff, "Attitudes," p. 344.

31. Solomon Sutker, "The Jews of Atlanta: Their Social Structure and Leadership Patterns" (Ph.D. dissertation, University of North Carolina, 1950), p. 74; *AC*, January 18, 1915, p. 1.

32. Thomas Gibson, "The Anti-Negro Riots in Atlanta," *Harper's Weekly* (October 13, 1906) 50:1457–58; "Results in Atlanta," *Independent*, (January 3, 1907) 62:52; Rainey, *Race Riot*, ch. 3; *Baltimore Morning Sun*, November 23, 1914, p. 3.

33. Miriam Kotler Freund, "Jewish Merchants in Colonial America" (Ph.D. dissertation, New York University, 1936), p. 96; Merle Curti, *The Growth of American Thought* (New York: Harper & Brothers, 1943), p. 51; Anson Phelps Stokes, *Church and State in the United States* (3 vols.; New York: Harper & Brothers, 1950) 1:854, 857; Jacob Rader Marcus, *Early American Jewry: The Jews of Pennsylvania and the South, 1655–1790* (Philadelphia: Jewish Publication Society of America, 1953), pp. 167, 228, 231, 333; Paul Masserman and Max Baker, *The Jews Come to America* (New York: Black Publishing Co., 1932), p. 88; Peter Wiernik, *History of the Jews in America* (New York: Jewish Publication Society of America, 1931), p. 127; Joseph L. Blau and Salo W. Baron, eds., *The Jews of the United States, 1790–1840* (3 vols.; New York: Columbia University Press, 1963) 1:17; Clement Eaton, *Freedom of Thought in the Old South* (New York: Peter Smith, 1951), p. 27; Thomas Jefferson to a New York Jewish editor, quoted in "Legislature of Maryland," *Niles' Register*, Supplement (1819) 15:10. Although voting and office holding were generally restricted to Protestants in all of the American colonies, the restrictions upon Jews tended to last longer in some of the southern states. See, for example, Jacob Rader Marcus, *Early American Jewry: The Jews of New York, New England and Canada, 1649–1794* (Philadelphia: Jewish Publication Society of America, 1951), pp. 103, 116.

34. Eaton, *Old South* p. 233; E. Merton Coulter, *The Confederate States of America* (Baton Rouge: Louisiana State University Press, 1950), p. 226; Rudolf Glanz, *The Jew in the Old American Folklore* (New York: Waldon Press, 1961), p. 54.

35. Rufus Learsi, *The Jews in America: A History* (Cleveland: World Publishing, 1954), p. 103; Margaret Case Harriman, *And the Price is Right* (Cleveland: World Publishing, 1958), p. 34.

36. Lucian Lamar Knight, *Reminiscences of Famous Georgians* (2 vols.; Atlanta: Franklin Turner Co., 1907), I, 512.

37. William M. Stewart, "The Great Slave Power," *Arena,* (May 1890)19:580; Carr quoted in Harry Golden, *A Little Girl is Dead* (Cleveland: World Publishing, 1965), 226.

38. Horace M. Kallen, "The Ethics of Zionism," *Maccabean* (August 1906)11:69; William J. Robertson, *The Changing South* (New York: Boni and Liveright, 1927), p. 99.

39. John Higham, "Social Discrimination Against Jews in America, 1830–1930," *Publications of the American Jewish Historical Society* (1957)47:1–33; Higham, "Anti-Semitism in the Gilded Age: A Reinterpretation," *Mississippi Valley Historical Review,* (March 1957) 43:559–78; Oscar Handlin, "American Views of the Jew at the Opening of the Twentieth Century," *Publications of the American Jewish Historical Society* (June 1951)40:323–44; John Higham, "American Anti-Semitism Historically Reconsidered," in Charles Herbert, ed., *Jews in the Mind of America,* Stember (New York: Basic Books, 1966).

40. No antisemitic remarks are attributed to any southern Populists *during the Populist era* in any of the following works: Richard Hofstadter, *The Age of Reform* (New York: Alfred A Knopf, 1955); V. C. Ferkiss, "Populist Influences on American Fascism," *Western Political Quarterly* (1957) vol. 10; Norman Pollack, *The Populist Response to Industrial America* (Cambridge: Harvard University Press, 1962); W. T. K. Nugent, *The Tolerant Populists* (Chicago: University of Chicago Press, 1963); C. Vann Woodward, "The Populist Heritage and the Intellectual," *American Scholar* (Winter, 1959–60) vol. 21; Frederic Cople Jaher, *Doubters and Dissenters* (New York: The Free Press, 1964).

41. Higham, *Mississippi Valley Historical Review* 43:572.

42. *Ibid.,* 559–78; Higham, "Social Discrimination," pp. 22, 47; Higham, *Jews in the Mind of America,* pp. 248–49. Although Atlanta was not a small town after 1900, in part, it did have a "small-town culture."

43. Benjamin Kendrick, "The Study of the New South," *North Carolina Historical Review* (January 1926), 3:10.

44. Robertson, *Changing South,* p. 99.

45. Elias Rivkin has written: "At every moment of economic or social crisis, especially since the 1890's, anti-Semitism has manifested itself [in the United States]. This antisemitism more and more linked the Jews with the sources of disintegration and decay and attempted to identify the Jews with the twin threat of international capitalism and international communism." Rivkin has also observed that "the position of the Jews in every society of the past has been as secure as the society itself. For every stress the Jews have been held essentially responsible; for every collapse they have been blamed." *Essays in American-Jewish History* (Cincinnati: American Jewish Archives, 1958), p. 60. In our own times, many southern Jews still feel defensive and hesitate to disrupt the status quo. Alfred O. Hero, Jr., a sociologist, has written that "small-town, Deep Southern Jews have feared especially that someone with a Jewish name would express controversial ideas and thus stimulate unfavorable reactions to Jews in general." *The Southerner and World Affairs* (Baton Rouge: Louisiana State University Press, 1965), p. 501. Hero's chapter, "Southern Jews," is the best historical discussion that I have seen on the subject.

46. *AC,* April 27, 1913, "extra," pp. 1, 2.

47. Henry A. Alexander, *Some Facts About the Murder Notes in the Phagan Case* (privately published pamphlet, 1914), pp. 5, 7.

48. *Augusta* (Ga.), *Chronicle,* May 2, 1913, p. 1.

49. *AC*, April 29, 1913, p. 4.

50. *AC*, April 28, 1913, p. 3. *Atlanta Georgian*, May 4, 1913, p. 2, hereinafter cited as *AG*.

51. Philip Waltner, "Municipal and Misdemeanor Offenders," in *The Call of the New South*, ed. James E. McCulloch (Nashville, Southern Sociological Congress, 1912), 110–11.

52. Hugh C. Weir, "The Menace of the Police," *World To-Day* (January, 1910), p. 52.

53. *Ibid.*, March, 1910, p. 174.

54. In regard to the conduct and competency of its policemen, Atlanta was typical of other American cities. "There is probably not a city in the South where the police do not make needless arrests." Waltner, "Offenders," *New South*, p. 107. Crime existed in every major city in the United States and the failure of police forces to control the widespread lawlessness evoked extensive comment. The Conference for Good City Government discussed the lack of competent policemen in 1906, 1909, and 1910. Delegates to these conventions argued that police reform could not be postponed. Better laws, better methods, and better men were essential to meet the needs of growing cities. In 1910 a national periodical ran a series of articles condemning police incompetence, inefficiency, and brutality. The author warned, "Gentlemen of the police, you are on trial." Edward M. Hartwell, "The Police Question," *Proceedings of the Atlantic City Conference for Good City Government*, 1906, p. 397. And see Augustus Raymond Hatton, "The Control of Police," *Proceedings of the Cincinnati Conference for Good City Government*, 1909, pp. 157–61; Leonhard Felix Field, "The Organization of Police Forces," *Proceedings*, 1910, p. 281; Weir, "Menace of the Police," p. 59.

55. Wytt E. Thompson, *A Short Review of the Frank Case* (Atlanta: n.n., 1914), p. 29.

56. *AC*, April 28, 1913, pp. 1, 2.

57. *AG*, April 28, 1913, p. 1. It was later made known that a microscopic test had not proven the hair to be Mary Phagan's.

58. *AC*, April 28, 1913, pp. 1, 2; April 29, 1913, pp. 1, 2; April 30, 1913, pp. 1, 2.

59. *New York Times*, August 26, 1913, p. 18; February 18, 1914, p. 3; *AC*, June 1, 1915, p. 4; *AG*, May 13, 1913, p. 2. Interview with Alexander Brin, a Boston reporter who covered the later stages of the Frank case, in Boston, August 19, 1964. Mr. Brin now publishes the *Jewish Advocate*.

60. *Savannah Morning News*, May 2, 1913, p. 1.

61. *AC*, May 2, 1913, p. 4.

62. "The Frank Case," *Outlook*, (May 26, 1915) 110:167.

63. L. O. Bricker, "A Great American Tragedy," *Shane Quarterly (April, 1943)* 4:90.

64. *AG*, April 30, 1913, p. 1; *Journal of Labor* (May 2, 1913) 15:4; "Accessory After the Fact," *Southern Ruralist (June 15, 1913)* 20:13.

65. English, *"Ethical Emphases," p. 219.*

66. Spain, *Attitudes*, p. 299.

67. Arthur G. Powell, *I Can Go Home Again* (Chapel Hill: University of North Carolina Press, 1943), p. 287.

68. Broadus Mitchell, *The Rise of Cotton Mills in the South* (Baltimore: The Johns Hopkins Press, 1921), p. 195.

69. *AG*, April 29, 1913, p. 3.

70. *AC*, May 9, 1913, p. 2; *AG*, May 8, 1913, p. 2; May 9, 1913, pp. 1, 2; *Savannah Morning News*, May 9, 1913, p. 1.

71. *AJ*, June 2, 1913, p. 9.

72. *AC*, May 11, 1913, p. 1; May 23, 1913, p. 1.

73. *AG*, May 11, 1913, p. 2; *Augusta Chronicle*, May 5, 1919, p. 2; *Baltimore Morning Sun*, November 19, 1914, p. 3; A. B. MacDonald, "Has Georgia Condemned an Innocent Man to Die?" *Kansas City* (Mo.) *Star*, January 17, 1915, p. 1; C. Thompson, *Short Reviews*, 25; C. P. Connolly, *The Truth About the Frank Case* (New York, 1915), p. 14; Abraham Cahan, *Blätter Von Mein Leben* (5 vols.; New York: Forward Publishing Co., 1931), 5:1, 494.

74. *AG*, July 27, 1913, p. 2.

75. *Frank* vs. *State, Brief of the Evidence*, pp. 54–57.

76. Quoted in *AJ*, August 4, 1913, p. 1.

77. *AG*, August 25, 1913, p. 1; August 26, 1913, p. 1; *AC*, August 26, 1913, p. 4; *Greensboro* (Ga.) *Herald-Journal*, August 29, 1913, p. 4; *Marietta Journal and Courier*, August 4; *Marietta Journal and Courier*, August 29, 1913, p. 2.

78. *AC*, June 22, 1915, pp. 1, 2, 9; *New York Times*, August 18, 1915, pp. 1, 3; August 19, 1915, pp. 1, 3; August 23, 1915, p. 5.

79. Daniel Bell has written: "Social groups that are dispossessed invariably seek targets on whom they can vent their resentments, targets whose power can serve to explain their dispossession." "The Dispossessed," in *The Radical Right*, ed. Daniel Bell (Garden City, N.Y.: Doubleday & Co., 1963), pp. 2–3.

80. *New York Times*, November 28, 1914, p. 5.

81. *Greensboro* (Ga.) *Herald-Journal*, August 29, 1913; Thompson, *Short Review*, 9; Connolly, *The Truth*, 11; "Frank's Prophesy of Vindication Comes True 10 Years After Georgia Mob Hangs Him as Slayer," *Jewish Advocate* (October 18, 1923), 42:20; *Minutes* of the executive committee of the American Jewish Committee, November 8, 1913 (located in the American Jewish Committee Archives, New York City).

82. Eric Hoffer, *The True Believer* (New York: New American Library, 1958), p. 92.

83. Alfred O. Hero, Jr. has written: "the newly urbanized Southern working class . . . seemed especially open to leadership by charismatic and authoritarian figures who would appeal to their anxieties and insecurities, with dogmatic, oversimplified 'solutions,' " *The Southerner and World Affairs*, p. 354.

84. Frederick Hansen Lund, "The Psychology of Belief," *Journal of Abnormal and Social Psychology* (1925) 20:194–95; Gordon W. Allport and Leo Postman, *The Psychology of Rumor* (New York: Holt 1947), p. 191; Melvin M. Tumin, *An Inventory and Appraisal of Research on American Anti-Semitism* (New York: Freedom Books, 1961), p. 115; Eunice Cooper and Marie Jahoda, "The Evasion of Propaganda: How Prejudiced People Respond to Anti-Prejudice Propaganda," *Journal of Psychology* (1947) 23:15; Mahlon Brewster Smith, "Functional and Descriptive Analysis of Public Opinion" (Ph.D. dissertation, Harvard University, 1947), 500, 507; George Cornewall Lewis, *An Essay on the Influence of Authority in Matters of Opinion* (London: Longmans, Green & Co., 1875), p. 10.

85. Quoted in William H. Nicholls, *Southern Tradition and Regional Progress* (Chapel Hill: University of North Carolina Press, 1960), p. 135.

86. Cash, *Mind of the South*, p. 310.

87. Quoted in *AG*, July 27, 1913, p. 2.

88. *AC*, May 25, 1913, p. 1; May 27, 1913, pp. 1, 2.

89. One bank teller, one bookkeeper, one real estate agent, one manufacturer, one contractor, one optician, one railroad claim agent, one mailing clerk, two salesmen, and two machinists. Garrett, *Atlanta* 2:622.

90. *AJ*, August 26, 1913, p. 1.

91. *New York Times*, February 23, 1915, p. 9.

92. Clipping from the morgue of the *Boston Herald-Traveller*, August 17, 1916.

93. *AG*, August 5, 1913, p. 4; Dalton (Ga.) *North Georgia Citizen*, August 28, 1913, p. 4; Lucian Lamar Knight, *A Standard History of Georgia and Georgians* (6 vols.; Chicago: The Lewis Publishing Co., 1917), 2:1190.

94. Frank Ritter, Jerry Thomson, and Robert Sherborne, "An Innocent Man Was Lynched," *The Tennessean* (Nashville), March 7, 1982, special news section; Clark Jack Freshman, "Beyond Pontius Pilate and Judge Lynch: The Pardoning Power In Theory and Practice as Illustrated in The Leo Frank Case" (unpublished thesis, Departments of History and Government, Harvard College, March, 1986), p. 4.

7

Southern Jewry
and the Desegregation Crisis:

1954–1970

Conventional opinion has it that Jews are one of the groups that consistently support civil rights causes and promote the welfare of minorities in the United States. To a considerable extent the available evidence supports this thesis. Jews have been prominent in the National Association for the Advancement of Colored People (NAACP), have participated in marches and protests along with blacks, and have used their legal acumen to help destroy the concept of second class citizenship. Even a cursory examination of financial contributions, active leadership, and organizational commitment to the civil rights movement finds large numbers of Jewish individuals and groups heavily represented.

Nevertheless, despite the participation of many Jews in the civil rights movement, the level of commitment has differed in various parts of the country. In the South, particularly, Jews have been more circumspect in their allegiance to equal rights for all citizens and, except for a few areas like Atlanta and some Hillel groups on college campuses, have been more guarded in their public postures. A significant division, for example, between northern and southern Jews occurred in 1954 when the United States Supreme Court, in *Brown* v. *Board of Education of Topeka, et. al.*, outlawed segregated school facilities. Most northern Jews applauded the Court's ruling; southern Jews met it with fear and trepidation.

"The segregation crisis has shaken Southern Jews more severely than any national event since the Civil War,"[1] Albert Vorspan, Social Action Director of the Union of American Hebrew Congregations wrote in 1959. For three centuries Jews had maintained harmonious relations with their Christian neighbors. They had carefully accepted regional customs as their own and even during the controversy over slavery few southern Jews publicly condemned the institution. In times of stress, however, Jews had often been singled out and blamed for whatever difficulties society might be undergoing. Hence during the Civil War blatant antisemitism (or, to use the nineteenth century expression, Judaeophobia) arose. The Jews as a group, and Judah P. Benjamin, the best known Jew in the Confederacy, were attacked.[2] As Bertram Korn has noted, "anti-Jewish prejudice was a characteristic expression of the age, part and parcel of the economic and social upheaval effectuated by the war."[3] During Reconstruction and the Populist eras there were again some examples of hostility to Jews but many fewer than had occurred during the Civil War. The Leo Frank case exacerbated Jewish-Christian relationships before the first World War but as the furor died down, southern Jews again relapsed into their normally quiet existence. The United States Supreme Court's decision in *Brown* v. *Board of Education,* though, set the stage for renewed tensions.

Jews in the South are, according to sociologist Alfred Hero, Jr., "the most cosmopolitan Southern ethnic group." They are, on the average, better off financially, better educated, concentrated in higher socioeconomic groups, and more urban than non-Jews.[4] Nevertheless they are not entirely secure in their positions and regardless of where they live shun controversy. That is because one of the region's cardinal virtues is conformity. As a former rabbi in Norfolk, Virginia, put it, "Probably nowhere [else] in America is the old principle of Jewish history, *Wie es Christel sich, so Judel sich'* (as the Christian do, so do the Jews) so apparent."[5]

The South, however, like every other region in the nation, is composed of different areas and the climate in some communities allows greater opportunities for diversity than in others. In general, though, the activities and thoughts of Jews below the Mason-Dixon line are in direct relationship to the sophistication of the city in which they reside. Where the gentiles are cosmopolitan the Jews are likely to be also. Where the Christians are more conservative, one finds Jews similarly inclined. Atlanta is perhaps the most cosmopolitan of southern cities and some Jews there have been among the most ardent advocates of integration. In more conservative Alabama few Jews have committed themselves. Norfolk Jews backed integration in the schools but Richmond's Jews were considerably more reserved. The small towns in the South are generally conservative. Jews in Shreveport and Charleston are more cautious publicly than those in New Orleans.[6] In Houston and Dallas the Jewish community divides between liberal and conservative factions but even one of the more reserved rabbis acknowledges, "The Jews, of course, take their place with those who advocate desegregation. . . ."[7]

Most southern Jews are merchants, highly dependent on the good will of their neighbors for sustenance. They therefore find it wise to fit in with the accepted customs of the community. This means, especially in the smaller towns, that they hold membership in the local temple, avoid public airing of controversial views, and claim as their own the community's standards of thought. They are particularly anxious to ingratiate themselves with the gentiles in their area and are "extremely sensitive to what non-Jews think about them." The Jew worries if another Jew is "identified with a position that is extremely unpopular" because he feels that all Jews will then be visited with economic reprisals or social ostracism.[8] When one central Virginia Jewish community heard, in 1958, that Arthur B. Spingarn, a New York Jew, was President of the NAACP, it received the news with "grim silence." "The knowledge that a Northern Jew was head of the leading organization for Negro rights," a commentator explained, "had shaken the security of this Virginia Jewish community."[9]

Religion is an important aspect of southern life. As a result, the minister or rabbi assumes a more esteemed role in the community than his counterpart in other regions. The rabbi of the

Reform congregation[10] in a southern community is well known
to his neighbors and is frequently asked to participate at Christian
interfaith meetings. To the extent that he does this job well his
own Jewish congregation applauds him. In fact, many Jews judge
their rabbi on the basis of the respect and esteem that he has in
the Christian community.[11] It is all the more important, therefore,
that the rabbi not arouse the ire of those in a position to harm the
Jews, like members of the Ku Klux Klan or White Citizens Councils or even ordinary consumers. When Rabbi Seymour Atlas
participated in a "Brotherhood Week" program in 1956, *Life* magazine carried the story and included a picture of the rabbi standing
next to a black man. The Board of Trustees of his Montgomery,
Alabama, congregation, asked Atlas to "demand" a retraction
from the national weekly, and to have *Life* inform readers in a
future issue that "Brotherhood Week" had nothing to do with
Negroes, Reverend Ralph Abernathy, the Supreme Court decisions
on segregation, or the Montgomery bus strike.[12]

The incident with Rabbi Atlas demonstrates how the 1954
Supreme Court decision alarmed southern Jews. Many of them
believed that it would threaten and erode the good relations that
they had tried to develop with their Christian neighbors. These
Jews thought that only by keeping absolutely quiet, or by saying
nothing about integration that would offend any southerner,
would they be able to continue living peacefully in the South.

Those who held such views were mistaken. Bigots, Ku
Kluxers, and members of the White Citizens Councils in many
southern communities used the integration crisis as a springboard
for the most vicious acts of antisemitism. In one year, from November 1957 through October 1958, eight southern Jewish temples were bombed[13] in communities undergoing stress because of
attempts at integration. The bombings that occurred took place
both in areas where some Jews had taken a stand as well as in
those where they had said nothing. Concomitantly there was an
increase in the distribution of antisemitic literature. Much of this
literature propagated the theme that "desegregation is a Zionist-
Communist plot to mongrelize the white race so that the Jews can
take over."[14]

Southern Jews, for the most part, reacted to the hostility

displayed not by castigating the White Citizens Councils or Ku Kluxers, whose activities probably fomented the attacks, but by denouncing northern coreligionists for making public efforts to promote racial equality. The southern Jews believed that the endeavors of their northern coreligionists, such as those in the American Jewish Congress and the Anti-Defamation League of B'nai B'rith, to achieve racial equality triggered the reactions of the southern bigots.[15]

When northern Jews marched in southern demonstrations to show their solidarity with the civil rights movement, local Jews often tried to stop them. One Birmingham teenager phoned a visiting rabbi and admitted, ''We are glad that you are doing what we would like to do but do not have the courage to do.'' Then he added, ''But, please, do not endanger us, do not get our synagogue bombed.''[16]

Other Jews reacted more vehemently. ''When a rabbi from New Haven, Conn., takes part in such demonstrations,'' a Macon Jew explained, ''you have no idea the position Jewry in our state is placed. . . . A rabbi from out of our area is detrimental to Jews in the South.'' ''For the probable success in organizing an effective Klan in Albany, Ga.,'' another Jew wrote to this same New Haven rabbi, ''you and your colleagues can take full credit.'' A Memphis attorney shouted in a closed session meeting of the American Jewish Committee, ''If only you Yankee Jews would keep your long noses out of our business,'' while an Alabama Jewish leader told a representative of a national Jewish agency: ''You're like Hitler. You stir up anti-Semitism against us.''[17]

Because Jews in the South have fears about being different from white Protestants, it is difficult to say how they really feel about segregation and desegregation. They always seem to consider first how the gentiles will react to their activities. Jews probably are more liberal than non-Jews on most issues and as Morton Gaba has pointed out

> Given the slightest evidence of Christian interest, Jewish leadership, both as individuals and as representatives of Jewish groups would emerge with the necessary manpower and financial backing in support of the Supreme Court decision as they have in a score of other communal endeavors.[18]

But that would not necessarily indicate how most of the individuals felt. Northern-based Jewish groups have been unstinting in their efforts to foster and develop civil rights throughout the nation even though many individual Jews not only are unconcerned with the issue but would actually prefer that blacks enjoy their civil rights in their own neighborhoods and not trespass among the Jews.

Allen Krause, who has examined the opinions of southern Jewish rabbis, believes that the vast majority of Jews below the Mason-Dixon line—he estimates 75 percent—are "somewhat ambivalent about the whole issue, but tending toward *thoughts* sympathetic to the Negro."[19] Perhaps this is the closest we can get to analyzing southern Jewish opinion on desegregation at the present time. But if at least their *thoughts* are on the side of civil rights, this differentiates them from most of their Baptist and Methodist neighbors.

One observer, Elijah E. Palnick, has written that "almost every Jewish community" in the South "is quietly working with the good Christians" to promote integration but "no Southern Jew boasts of it."[20] Bill Kovach, a reporter for *The New York Times*, but formerly with *The Nashville Tennessean*, wrote the author that after "following the trial of civil rights workers" he "was personally impressed with the number of Jews who acted as individuals in support of the [black man's] pursuit of equal rights." He then went on to name specific individuals: the owner of a department store in Fayetteville, which he characterized as a "very small, rural town with the traditional Southern prejudice against Jews and Negroes," an attorney in East Tennessee, and a host of individuals in Nashville.[21]

But these observations are a far cry from the remarks of others who claim that there has been a "conspiracy of silence" or a "pronounced and emphatic" silence among Jews in regard to desegregation. Probably both opinions are accurate. Most Jews in southern communities have done little to promote equal rights openly but at the same time there have been a few individuals who have worked, overtly or covertly, to see that Negroes are treated justly. Nevertheless one must not minimize the consequences for many Jews who enter the fray. Only if the southern Jew "has a strong moral sense of justice combined with a disregard for the physical safety of himself and his family," Daniel Snowman emphasized in 1964, "will he throw in his lot openly with the various civil rights groups."[22]

Participation figures vary from city to city. Rabbi Perry Nussbaum estimated that in Jackson, Mississippi, no more than five of the 150 Jewish families did anything to help the movement and those five were only "moderately active."[23] On the other hand Rabbi Malcolm Stern wrote that "the overwhelming majority of Norfolk Jews have whole-heartedly supported in every feasible way the local attempts by the School Board and others to comply with the Supreme Court decision."[24] Jackson and Norfolk are probably the extremes with most other southern Jewish communities falling in between but not necessarily in the middle. In the early 1960s Alfred Hero found that southern Jews kept their views "so quiet on controversial issues, including race, that southern Gentiles . . . greatly underestimated their real divergence from Protestant thinking on public and social questions."[25]

Almost all of the articles that have been published about the reactions of southern Jews avoid naming specific communities. Hence one reads of "Southern City," "Deltatown," "Antebellum Town," etc. Individuals are similarly protected. It is therefore difficult to pinpoint what specific individuals have done. There is one group of southern Jews whose opinions on desegregation have been examined and analyzed—the rabbis.[26] More often than not these men reflected the views of their congregations in their public (and private) utterances.

Most of the rabbis were cautious, shunned the limelight, and followed a moderate approach to desegregation. "I don't see how we can do much," a New Orleans rabbi wrote, "until the Protestant ministry avows a more positive stand. They could change the situation overnight." From South Carolina another acknowledged "While I have spoken against segregation and in favor of integration from my pulpit from time to time—to the great discomfiture of my members—I have put nothing in writing [because] we have a dangerous powder keg in Florence which might explode at any time." A Tennessean sermonized, "as a Southern Congregation, we need not initiate or take an overly conspicuous role in advocating integration." A North Carolinian used a Jewish holiday as an occasion to present his views obliquely, "The festival of Purim teaches us that we must oppose all attempts at stifling man's freedom and his right to enjoy that freedom. The problem of desegregation, with which we of the South are confronted today, takes on another light if we apply the lesson of Purim." And another rabbi, in West Tennessee, advised his followers: "we must move slowly and gradually. . . ."[27]

Perhaps six to ten rabbis in the South worked diligently to promote the cause of civil rights. Two or three had the support of a significant number of their congregants. Others worked quietly, behind-the-scenes; and even though some Jews in their community knew of their activities their discretion allowed these individuals to continue with their work. The most notable among them include Rabbis Jacob Rothschild of Atlanta, Emmet Frank of Alexandria, Virginia, Perry Nussbaum of Jackson, and Charles Mantinband of Alabama, Mississippi, and Texas.

During the height of the civil rights controversy in the early 1960s, Mantinband ministered to the Jews of Hattiesburg, Mississippi. He engaged in civil rights activities openly even though most of his congregation frowned on such work. He claimed that too many Jews of his acquaintance both chanted and believed

> Come weal
> Come woe
> My status
> Is quo

His Board of Trustees considered the rabbi "crazy" and "ahead of his times" in the area of civil rights. They told him "in no uncertain terms" that they preferred him to remain silent on the issue but he ignored their wishes. At home he entertained guests of his own choosing and on one occasion the sight of black people entering his house by the front door so unnerved a neighbor that he later demanded, "Who are those people?" "Some of my Christian friends," the rabbi replied coolly.

Mantinband did curtail some of his activities because of community pressure. His congregants' fears were so great that he avoided some biracial meetings—although he spoke on many occasions at Negro colleges—and shunned press publicity for his efforts. One Christmas the Taconic Foundation of New York sent a check of $2500 to his congregation in honor of Mantinband's "sane approach to the race question." The gift threw the congregation into a panic. A committee investigated for months, and not until it was discovered that others, including Christian groups, had received similar bequests did the congregation finally accept it.[28]

Another southern rabbi advocating civil rights causes is Jacob Rothschild of Atlanta. Rothschild spoke out for Negro equality long before it became fashionable and almost a decade before the Supreme Court's decision on the subject. During the 1948 presidential campaign, in which the Dixiecrats bolted from the Democratic Party over the civil rights program proposed by Harry S. Truman, he decried the growing race hatred that threatened the South and urged his people to "be among those who are willing to *do* something" to reverse the tide. He invited Negroes to his home and he visited theirs. In his temple he held integrated workshops, forums, and discussion groups. In 1957 he joined with seventy-nine other Atlanta clergymen in issuing the "Atlanta Manifesto" which demonstrated clerical support for the civil rights movement. Unlike Mantinband, Rothschild had considerable support from local Jews. When one member of his congregation resigned from the temple because she was incensed at seeing Rothschild's daughter with a Negro friend in a restaurant, the Board of Trustees wrote her a letter regretting that she had failed to "learn the lesson of Judaism taught by our rabbi in word and deed."[29]

The most dramatic southern Jewish supporter of the civil rights movement, Rabbi Emmet Frank of Alexandria, Virginia, chose the holiest night of the Jewish year—the eve of the Day of Atonement—to denounce the most powerful political figure in the state in 1958—Senator Harry Byrd. Rabbi Frank, who had spoken on the subject both before and after that September evening, insisted that "the Jew cannot remain silent to injustice." He excoriated those who advocated "massive resistance" to integrated public schools and then continued:

> Let the segregationists froth and foam at their mouth. There is only one word to describe their madness—Godlessness, or to coin a new synonym—Byrdliness. Byrdliness has done more harm to the stability of our country than McCarthyism.

Frank received nationwide publicity for this sermon and his attitudes at that time. Judging from the amount of letters that he received, most of his correspondents, as well as his congregants, supported the stand that he took although a minority did not. "As the years go on," one of his detractors wrote, "you will reflect on the damage you have done those to whom you were supposed to be a religious leader."[30]

The fourth rabbi is Perry Nussbaum of Jackson. Unlike Mantinband, Rothschild and Frank, Nussbaum tried to be circumspect in his actions. Had he publicized his early activities he probably would never have had an opportunity to engage in later ones from a Mississippi pulpit. Unlike Rothschild and Frank he could not count on any significant support from his congregation. He made quiet efforts in the 1950s to see what he could do to promote integration and in 1961 he instituted a chaplaincy program for the arrested freedom riders of all denominations (many were Jewish) who were jailed by Mississippi officials. Fortunately, as he acknowledges,

> the newspaper people understood the sensitive nature of the program, so that nothing was publicized locally. This would have been the last straw for my own people. If it became generally known, for instance, that I conducted worship services regularly at the Penitentiary, the reactions from many of my own people and certainly from the White Citizens Councils would be tremendous!

During the next few years the rabbi's views on desegregation received greater circulation and the retaliations against him began in earnest. A bomb exploded just outside his temple study in

September 1967, and two months later his home was bombed. On both occasions he escaped with his life only through luck.[31]

It is interesting that of the four rabbis about whom we have the most information, three are not native southerners. Mantinband was born in New York, reared in Norfolk, but attended college in the North. Rothschild was born and raised in Pittsburgh and attended college in Cincinnati. Nussbaum comes from Canada. The only native Southerner, Emmet Frank, was born and spent his early years in New Orleans, one of the South's more cosmopolitan cities, and attended college in Houston. Further study might show that the few southern Jews who tried to promote integration were first or second generation southerners to whom the southern heritage meant little.

Since the 1970s, more southerners have accepted desegregation and this has eased the strain within the various Jewish communities. School integration is proceeding at a pace that only a few years ago would have been considered impossible, and Jews now feel less uncomfortable about the expressions of coreligionists on the subject. National defense organizations like the American Jewish Committee and the Anti-Defamation League are experiencing a regional revival following more than a decade of resignations and protests about northern lack of sympathy for the southern Jew's situation. The KKK and White Citizens Councils— with their antisemitic outbursts—have toned down considerably. And even in Mississippi the unthinkable has come to pass with hardly any notice: Rabbi Nussbaum attended an integrated meeting of the Freedom Democratic Party in a Jackson hotel and sometime later participated in an integrated protest rally against the Vietnamese war on a local college campus. In 1965 or 1966, Nussbaum claims, such activities would have been "unthinkable."[32] But now the "power structure" in Mississippi, Nussbaum contends, will no longer tolerate the excesses of the past. For the southern Jew this means that he no longer has to fear obeying the law of the land or acknowledging that perhaps integration and equal rights for all people are not as dreadful as they may have seemed only a decade ago.

Notes

1. Albert Vorspan, "The Dilemma of the Southern Jew," *Reconstructionist* (January 1959) 24:6. See also Murray Friedman, "Virginia Jewry in the School Crisis," *Commentary* (January 1959) 27:17.

2. Bertram W. Korn, *American Jewry and the Civil War* (Philadelphia: The Jewish Publication Society of America, 1951), p. 17.

3. Ibid., p. 156.

4. Alfred O. Hero Jr., *The Southerner and World Affairs* (Baton Rouge: Louisiana State University Press, 1965), p. 477.

5. Malcolm Stern, "Living the Norfolk Story," speech delivered to Congregation Rodeph Shalom, Philadelphia, February 27, 1959. Copy in American Jewish Archives, Cincinnati (hereafter AJA).

6. Hero, *Southerner and World Affairs*, ch. 13.

7. William S. Malev, "The Jew of the South in the Conflict on Segregation," *Conservative Judaism* (Fall 1958) 13(1):42.

8. Charles Mantinband, "Mississippi, The Magnolia State," October 1961, unpublished essay in AJA, pp. 4, 6–7; Hero, *Southerner and World Affairs*, p. 476; Joshua A. Fishman, "Southern City," *Midstream* (Summer 1961) 7(3):48; Joel Dobin, "Portrait of a Southern Community," *Congress Weekly*, April 28, 1958, p. 7; Perry E. Nussbaum, "And Then There Was One—In the Capital City of Mississippi," *CCAR Journal* (October 1963) 11(3):15.

9. Vorspan, "Dilemma"; James A. Wax, "The Attitude of the Jews in the South Toward Integration," *CCAR Journal* (June 1959):18.

10. Over 10% of Southern congregations are Reform. Conservative and Orthodox rabbis have played a much less conspicuous role in interfaith activities and in desegregation. P. Allen Krause, "Rabbis and Negro Rights in the South, 1954–1967," *American Jewish Archives* (April 1969) 221:42–43.

11. Perry Nussbaum to Rabbi Jacob J. Weinstein, October 29, 1958, AJA, box 2800; Hero, *Southerner and World Affairs*, p. 500; Fishman, "Southern City," p. 43.

12. Harry L. Golden, "A Rabbi in Montgomery," *Congress Weekly*, May 13, 1957, p. 7.

13. *Facts* (October-November 1958) 13:131–33; clipping in "Southern States" folder at the American Jewish Committee Library, New York City.

14. Friedman, "Virginia Jewry," p. 19; Hero, *Southerner and World Affairs* p. 496; Nathan Perlmutter, "Bombing in Miami," *Commentary* (June 1958) 25(6):502–3; Arnold Forster, "The South: New Field for an Old Game," *The ADL Bulletin* (October 1958) 15:1–3.

15. Vorspan, "Dilemma"; see also James Lebeau "Profile of a Southern Jewish Community: Waycross, Georgia," *American Jewish Historical Quarterly* (June 1969) 58(4):434–35, 442.

16. Jack Bloom to Leonard Dinnerstein, May 15, 1971; Rabbi Richard W. Winograd, "Birmingham—A Personal Statement," 1963 copy in AJA.

17. Alfred M. Koplin to Rabbi Richard J. Israel, August 31, 1962; Lee Sterne to Rabbi Richard Israel, September 4, 1962; Charles Mantinband to Jacob Marcus, December 9, 1960, all in AJA; Vorspan, "Dilemma," p. 7.

18. Morton J. Gaba, "Segregation and a Southern Jewish Community," *Jewish Frontier* (October 1954) 21(10):13.

19. Krause, "Rabbis and Negro Rights," p. 23.

20. Elijah E. Palnick, "Southern Jewry and Civil Rights," *CCAR Journal* (June 1965) 13(2):62.

21. Bill Kovach to L.D., October 28, 1968.

22. Friedman, "Virginia Jewry"; Mantinband to Marcus, December 9, 1960, AJA; Perlmutter, "Bombing in Miami"; sermon of Herbert M. Baumgard, Holy Days, 1959, delivered at University of Miami for South Dade Jewish Center, copy in box 2143, AJA; Daniel Snowman, "Southern Jews and Civil Rights," *Jewish Chronicle,* October 23, 1964, clipping, "Southern States" folder, American Jewish Committee.

23. Jack Nelson, "Terror in Miss. Focuses on Jews," *New York Post,* December 6, 1967, p. 52.

24. Malcolm Stern to Albert Vorspan, October 2, 1958, AJA.

25. Hero, *Southerner and World Affairs* p. 496.

26. In 1957, Jacob R. Marcus, Director of AJA, began soliciting the views and sermons of southern rabbis on desegregation. Most of the people to whom he wrote responded, and the bulk of this information is still restricted. Later on, in the 1960s, a graduate student at Hebrew Union College, Allen Krause, interviewed more than a score of southern rabbis on the topic. The tapes of these interviews are also at AJA. Krause based his dissertation on the information gathered and summarized it in his article "Rabbis and Negro Rights" (see note 10).

27. J. E. Feibelman to J. R. Marcus, January 17, 1956, Nearprint file, AJA; *The New York Times,* July 8, 1959, p. 20; Rabbi Avery J. Goosfield to J. R. Marcus, March 19, 1957; Louis M. Tuchman to Marcus, March 28, 1957; sermon of Rabbi James A. Wax, February 17, 1956, p. 4—all in AJA, box 2143; Malev, "The Jew of the South."

28. Mantinband to Marcus, December 9, 1960; Allen Krause interview of Mantinband, June 23, 1966, tape 440; *National Jewish Post and Opinion,* March 1, 1963, p. 3—all in AJA; "The Southern Rabbis Face the Problem of Desegregation," *CCAR Journal* (June 1956), p. 4; Mantinband, "Rabbi in the Deep South," *ADL Bulletin* (May 1962) 19:8; Krause, "Rabbis and Negro Rights."

29. Jacob Rothschild's sermons, microfilm 1032, AJA; *CCAR Journal* (June 1965) 13(2):59; Rothschild, "A Rabbi in the South," speech given at Hebrew Union College, Cincinnati, January 9, 1970, copy in AJA; Krause, "Rabbis and Negro Rights," p. 38; Vorspan, "Dilemma," p. 8.

30. Box 2335, AJA, contains the letters Frank received in response to his views on desegregation. The majority of these letters commend him for his stand. There are also newspaper clippings and sermons in box 2335. Box 2143 has other of his sermons. Sidney Weil to Emmet Frank, January 26, 1959, box 2335. See also Krause, "Rabbis and Negro Rights," p. 31; Friedman, "Virginia Jewry" p. 21; and Vorspan, "Dilemma," p. 9.

31. Correspondence and Miscellaneous Items Relating to "Freedom Riders" 1961, AJA; Perry Nussbaum, autobiography, April 1967, Nearprint file, AJA; Nussbaum, "Rabbis Under Fire," paper sent to L.D. by Rabbi Nussbaum; Nussbaum, "And Then There Was One," pp. 16–17; *New York Post,* December 6, 1967, p. 52.

32. Nussbaum, "Rabbis Under Fire"; speech by Nussbaum, "The Jew in the South," November 8, 1968, copy of which was sent to L. Dinnerstein by Rabbi Nussbaum

Part III
Antisemitism in the United States

8

The Funeral
of Rabbi Jacob Joseph

The funeral of Rabbi Jacob Joseph on New York City's Lower East Side on July 30, 1902, culminated in the worst antisemitic police riot witnessed in America. Neither before nor since has any organized group of public officials displayed such animosity and wanton cruelty toward Jews in this country. Under the guise of maintaining order, the police went berserk. Thus, the riot highlighted not only the ineptness of the force in handling disturbances among large crowds but it underscored, as well, the severely antagonistic relationship that existed between the new Jewish immigrants and the officers of the law. Furthermore, it reflected the tensions extant in the city between the Jews and the Irish. Although the history of the police in the United States is replete with incidents of brutality and disrespect for the rights of minorities, laborers, strikers, civil rights advocates, and students, the antisemitic component in this one makes it stand out from all the rest.[1]

The turn-of-the-century influx of immigrants to the United States threatened many New Yorkers ensconced in their own communities, especially the Irish.[2] Since the early decades of the nineteenth century, the city never had the opportunity to achieve social stability or to assimilate its newcomers. There were always more economic changes, additional technological innovations, and flocks of people to be absorbed. "The institutional structure

of the city," James Richardson has informed us, "had great difficulty meeting the challenge put upon it by the rapid rate of social
change." In May 1902, the *New York Times* observed, "So far the
year of 1902 has broken the record of the past decade for immigrants landing at this port." In August it commented, "the volume
of immigration pouring into this country is larger than it has ever
been before, with the exception of two years—1881 and 1882."
The following January, however, the paper noted that 551,645
immigrants landed at Ellis Island in 1902, and that total broke all
records since the government began keeping them in 1819.[3]

The figures for Jews came to about 10 percent of the total.
Although the peak year for Jewish immigration had been 1892,
when 73,636 people arrived in the United States, the numbers for
1900 (60,764), 1901 (58,098), and 1902 (57,688) ranked just
below the all-time high to that date, and the three-year combination exceeded the total for any other three consecutive years to
that point. At least 75 percent of these Jewish newcomers moved
into the Lower East Side ghetto.[4]

The Irish, and this included the police, resented the Jewish
tenement dwellers crowding into the ghetto and, for several years,
had been attacking them. Along with the Germans, the Irish felt
intruded upon by these newcomers. The Germans had started to
move out of the Lower East Side and up the social ladder more
quickly than the Irish had, so their hostility toward Jews possessed
a lesser intensity than did that of the Irish. Moreover, Germans
had never entered the police force in numbers as great as the Irish,
thereby precluding another area of daily friction. During the 1890s
Jewish publications commented upon the accumulation of insults
and assaults against their brethren in the larger urban areas
throughout the country. Irish and German gangs preyed upon
Jews but the police rarely intervened to protect the victims.[5]

The source of this hostility is difficult to pinpoint. One
historian, Gerald Kurland, concluded that the "pervasive intergroup conflict seems less traceable to circumstances in the United
States than to attitudes or traditions going back to their history in
Ireland." Kurland also noted that in the old country, "those whom
an Irishman encountered in centuries past could be readily cate-

gorized as either (1) another Irishman or (2) a bitter enemy. . . ."
As Christians, of course, the Irish had imbibed the tale of the Jew
as Judas and Christ-killer from religious teachings, and they knew,
too, about the image of Shylock, or the Jew as the representative
of money and power. Anti-Jewish outbreaks occurred in Ireland
from 1884 through the end of the century as the exodus from
Russia began to make an impact on that nation's largest cities. If
humorist Finley Peter Dunne accurately captured the essence of
Irish-American views in his fictional essays about "Mr. Dooley,"
they were instinctively, and without reason, antisemitic. For example, in 1899, during the retrial for treason of the French Captain
Alfred Dreyfus, one of Dunne's characters, "Mr. Hennessy,"
reached his verdict before hearing the evidence. "I don't know
anything about it [the Dreyfus affair], but I think he's guilty. He's
a Jew."[6]

Intergroup tensions and hostilities arose frequently, not
only between Jews and Irish, but among the Irish and several
other peoples as neighborhoods engaged in the process of transition. "Most of the immigrants who arrived after the Civil War,"
historian James Richardson noted, "moved into slums formerly
dominated by the Irish. Italians, Jews, Chinese, and Negroes found
that to the Irish beating up newcomers was a kind of sport. Too
often the predominantly Irish police force arrested the victim
rather than the aggressor or joined in on the Irish side."[7] Why the
Irish, in particular, had such conflict with so many others is perplexing. Throughout much of the period between their arrival in
America before the Civil War and the end of World War II, group
antagonisms, rather than cooperation, seem to have been the
norm for them even though the leading Irish-American politicians
had the facility for getting on with members of practically all other
ethnic groups.[8]

Irishmen represented a significant percentage of the members of the police forces in the urban northeastern quadrant of the
nation, and a majority of those in New York City. As police officers,
they displayed little of the politicians' finesse in dealing with other
peoples. The cops routinely dispensed "curbside justice," using
their clubs indiscriminately on peddlers and other lower-class

immigrants who offended their sensibilities or challenged their authority.[9] As police officers, the Irish behaved in a manner similar to those in the same occupation nationally so it is difficult to distinguish on many occasions whether their behavior stemmed from ethnic association or occupational ethos. When their professional interests coincided with Irish prejudices, as they did during the riot that occurred during Rabbi Joseph's funeral, they positively exploded.

The Irish police looked down upon the Jews because of their immigrant status and low-class position, but they also harbored other resentments. The East European Jews tended to be more socialistically inclined than were the Irish and favored reforms in society to uplift the working classes. The Irish had been brought up to oppose socialism and to accept the status quo while the police were trained to uphold law and order. "The rank and file of the police department," Richardson tells us, "were every bit as anti-labor and anti-radical as the department's civilian heads."[10] Police officers, as well as devout Irish Catholics, lived in an authoritarian world with a multiplicity of rules that governed their lives. Order was a key word for both of them. The endless labor disputes on the Lower East Side between Jewish laborers and Jewish entrepreneurs exasperated the officers in blue. Thus, during strikes and labor conflicts, the police invariably supported the employers, which heightened the tensions between them and the Jewish immigrants.[11]

In 1901, the Jews on the Lower East Side rebelled against police harassment and general corruption, and voted "en masse" for the Reform administration promised by patrician Seth Low. The Reform ticket won and the police had another reason for opposing the ghetto Jews. The accumulated venom of the Irish officers and patrolmen toward the Jews then erupted at the most unexpected time—during the course of a rabbi's funeral.

Jacob Joseph, born in Krozh, province of Kovno, Russia, in 1840, studied Talmud his entire life. His intellectual gifts were recognized early and the local Jewish community supported him while he steeped himself in Talmudic lore. As an adult, he lived in Vilna, then known as the "Jerusalem of Lithuania and the greatest center of Talmudic scholarship in the world," and his fame spread throughout the Jewish quarters of eastern Europe and reached as far west as the orthodox circles of American Jews. In 1888, when prominent Jews on the Lower East Side sought to enhance the prestige of their community, a federation of several local synagogues asked the renowned spiritual leader to come to America as "chief rabbi" and to preside over the inauguration of what was hoped would be a new era in the history of American Jewry. Leaping at the opportunity presented by the challenge in the New World, "the greatest Rabbi that ever came to this country" accepted the offer and arrived in New York City on July 7, 1888.[12]

Joseph's career in America proved a terrible disappointment both to him and to the people who brought him. The most serious problem stemmed from the fact that Orthodox Jewry has no formal procedure for recognizing a "chief rabbi"; other rabbis in America saw no need to subordinate their views to his authority despite his superior erudition. His Old World sermons and customs seemed quaint in New York where people dressed and behaved differently than they had in Europe, and where they tried desperately to adapt to life in the United States. American Jews read secular newspapers, attended theaters and public schools, and strove for success. The learned rabbi never could accept the changes he saw about him. To Abraham Cahan, editor of the popular Yiddish newspaper, the *Forward,* Joseph always seemed "the man of the third century." "The very notion of a man and his wife taking a walk together, like a Gentile couple," Cahan continued, "would have shocked [the rabbi's] sense of decency." He also opposed labor unions, which infuriated the Jewish workers. His views, his manner, his dress, almost everything about him, in fact, showed the gulf between him and other American Jews. Soon people drifted away from this antiquated scholar and the rabbi found increasing solace in reading his Holy Books.[13]

For several years before his death on July 28, 1902, Rabbi Joseph dwelt quietly with his wife, practically ignored by the community. Bedridden with paralysis, his last years were as bleak as his early ones were brilliant. When the eminent Talmudist died, "like a flower transplanted to uncongenial soil," a wave of remorse spread over the ghetto. Perhaps feeling guilty over having rejected traditional Judaism and/or because they wanted to make up for all of the years that they had ignored and humiliated the great rabbi, thousands of people who had never laid eyes upon Joseph, but who knew of his reputation for scholarship and piety, gathered in front of his house at 263 Henry Street and "wept and moaned at his door." His portrait, which had not been seen on the streets for six or seven years, appeared in store windows "heavily draped in mourning." The East Side teemed with stories of his erudition, his greatness, and his philanthropy. The *Jewish Messenger* commented, "The irony of fate has again been illustrated in the case of Rabbi Joseph. The neglect to which he was subjected in his lifetime has been followed by a kind of apotheosis; and while a few weeks ago the great mass of American people were in absolute ignorance of his existence, now his name has appeared in every newspaper."[14]

Plans were made to conduct the most solemn and impressive Jewish funeral yet seen in America. Several congregations vied for the honor of burying the rabbi. Since the great man left no estate, the "prize" fell to congregation Beth Hamedrash Hadol which offered the widow $1,500 in cash and $15 a week for life. This act, called "buying a mitzva," or good deed, was supposed especially to please God and to help smooth the path to eternal happiness for all who contributed. At the same time, the synagogue lost no money. A Canal Street merchant offered $5,000 to purchase the burial plot next to the rabbi's grave and several families indicated their willingness to pay huge sums for the privilege of lying nearby in the cemetery.[15]

On the morning of July 30, 1902, sixty-two persons, including prominent rabbis from as far away as Boston and Philadelphia along with members of the family, gathered in the Joseph apartment to wash the body and dress it in the traditional shroud and prayer shawl before putting it, according to Orthodox tradition, in a plain pine box. Before removing the casket to the hearse, the men present conducted religious services and chanted the prayer for the dead. As the police and pallbearers carried the box out of the building, shortly after 11 A.M., they had to struggle against crowds of mourners who surged forward trying to touch the coffin and pay homage to the dead man.[16]

Once the bier was securely placed, Captain William Thompson of the 7th Precinct (who had already called ahead to the police in Brooklyn to warn them that this was no ordinary procession and advised that they be adequately prepared when the Grand Street ferry carrying the cortege docked early in the afternoon) moved to the front while a solid line of officers framed the hearse on all sides. Two hundred carriages carrying members of the family, distinguished mourners, and those wealthy enough to ride, attempted to follow, but the crowds rushed in between and the carriages made their way to the ferry as best they could. Directly in front of the horses and wagon pulling the hearse, hundreds of beardless youths from the religious schools in Manhattan, the Bronx, and Brooklyn, walked slowly while solemnly chanting the *Thillim,* or "Promise of David." Tears filled their eyes.[17]

The police had not anticipated the huge throngs, estimated by observers to be between 50,000 and 100,000 people. Mourners stood shoulder to shoulder across most of the Manhattan streets upon which the funeral cortege would proceed on its journey to the rabbi's final resting place. Hundreds of stores on the Lower East Side closed for the funeral and thousands of mechanics, laborers, peddlers, pushcartmen, and shop keepers gave up a day's wages to pay homage to the memory of Rabbi Jacob Joseph. "No Orthodox Jew was too old or too feeble to join" the throng, the *Sun* informed readers the next day.[18]

The previous night one of the men who had arranged the funeral sought a police permit allowing the hearse and attendant mourners to parade through the streets. He suggested that perhaps 20,000 persons would be present and he thought that an escort of twenty to twenty-five policemen would be enough to handle the crowds. The sergeant on duty at the station granted the permit. Later in the evening the police received a telephone call from a reporter at one of the Yiddish newspapers stating that the crowds would be enormous and that twenty-five police officers could not handle them. No attention was paid to the reporter's warning.[19] Police procedures dictated that the inspector in charge be informed when large public demonstrations were scheduled to occur. In this case Adam A. Cross, the responsible official, was not told by the sergeant who received the petition. Cross, temporarily in command because of another officer's leave, was also the key deputy to Police Commissioner John N. Partridge.[20]

Before the procession left the dead man's home, the police on duty that morning knew that they would need reinforcements and called for assistance. Although the exact number of police in the streets and protecting the cortege at first was not ascertained, there were at least fifty men on the job. Ten more were sent at 10:15 A.M.; then at 10:40 reserves were called out from four additional precincts; ten minutes later a call for more officers brought forth police from the 2nd, 6th, 9th, 10th, 15th, 16th, 17th, 18th, 19th, 20th, 21st, 22nd, 24th, and 25th precincts, along with increased supervisory personnel. In all, between 10 and 11 A.M. two sergeants, four roundsmen (supervisors of the foot patrol), and 102 patrolmen were dispatched. As events later proved, this was still not enough.[21]

The funeral cortege proceeded slowly from Joseph's home to synagogues on Madison, Pike, Eldridge, Forsyth, and Norfolk Streets. In front of each building rabbis recited the prayer for the dead. The intention had been to remove the casket at each synagogue, but with people wailing, sobbing, and chanting from curb-to-curb, all waiting to pay final respects and most hoping to touch the bier, the plan was altered. Unceasing lamentations were pierced by wails and screeches as the funeral procession meandered through the Lower East Side.[22]

Fortunately, at first no major disturbances arose to tax the energies of the police. To be sure, there had been some difficulty getting the procession reorganized again after the prayers had been finished in front of the last synagogue stop on Norfolk Street. The sergeant in charge, however, ordered his men to clear the block and admonished them, "But don't forget that this is a funeral and not a riot. No clubs." The patrolmen did as ordered, and many of the Jews present were astonished at the gentleness of police treatment. Within five minutes the street was cleared and the hearse began moving toward the Grand Street ferry, its final destination in Manhattan.[23]

As the procession turned east from Norfolk onto Grand Street shortly before 1:00 P.M., one could see the Hoe and Company printing press manufacturing factory, a massive building which occupied the block bound by Grand, Sheriff, Cannon, and Broome Streets. More than 1,800 people, mostly of Irish descent, worked there. Very few Jews were on the payroll. (Estimates ran from one to fifty Jewish employees, but even if one accepts the highest figure it still meant that over 97 percent of the workers were non-Jews.) On several occasions in the past few years male factory employees had insulted, terrorized, and assaulted neighborhood Jews, especially during the noon lunch break. The police and the Hoe management had received several complaints about the behavior of the young men but little had been done to curb their actions; nor had much newspaper publicity been given to the unpleasant incidents. Robert Hoe, Jr., the owner, later admitted that "some of the boys" disliked Jews and had harassed them in the past but he also indicated that he had asked them to discontinue such activities. In fact, management posted a notice in February 1901 ordering "boys throwing snowballs and other missiles at passersby on the street" to stop; the message was neither observed nor enforced. After the funeral Hoe would speculate that perhaps he had not been as strict with about 300 of these "mischievous boys" as he should have been.[24]

The police knew about the hostility that existed between the Hoe workers and the Jews (several officers admitted afterwards that the strained relations between the two groups was "common knowledge") but law enforcers sympathized with, and engaged in actions remarkably similar to, those of the Irish workers. Most policemen were of Irish descent and they had, as John Higham has written, "a reputation for brutal treatment of East Side Jews." Their rough and uncivil handling of the neighborhood people was "inexcusably common," the mayor's investigating committee would later report. Complaints about their behavior often resulted in only slight fines or reprimands from their superior officers, also usually of Irish ancestry. The *New York Times* would editorialize after the mayor's investigating committee report appeared that "the police," or a considerable portion of them, regard the Jews of the Lower East Side not as claimants for protection but as fit objects of persecution. These unhappy Jews are not only not protected by the police, they are in need of protection against the police."[25]

It is not surprising, therefore, that the advance warnings of a Jewish undertaker to Captain Thompson of the 7th Precinct went unheeded. The undertaker informed the police captain that he had never taken a Jewish funeral procession past the Hoe factory without trouble occurring. Only three weeks earlier, the undertaker explained, a driver of his had been struck in the face by an apple core thrown from one of the factory windows.[26]

As the procession made its way down Grand Street toward the ferry, one heard more clearly the shouting and jeering of the Hoe workers; as soon as the hearse passed in front of the factory, the assaults began. A stale loaf of bread hit the coachman of the wagon carrying the bier while pieces of iron and screws showered down upon the casket. An oil-soaked rag fell into the carriage behind the coffin, shocking four of the rabbis who had participated in the services that morning. Then, in a sequence which observers found difficult to recall exactly, iron bolts, blocks of wood, screws, melon rinds, and sheets of water from buckets and hoses rained out of the windows, pummeling and dousing the people in the streets. The mourners had not anticipated such a torrent of debris or such disrespectful behavior and they lost their composure. Some hurled back the same objects that had been thrown at them. Others ran into the downstairs offices of the factory to protest the demonstration.[27]

The office workers below, unaware of the happenings on the upper floors and in the streets, panicked when a mob of people, many babbling hysterically in Yiddish, surged through the front doors. Hoe officials immediately telephoned the police station requesting protection while at the same time telling the protestors, "in no doubtful language," to get out of the building. (One individual later testified that when he ran into the office and asked to have the hoses turned off he heard the response, "Get out, you sheenies, we'll soak you.") As the first committee of mourners turned to leave, another group of complainants entered. Some of the outsiders even tried to rush the stairs but were repelled when the factory superintendent, after first glancing at Mr. Hoe and getting a nod of approval, pulled the fire hose off the wall and set forth a four-inch stream of water upon those trying to reach the upper floors. This force of water along with concerted efforts of Hoe employees chased the protestors out of the building. According to the later report of the mayor's investigating committee:

> either during the struggle before the closing of the gates or imme-
> diately thereafter, the first hose on the office floor was run out and
> a stream of water was discharged therefrom, not only on those just
> ejected, but indiscriminately on the spectators in street cars and in
> the street, on the mourners in the procession and into the house
> on the opposite side of the street. Some people in the street in their
> resentment thrust their umbrellas through windows on the ground
> floor, and a fusillade of missiles sprang up on both sides, the people
> in the street supplying themselves from the heaps of stones and
> broken brick under the new East River Bridge Structure, a block
> and a half away, while the occupants of the building used whatever
> came to hand, particularly a number of large iron bolts and nuts.
> . . . At an early stage of the difficulty water was thrown out to the
> streets from the upper windows of the Hoe factory and also from
> the Sheriff Street entrance of the office floor and used in a reckless
> manner. Large numbers of people in the adjoining streets were
> drenched with this water, which penetrated a house across the
> street, and the water was cast in all directions.[28]

When the riot began observers saw four policemen stationed in front of the Hoe factory. None of them attempted to halt the disruption or curb the assailants. Had even one of the policemen "cared to perform his duty," the Yiddish newspaper, the *Jewish Gazette* noted, "this outrage could have been stopped."[29]

The rioting at the factory and in the streets apparently peaked when the hearse reached the Grand Street ferry. Those people and carriages immediately behind also remained part of the cortege. Captain Thompson had deployed about 100 men to the ferry, and they smoothed the path for a quick boarding and departure across the East River.

Three hundred policemen and another 15,000 mourners awaited the boat in Brooklyn. To avoid further demonstrations the police altered the planned route, but an altercation developed anyway at Kent Avenue and South 6th Street where some factory workers hooted, jeered and threw things from the window. The police in Brooklyn ended the demonstration swiftly. The cortege then moved slowly on its way to the cemetery where, according to the *New York Times*, crowds "trampled over graves, jumped fences, hung to the horses' heads, and rushed past the few policemen who had been sent out with the procession." Under a fierce sun, sixty-two rabbis took more than an hour chanting the appropriate prayers. Then the men began digging the grave; when ready, they deposited the coffin and covered it over with the earth they had just removed. It was almost night when the last of the mourners left the cemetery.[30]

Meanwhile, by 1:20 P.M. when the police arrived at the Hoe factory, the melee in Manhattan had begun to subside. Responding to the call from factory officials, and perhaps from others as well, about 200 additional policemen and six patrol wagons, under the command of Inspector Cross, came upon the scene. "Without a word of warning or any request to disburse," the mayor's committee wrote afterwards, the reserves "rushed upon the remnant of the gathering, some of them with great roughness of language and violence of manner." As the *New York Times* observed, "It was evident from the actions of the officers that they considered the mourners in the wrong."[31] Given the values and expectations of the police, their conclusions were, in retrospect, understandable. "Usually contemptuous of civil liberties unless the people they were dealing with were of sufficient social and political status to make trouble for them,"[32] the police had been called by a representative of the neighborhood's largest employer to complain about an unruly Jewish mob about whom the men in blue were prepared to believe any accusation. Further inquiry as to what had happened seemed unnecessary. The police viewed their responsibility as one in which they had to disperse the gathering and restore order.

Leading the way, Inspector Cross charged the crowd yelling as he slashed his club this way and that, "Kill those Sheenies! Club them right and left! Get them out of the way!" Since, as a later police commissioner wrote, the inspector "sets the pace and gives the tone" to the activities of his subordinates, it is not difficult to imagine what occurred next. The patrolmen also ran into the assemblage swinging their sticks with abandon, "shouting as they waded through the dense gathering, and shoving roughly against men and women alike. . . ." Heads were bloodied and eyes slashed as people tried to run from uniformed officers who had apparently gone crazy. Owners of carriages could not control their horses that, along with people scurrying for cover, trampled over the weaker and smaller members of the crowd as they tried to escape the scene.[33]

In the thirty minutes it took to disperse the gathering, hundreds of Jews were injured. An insurance man who witnessed the riot from his office half a block away saw policemen pursue those trying to get away, clubbing them on their heads, shoulders, and backs. Some of the Hoe employees who had started the trouble poured into the streets to aid the police. One Jew testified that as he tried to get out of the way an officer knocked him senseless. A second claimed that after being beaten without cause and thrown into a patrol wagon, he was choked by several other patrolmen. Another accused a cop of knocking his head against the wagon and then choking him. "As the man told the story," the *New York Times* reported, "his face looked as though he had been the loser in a prizefight." Doctors worked on the scene for over an hour. More than 200 people required medical attention while others ministered to their own wounds. The *Sun* reported that "several hundred" Jews had been clubbed by the police. Three of the detectives also needed medical aid. One had been hit by a stone and lost consciousness.[34]

On the afternoon of the riot, the police tried to bring the alleged culprits to justice. They arrested eleven Jews and one Hoe employee and took them to the Essex Market Court. The Jews, despite the protests of their attorneys—who included Congressman Henry Goldfolgle—that they were the victims and not the offenders, were fined $5 or $10 each for their activities that afternoon. The magistrate ordered two of the Jews held for $1,000 bail and charged them with inciting others to riot. The Hoe employee had, unfortunately, sprayed a policeman with his hose. In court he claimed that he had acted upon orders from his foreman and had not meant to douse the officer.[35]

The Hoe company and its employees also suffered from the riot. More than 200 glass window panes had been shattered, offices had been soaked, and office furniture destroyed. The factory damage totaled about $1,200. The sidewalks in front of the building on Grand Street were cluttered with sticks, stones, bits of scrap iron, bolts, barrels, and other debris. Policemen patrolled the factory during the rest of the afternoon and at 5 P.M. ordered the employees to leave in a single file. They then escorted the workers out of the neighborhood.[36]

The entire incident shocked the Lower East Side Jewish community. One Jew could not believe that after being victimized by the factory workers, the police "who should have protected us, clubbed us into insensibility." Another reflected that "it was a thing that even a Russian, with all his dislike of our people, would have been ashamed of." That evening and during the next few days protest meetings were held throughout the Jewish quarter and in other areas of the city. Resolutions were passed criticizing Hoe employees, demanding Inspector Cross's removal, denouncing police brutality, and calling for a thorough investigation of the events.[37]

East Side Jews considered the behavior of the police during the riot not as an ephemeral outburst but as part of a systematic and persistent persecution. In fact, one of the resolutions adopted at a protest meeting specifically attributed the occurrences during the rabbi's funeral to a "smoldering anti-Semitism which, if uncrushed, will lead to anarchy." Hostilities between the police and the Jews had been the norm for several years. The ghetto residents firmly believed that they would not get adequate protection from the men in blue and that they had to be wary of them.[38]

Inspector Cross received the most severe vilification. One protester characterized him as "not fit to be a butcher, much less to command 200 policemen," and others made equally harsh evaluations. Delegations of Jews went both to the mayor and the police commissioner requesting that the inspector be relieved immediately of his duties and brought up on charges. The next day Cross was transferred to the Bronx. That exile did not satisfy the ghetto residents. Cahan of the *Forward* told an enthusiastic gathering that the inspector should have been sent to Siberia.[39]

Mayor Seth Low assured the Jews that a full investigation would be made. Low had campaigned for office in 1901 under the banner of reform and primarily on the issue of police corruption. He had promised to clean up the department and rid it of its "rapacity and inefficiency." The police actions during the funeral obviously embarrassed City Hall.[40]

During the previous administration, dominated by Tammany Hall, Bill Devery had run the police department. Although newspapers clamored for his removal, Mayor Robert A. Van Wyck, a stooge of Tammany boss Richard Croker, refused to do so. He had even proclaimed Devery "the best Chief of Police New York ever had," even though Devery had openly associated with known gamblers and conducted business on a street corner in front of a saloon which remained open long after its legal closing time. (When reporters had questioned Devery about allowing the saloon to remain open after it should have been shut, the police chief responded that although he saw men going in and coming out of the building, he did not know whether it was a saloon.)[41]

Van Wyck's refusal to discharge Devery, despite his open flouting of the law, had so infuriated the Republican state legislators in Albany that they abolished the position of New York City chief of police. The Mayor had consulted Tammany boss Croker, then living in England but still managing Democratic politics in New York City, about how to handle the situation. Croker wired back that a new post, "Deputy Police Commissioner," should be created with Devery named to it. Van Wyck did as he was told.[42]

When the municipal election of 1901 approached, Richard Croker and several of his associates realized that Devery's antics had served them ill and that the police chief's mingling with known criminals reflected poorly upon the city's Democratic party. Seth Low, formerly Mayor of Brooklyn, had led a coalition of reformers, which included William Travers Jerome as candidate for district attorney, against the incumbents. Low spoke softly but Jerome struck the theme for the election by railing against existing prostitution and political graft. The Reform ticket had won the election and was committed to end the corruption that existed in the police department.[43]

As his first move, Low had chosen Colonel John N. Partridge, his Brooklyn police commissioner twenty years earlier, as New York City's chief of police. Partridge knew little about what had been going on in the police department before his arrival and showed this ignorance almost immediately by selecting as "his principal uniformed advisor Inspector Cross . . . whose reputation among policemen and others familiar with the affairs of the force was the worst." Five months into the new city administration, complaints about lax discipline and unchecked police blackmailing activities continued as if nothing had changed.[44]

Thus the charges made against the police, and especially against Inspector Cross, after their discreditable performances on the day of Rabbi Joseph's funeral, came before a mayor sensitive to the misdeeds of the force. Even without a background of police bumbling and corruption, an investigation would have been expected, but in light of the suspicions that press and public already had of Partridge's operations and Cross's activities, a thorough police department inquiry was ordered by the mayor. A few days later Low expanded the investigation by asking a distinguished group of citizens to conduct their own investigation and report directly to him.[45]

The result of the police inquiry was presaged on the very day of the riot when, after the funeral, Colonel Partridge requested an immediate report from Cross. That afternoon the inspector, having spoken only with Hoe officials about the causes, quickly summarized his findings for the chief. When newspapermen queried Cross about whether he would also seek information from "East Side Hebrews," the following exchange occurred:

> *Cross:* "No, I am not sending out invitations to people to come here and tell me their troubles. If anyone has a grievance I expect him to call on me. I have never found people bashful under those circumstances."
>
> *Reporters:* "Then you do not intend to solicit such complaints?"
>
> *Cross:* "No, why should I?"
>
> *Reporters:* "How, then, do you expect to get at the facts?"
>
> *Cross:* "Never you mind. Leave that to me."[46]

The police department released Cross's report to the public. The document stunned both participants in, and spectators at, the riot. According to the police inspector, huge crowds had not been anticipated and therefore a smaller number of policemen were assigned than might otherwise have been the case. He also claimed that "no clubbing was done in front of the Hoe factory after I got there, and the men told me that they had not seen any previous to that time. . . . If there were isolated instances of clubbing, however, I was in no way responsible for them." Then Cross made what the *Sun* called a "remarkable assertion." He stated that the mourners came armed with stones, nuts, and bolts, and had deliberately flung them at the factory windows thereby precipitating the riot. "Those who broke the windows and destroyed the property of Hoe and Co.," the report read, "came there prepared to do what they did, showing at the time that the attack on Hoe and Co. was premeditated."[47]

The police department's investigation of the riot was obviously a travesty. "The inherent belief of all the police force from top to bottom," a later commissioner would write, is "that the press and public are prejudiced against them, and that the courts are their enemies instead of their friends. . . ." In times of crisis, the police of 1902, just as those in other eras, shielded each other.[48] Accordingly, no officer could be found to make incriminating remarks about another or break ranks when confronted by outsiders. William McAdoo, the police commissioner who would make the assertions, attributed these characteristics to the strong Irish heritage of the police. An Irish mother would rather see her child dead than see him "inform." McAdoo then quoted a policeman of Irish ancestry who told him, "I would be ashamed to look my children in the face if I turned informer." In a broader study of the Irish and their cultural ethos, Daniel Levine would write, "The Irish policemen exercised wide discretion in apprehending violators—and upholders—of the law. They interpreted the law with the latitude and flexibility appropriate to their interests. . . ." Mutually reinforcing occupational and cultural traditions ensured that the police inquiry into their own behavior vis-à-vis a local outgroup—the Jews—would not lead to the exposure or punishment of any of the culprits.[49]

The independent citizens committee that the Mayor appointed, however, included individuals more distinguished and impartial than the members of the police force. Low chose five men renowned for their independence and public service. They included William H. Baldwin, president of the Long Island Railroad and chairman of a former citizens committee which had unearthed previous maladministration in the police department when Tammany Hall had controlled the city government; Thomas Mulry, a well-known Catholic banker and philanthropist; Edward B. Whitney, a prominent attorney and former member of the New York State Tenement House Commission; and two highly regarded Jews, Louis Marshall and Nathan Bijur. The members elected Whitney as chairman, and a Jew, Bernhard Rabbino, vice-president of the East Side Civic Club, as clerk. The composition of the committee pleased the Lower East Side ghetto residents. The *Jewish Gazette* observed, "If the Mayor had carefully scrutinized every Jew in New York City, he could not have secured two more representative men" than Marshall and Bijur. The Christians on the committee, the editorial continued, "are men who are known throughout the city as possessing rare culture and education and men possessing a high sense of American fairness. We feel that if this committee really has power it will do the East Side justice."[50]

The committee possessed few legal powers. It could not subpoena witnesses nor penalize those who refused to cooperate, but its members had prestige as well as the respect of a large majority of the Lower East Side Jews. This meant that the committee's report would probably be received by the Jews, the Mayor and his associates, and others in the city with appropriate recognition and appreciation. The *Jewish Gazette* even engaged in some wishful thinking and speculated that the committee investigation might lead to "the relief from the petty persecutions and picayune tyrannies to which the East Side has been subjected for so long."[51]

The group met for the first time on August 12, 1902, at 61 Rivington Street in the heart of the ghetto. Through August 20 the members heard testimony that, for the most part, unearthed no information about the riot that had not already been published. One of the committee's functions, it seems, was to provide a forum for the expressions of accumulated grievances that the Jews had been harboring toward the police. Most of the witnesses related their own horrible experiences and repeated stories about long-time police brutality in the neighborhood. People told of a boy being beaten by a policeman for loudly reciting poetry in the park, of Jews and Jewish funerals being regularly attacked in front of the Hoe premises, and of the police shutting their eyes when the victims happened to be Jewish. Furthermore, many of the people spoke of the inability of a Jew to get justice in the station house or in the local magistrate's court. One man explained to the committee that until "5 or 6 years ago" there had been few Jews in the area of the Hoe factory, but that recent immigration had changed the composition of the neighborhood. The man continued, "There has been a certain amount of race feeling in that locality for years." A physician claimed that he had been a resident of the area for 26 years and had seen many outrages perpetrated by the Gentiles and the police upon the Jews but had not bothered to complain because experience had taught him that such protests "would do no good."[52]

The mayor's committee also invited Hoe workers and supervisors to appear. Their testimony contradicted that given by the Jews. One foreman claimed that the riot had been planned in advance and began when a fracas developed in the street between cigarmakers and cloakmakers. He also asserted that no water could have emanated from the factory windows because the hoses stopped ten feet in front of them. More than twenty Hoe workers stated that no iron bolts like those found in the streets were used in the factory; therefore they must have been thrown first from the outside before being hurled back. A foreman even asserted that he had observed a woman with an apron full of stones supplying the men with missiles used to bombard the factory. Hoe employees also told the committee members that no hot water existed in the building and therefore they could not have scalded anyone outside. (Committee members Marshall and Mulry later toured the factory and found hundreds of bolts such as those that had been flung from the windows and also tested the water and discovered that it was hot.) The attorney for the Hoe firm told committee members on the last day of the hearings that the owners of the factory would not testify because they had nothing to add to the declarations that had already been made.[53]

Several policemen also had an opportunity to speak before the committee. They confirmed that tensions existed between Hoe workers and Jewish area residents. Inspector Cross reiterated his belief that the mourners had come armed and had determined beforehand to attack the factory. He also admitted that he had obtained the information for his report primarily from the people at the Hoe factory and had not spoken to even one Jew until more than two hours after he had arrived at the scene of the riot. In addition to the public hearings, the members heard some witnesses in private and had access to the records of the police commissioner as well as to affidavits given to the district attorney.[54]

Less than three weeks after the hearings the committee delivered its unanimous report. Although temperate and even understated, the findings devastated the police and Hoe workers alike. The document asserted, "It is universally conceded that those who actually took part in the funeral procession are entirely without fault." Inspector Cross's attempt to put blame upon the bystanders was "without any basis of justification." The primary responsibility for the disturbances rested with the Hoe employees. Although the factory employers were not held responsible for the riot, they were censured for failing to identify or reprimand the perpetrators. "To us," the report read, "there seems to be every indication of a concerted effort to hush up the affair and to protect all the inmates of the factory from discharge or prosecution." Several Hoe executives refused to speak with the committee and also prohibited those who had been assaulted from going into the building to identify the culprits. Simply because few Hoe workers chose to come before the committee did not mean that they were in the wrong, the report noted, "though we cannot but be affected in our judgment of the whole affair by the fact that so many desisted from inquiry into its cause where the temptation to inquire would naturally be so strong."[55]

Another section of the conclusions addressed itself to the negligence of the police. The committee members reprimanded those at police headquarters who had accepted a layman's analysis of how many patrolmen would be needed for the funeral and rejected the advice of a late-evening caller telling them that the anticipated crowds would demand a huge patrol. In private conversation with the committee members, police authorities actually acknowledged that 400 patrolmen should have been assigned along with a suitable number of ranking officers. Those police officers charged with escorting the funeral procession and controlling the crowds, committee members concluded, did not conduct themselves in a professional manner. "Through the day," the findings stated, "the mourners and spectators were treated by the police with marked incivility and roughness." The committee members also commented on the general relations between the police and the ghetto dwellers. For a period of years, they observed, there seems to have been "a complete lack of sympathy between the policemen and the residents of the East Side."[56]

The leading daily and Jewish newspapers applauded the committee's conclusions. The *Tribune* editorialized that not only did the report confirm the impression that the police "failed disgracefully" in their duty to protect the mourners but observed as well that since the riot "the police authorities have been most lenient to policemen charged with ill treating the abused mourners." The editorial sharply depicted the attitudes that existed among the Irish toward other groups in the city: "It is evident that a great number of rank and file of the force, as well as many of the sergeants and captains, sympathize with the rowdies and are rather glad to see them give vent to race prejudices. The fact is the 'tough' spirit is strongly intrenched in the police force. The rowdies who think it smart to pummel 'niggers,' stone poor Russian Jews, kick over Syrians' fruit stands, annoy industrious 'Dagos,' pull the pigtails of the 'Chinks,' and trample under foot plain citizens of American blood are generally the friends of the policemen." The *New York Times* called for the "very sternest administration of justice . . . upon such policemen as are proved to have persecuted the people they were bound to protect." The *Jewish Messenger* approvingly admitted that "it was rare" for the police department to have been so "vigorously condemned," while London's *Jewish Chronicle* stated: "The report forms the most telling arraignment of the police administration made since Mr. Low came into office. . . ."[57]

Mayor Low, after being told by District Attorney Jerome that the committee's conclusions coincided with reports made to him by subordinates, ordered those culpable for malfeasance brought to trial. The Mayor's immediate and forthright response brought praise from the *Jewish Messenger*. Low "has done his full duty," the paper wrote; "we don't have enough words of praise for him." Then it added, prophetically, that Colonel Partridge had "very few" days left as police commissioner.[58]

In the time allotted, Partridge further demonstrated his inadequacies. He followed the Mayor's orders in having charges brought against Inspector Cross for failing to assign an adequate number of officers to the procession, for permitting patrolmen to use their clubs on the crowds, and for conduct unbecoming an officer in making a misleading and untrue report of the riot; against Captain John D. Herlihy for failing to provide an adequate escort for the funeral and for permitting a sergeant to disregard a warning that there would be at least 100,000 persons at the funeral; and against Captain Charles Albertson for going out to lunch while the procession was passing in front of the Hoe factory and for not informing him of the need for preserving order during the course of the funeral. Two others charged resigned from the force before the trial while those indicted by the district attorney's office later won acquittal in the courts. The officers tried by the police department also escaped without punishment. Commissioner Partridge judged all of the accusations against his men to be "without foundation" and concluded that the evidence produced did not sustain the charges.[59]

Partridge's decision was not surprising. Historically, both before and after 1902, policemen throughout the country have generally closed ranks and protected one another when attacked by persons outside of the department. The literature on this subject indicates that it is neither an "Irish" nor a "New York" phenomenon. "To maintain the morale of their organization," Richardson wrote in his study of the New York police, "commissioners tended to accept the policeman's word against that of a civilian complainant unless the civilian had social or political influence." Moreover, since there were no institutional sanctions against it, "police perjury was commonplace."[60] The policemen simply lied to protect themselves and their superiors chose to believe them.[61]

The exoneration of those officers tried for their culpability for the riot came in late December, two weeks after Partridge submitted his resignation, effective January 1, 1903. The attacks made upon him personally, as well as in his professional capacity, left no doubt that he had not accomplished what the Mayor had originally promised. One of Low's biographers later wrote that Partridge's "customary inactivity in the wake of the Rabbi Joseph riot sealed his fate as Police Commissioner." The City Club, a good-government organization, investigated the police department and found that "the connection of the members of the police force with illicit business that characterized the last administration have not been adequately diminished." On December 12, 1902, the day that the City Club intended to send a delegation to the Mayor requesting him to dismiss the Police Commissioner, Partridge resigned.[62]

Neither the Commissioner's departure, the report of the mayor's committee, nor the riot led to any significant changes. Low's next appointee, Francis V. Greene, tried to improve the quality of police work, and, in fact, had charges of neglect of duty and conduct unbecoming an officer brought against Cross. The accusations were sustained in a department trial, and after the conviction Green dismissed Cross from the force.[63] Police harassment of Jews continued, however. Commissioners came and went at the Police Department, and Tammany Hall unseated Low at the next election thereby regaining control of the city government, which it held onto for the better part of the next thirty years.

In September 1908, only six years after the riot at Rabbi Joseph's funeral, New York City Police Commissioner Theodore A. Bingham announced that Jews constituted 50 percent of the city's criminals. The furor that arose by this assertion forced Bingham, who could not factually substantiate his remarks, to retract them two weeks after they appeared in print.[64] The original assertion indicated that police prejudices toward Jews continued unabated and that whatever impact the report of the mayor's investigating committee might have made in 1902, its effect had been entirely dissipated by 1908.

In retrospect, it seems that the outstanding significance of the riot was not to unveil police brutality—which was and remained a fairly common occurrence in most cities of America throughout the century—but to highlight the friction that existed between minority groups in the growing cities of industrial America. The Irish resented the Jews, and those feelings reflected themselves in the policemen's attitudes. As William McAdoo, who succeeded Greene as police commissioner, wrote, "Irish traditions and feelings have been incorporated into the very organization of the police."[65] Thus one must consider the ways of the policemen and their actions not only as those of officers of the law but also as expressions of group feeling.

A specific example, commented upon by contemporaries, of the differing attitudes of the New York City police toward one of their own in contrast with an outsider was the comparison of their performances after the deaths of two religious figures. Archbishop Michael A. Corrigan, son of Irish immigrants, died in May 1902. He had been the reigning prelate in the city's Roman Catholic Church since his consecration in 1885. For the Archbishop's ceremonies at St. Patrick's Cathedral, where more than 100,000 people passed by the bier in two days, about 500 policemen were assigned. No unseemly behavior occurred. The police arrangements were even singled out by the *New York Times* for being "excellent both in plan and execution." The corresponding lack of respect for a Jewish leader, however, was striking. Although Corrigan, a major ecclesiastical figure in the community, had, unlike Joseph, maintained his dominant position and the respect of his congregants throughout the seventeen-year period that he headed the Roman Catholic Church in New York City, the *Jewish Messenger* asserted, "The contrast between the funerals of Archbishop Corrigan and Rabbi Joseph could not be glossed over." The *New York Times* echoed the Jewish journal's conclusions: "The contrast" between the two funerals "explains the whole business. . . ."[66]

Thus the riot at the funeral resulted not only because of inadequate police protection and Inspector Cross's viciousness, but also because of the total insensitivity of the police to minority rights as well as to the intense interethnic animosity which had developed in the city with the huge influx of Jews (there were about 600,000 of them in New York in 1902, with about two-thirds of these people having arrived during the previous decade).[67] The funeral of Rabbi Jacob Joseph, therefore, must be seen in the context of developing antagonisms caused by an older and established ethnic group—the Irish—feeling overwhelmed and encroached upon by a newer one—the Jews—whose numbers appear unlimited. The Jews did change the character of the Lower East Side just as the Irish feared they would, and the continued and expanded immigration during the next two decades precluded any peaceful resolution of conflict between the two groups. Not until well into the twentieth century, when both the Jews and the Irish ceased competing with one another for a secure place in American society, did their animosity begin to subside. By that time there were other ethnics in the city experiencing the same tensions that the Jews and Irish had overcome, and charges of "police brutality" and insensitivity to minority needs were hurled by blacks and Hispanics who had replaced the former groups at the bottom of society.

Notes

Financial assistance to do this research was provided by grants from the American Philosophical Society and the University of Arizona Humanities Fund.

1. Moses Rischin, *The Promised City: New York's Jews, 1870–1914* (New York, 1970), p. 91; John Hingham, *Send These to Me* (New York, 1975), p. 136; see also Robert M. Fogelson, *Big City Police* (Cambridge, Mass., 1977), p. 34; Samuel Walker, *A Critical History of Police Reform* (Lexington, Mass., 1977), p. 17.

2. Ronald H. Bayor, *Neighbors In Conflict* (Baltimore, 1978), p. 3.

3. James F. Richardson, *The New York Police: Colonial Times to 1901* (New York, 1970), pp. 165–66; *New York Times*, May 4, 1902, p. 6, Aug. 17, 1902, p. 6, Jan. 1, 1903, p. 5.

4. Edward A. Steiner, "The Russian and Polish Jew in New York," *Outlook* (1902) 72: 532; Leonard Dinnerstein and David M. Reimers, *Ethnic Americans*, 2nd ed. (New York, 1982), p. 163.

5. Rischin, *The Promised City*, p. 91; Higham, *Send These to Me*, pp. 134–35; Philip Cowen, *Memories of an American Jew* (New York, 1932), p. 289; *American Israelite* (Cincinnati), July 13, 1899, p. 4; *B'nai B'rith Messenger*, May 20, 1899, p. 4; Morris D. Waldman, *Nor By Power* (New York, 1953), pp. 297–98; Rose A. Halpern, "The American Reaction to the Dreyfus Case" (unpublished Master's thesis, Columbia University, 1941), pp. 85, 88–89.

6. Gerald Kurland, *Seth Low: The Reformer in an Urban and Industrial Age* (New York, 1971), p. 41; Rudolf Glanz, *Jew and Irish* (New York, 1966), pp. 12–13, 22, 106, 128–29; Finley Peter Dunne, *Mr. Dooley At His Best* (New York, 1938), p. 136.

7. Richardson, *New York Police*, p. 167.

8. Kurland, *Seth Low*, pp. 39, 40, 41, 118.

9. "Hard On The Jews," *Life* (Sept. 25, 1902) 40: 266; Richardson, *New York Police*, pp. 158, 189, 193, 201; Higham, *Send These to Me*, p. 136; Walker, *A Critical History of Police Reform*, pp. 15, 17.

10. Richardson, *New York Police*, p. 200; see also Fogelson, *Big City Police*, p. 34.

11. Walker, *A Critical History of Police Reform*, p. 17; Richardson, *New York Police*, pp. 172, 199, 200, 201.

12. Abraham Cahan, "The Late Rabbi Joseph, Hebrew Patriarch of New York," *American Review of Reviews* (Sept. 1902), 26: 312–13, 316; Stanley Feldstein, *The Land That I Show You* (Garden City, N.Y., 1978), p. 179; Paul Masserman and Max Baker, *The Jews Come to America* (New York, 1932), pp. 253–54; Peter Wiernik, *History of the Jews in America* (New York, 1912), p. 278; Abraham Cahan, "The Late Rabbi Joseph," *American Hebrew* (Aug. 1, 1902): 302; see also Abraham J. Karp, "New York Chooses a Chief Rabbi," *Publications of the American Jewish Historical Society* (Mar. 1955) vol. 44.

13. Masserman and Baker, *The Jews Come To America*, pp. 253–54; Cahan "The Late Rabbi Joseph," p. 313.

14. Cahan, "The Late Rabbi Joseph," pp. 311, 314; *American Hebrew* 71: 302; *New York Times*, Aug. 10, 1902, p. 25; *Jewish Messenger* (New York), Aug. 15, 1902, p. 6.

15. *American Israelite*, Aug. 7, 1902, p. 4; *New York Times*, July 31, 1902, p. 2; Harry Simonhoff, *Sage of American Jewry, 1865–1914* (New York, 1959), p. 199.

16. *New York Sun*, July 31, 1902, p. 2; *New York Times*, July 31, 1902, p. 2; Cahan, "The Late Rabbi Joseph," p. 312.

17. *New York Times,* July 31, 1902, p. 2; *New York Sun,* July 31, 1902, p. 2; Cahan, "The Late Rabbi Joseph," p. 312.

18. *New York Sun,* July 31, 1902. p. 2.

19. *New York Times,* July 31, 1902, p. 2; *New York Tribune,* July 31, 1902, p. 3; Cahan, "The Late Rabbi Joseph," p. 312; *Jewish Messenger,* Aug. 8, 1902, p. 6.

20. "The Report of the Mayor's Committee," *American Hebrew* (Sept. 19, 1902) 71: 497; *New York Times,* Oct. 21, 1902, p. 16; letter from John N. Partridge to Seth Low, July 31, 1902, in "Scrapbook, 1902," p. 116, in Seth Low MSS., New York City Municipal Archives.

21. Partridge to Low, July 31, 1902, Low MSS.; "Report of the Mayor's Committee," p. 497.

22. *New York Times,* July 31, 1902, pp. 1, 2; *New York Sun,* July 31, 1902, p. 2; *New York Tribune,* July 31, 1902, p. 1.

23. *New York Sun,* July 31, 1902, p. 2.

24. *New York Sun,* July 31, 1902, p. 1, Aug. 1, 1902, p. 1, Aug. 3, 1902, p. 4; *New York Times,* July 31, 1902, p. 1, Aug. 1, 1902, p. 4, Aug. 3, 1902, p. 3, Aug. 14, 1902, p. 9, Sept. 16, 1902, p. 2; *New York Tribune,* July 31, 1902, p. 1, Aug. 1, 1902, p. 3; *American Israelite,* Aug. 7, 1902, p. 7.

25. *New York Times,* Aug. 26, 1902, p. 14, Sept. 16, 1902, p. 8; Higham, *Send These to Me,* p. 136; "Report of the Mayor's Committee," p. 498; see also William McAdoo, *Guarding a Great City* (New York, 1906), p. 262; *Life* (Sept. 25, 1902) 40: 266.

26. *New York Times,* Aug. 1, 1902, p. 4, Aug. 19, 1902, p. 7; see also Higham, *Send These to Me,* pp. 135–136.

27. *Jewish Gazette* (New York), Aug. 15, 1902, p. 1 (English Supplement; all references to this newspaper are to its English Supplement); *New York Sun,* July 31, 1902, p. 1; *New York Times,* July 31, 1902, p. 1, Aug. 19, 1902, p. 7.

28. *New York Times,* July 31, 1902, p. 1; *New York Tribune,* July 31, 1902, p. 1, Aug. 6, 1902, p. 4; *New York Sun,* July 31, 1902, p. 1; "Report of the Mayor's Committee," p. 497.

29. *Jewish Gazette,* Aug. 15, 1902, p. 2.

30. *New York Sun,* July 31, 1902, p. 2; *New York Times,* July 31, 1902, pp. 1, 2.

31. "Report of the Mayor's Committee," pp. 497–98; *New York Times,* July 31, 1902, p.1.

32. Richardson, *New York Police,* p. 194.

33. McAdoo, *Guarding A Great City,* p. 22; *New York Times,* July 31, 1902, p. 1, Aug. 1, 1902, pp. 1, 14, Aug. 2, 1902, p. 2, Aug. 3, 1902, p. 3; *New York Sun,* Aug. 1, 1902, pp. 1, 14; *American Israelite,* Aug. 7, 1902, p. 7.

34. *New York Times,* July 31, p. 2, Aug. 2, 1902, p. 2, Aug. 14, 1902, p. 9; *New York Sun,* July 31, 1902, Aug. 2, 1902, p. 10; *New York Tribune,* Aug. 5, 1902, p. 3; *Jewish Gazette,* Aug. 15, 1902, p. 1; *American Israelite,* Aug. 14, 1902, p. 7.

35. *New York Tribune,* July 31 1902, p. 3; *New York Times,* July 31, 1902, p. 2, Aug. 1, 1902, p. 14.

36. *New York Times,* July 31, 1902, pp. 1, 2; *New York Tribune,* July 31, 1902, pp. 1, 3; *New York Sun,* July 31, 1902, p. 2.

37. *New York Times,* July 31, 1902, p. 2, Aug. 1, 1902, p. 14, Aug. 2, 1902, p. 2, Aug. 7, 1902, p. 14; *New York Sun,* Aug. 1, 1902, p. 1; *New York Tribune,* Aug. 1, 1902, p. 3, Aug. 6, 1902, p. 4.

38. *New York Times,* Aug. 2, 1902, p. 2, Aug. 3, 1902, p. 3, Aug. 7, 1902, p. 4;

Jewish Chronicle (London), Aug. 8, 1902, p. 17; *New York Sun*, July 31, 1902, p. 2; *New York Tribune*, Aug. 1, 1902, p. 3.

39. *New York Times*, Aug. 1, 1902, p. 14, Aug. 2, 1902, p. 2; *New York Sun*, Aug. 2, 1902, p. 10.

40. *New York Tribune*, Aug. 1, 1902, p. 3; *New York Sun*, Aug. 5, 1902, p. 10; *Jewish Messenger*, Aug. 8, 1902, p. 6.

41. "A Serious Matter," *American Hebrew* (Aug. 1, 1902), 71:92.

42. Ibid.

43. Gustavus Myers, *The History of Tammany Hall* (New York, 1917), pp. 473, 487.

44. Kurland, *Seth Low*, p. 145; Myers, *History of Tammany Hall*, p. 303; *New York Times*, Mar. 1, 1903, p. 2; Francis Vinton Greene, *The Police Department of the City of New York* (New York, 1903), pp. 50, 52, 53–54; "The Police Failure," *Nation* (May 29, 1902) 74:420; Steven C. Swett, "The Test of a Reformer: A Study of Seth Low, New York City Mayor, 1902–1903," *New York Historical Society Quarterly* (Jan. 1960) 44:35.

45. *New York Sun*, Aug. 1, 1902, p. 1; *New York Times*, Aug. 1, 1902, p. 1, Aug. 7, 1902, pp. 2, 14; *New York Tribune*, Aug. 1, 1902, p. 3; *Jewish Gazette*, Aug. 15, 1902, p. 1.

46. Jewish Gazette, Aug. 22, 1902, p. 5; *New York Times*, Aug. 1, 1902, p. 14.

47. *New York Tribune*, July 31, 1902, p. 2, Aug. 1, 1902, p. 3; *New York Times*, Aug. 1, 1902, p. 14, Aug. 2, 1902, p. 2; *New York Sun*, July 31, 1902, p. 2.

48. Mark H. Haller, "Historical Roots of Police Behavior: Chicago, 1890–1925," *Law and Society Review* (Winter 1976) 10: 320, 321; Harlan Hahn, "A Profile of Urban Police," in *The Police Community*, ed. Jack Goldsmith and Sharon S. Goldsmith (Pacific Palisades, Calif., 1974), pp. 19, 20; Egon Bittner, "Espirit De Corps and the Code of Secrecy," in *The Police Community*, ed. Goldsmith and Goldsmith, pp. 237, 238.

49. McAdoo, *Guarding a Great City*, pp. 268, 271–272; Edward M. Levine, *The Irish and Irish Politicians* (Notre Dame, Ind., 1966), pp. 122–23.

50. *New York Times*, Aug. 7, 1902, p. 14; Jan. 6, 1911, p. 9; Mar. 11, 1916, p. 11.

51. *Jewish Gazette*, Aug. 22, 1902, p. 5.

52. *New York Times*, Aug. 13, 1902, p. 4, Aug. 21, 1902, p. 5; *New York Tribune*, Aug. 13, 1902, p. 2.

53. *Jewish Gazette*, Aug. 29, 1902, p. 4; *New York Times*, Aug. 19, 1902, p. 7, Aug. 21, 1902, p. 5, Aug. 26, 1902, p. 14.

54. *Jewish Gazette*, Aug. 19, 1902, p. 4; *New York Times*, Aug. 26, 1902, p. 14; "Report of the Mayor's Committee," p. 497.

55. "Report of the Mayor's Committee," p. 497.

56. Ibid., pp. 497–99.

57. *New York Tribune*, Sept. 17, 1902, p. 10; *New York Times*, Sept. 16, 1902, p. 8; *Jewish Messenger*, Sept. 19, 1902; p. 5; *Jewish Chronicle*, Sept. 19, 1902, p. 8; see also n. 54.

58. Kurland, *Seth Low*, p. 159. *New York Times*, Sept. 18, 1902, p. 1; *Jewish Gazette*, Sept. 26, 1902, p. 1.

59. *New York Times*, Oct. 1, 1902, p. 16, Dec. 25, 1902, p. 2; *New York Tribune*, Oct. 21, 1902, p. 4; Louis Marshall to the editor of the *Jewish Gazette*, Dec. 29, 1902, in *Louis Marshall: Champion of Liberty*, ed. Charles Reznikoff, 2 vols. (Philadelphia, 1957), 1:11.

60. Richardson, *New York Police*, p. 203.

61. See Haller, "Historical Roots of Police Behavior," *Law and Society Review* 10:320, 321; Hahn, "Urban Police," p. 19, and Bittner, "Espirit de Corps," p. 237, both in *The Police Community*, ed. Goldsmith and Goldsmith.

62. *New York Times,* Nov. 21, 1902, p. 2, Dec. 13, 1902, p. 1; Kurland, *Seth Low,* p. 159; *Nation* (Dec. 18, 1902) 75:473.

63. *New York Times,* Mar. 1, 1903, p. 1, Mar. 7, 1903, p. 3, Mar. 21, 1903, p. 16, Apr. 10, 1903, p. 5, Apr. 18, 1903, p. 2, May 7, 1903, p. 1.

64. Arthur A. Goren, *New York Jews and the Quest for Community* (New York, 1970), pp. 24, 34.

65. McAdoo, *Guarding a Great City,* p. 261.

66. *New York Times,* May 9, 1902, p. 3, May 10, 1902, p. 3, Aug. 3, 1902, p. 3, Sept. 16, 1902, p. 8; *Jewish Messenger,* Sept. 19, 1902, p. 6.

67. Isaac Max Rubinow, "The Jewish Question in New York City (1902–1903)," *Publications of the American Jewish Historical Society* (Sept. 1959) 44:92; Dinnerstein and Reimers, *Ethnic Americans,* p. 63.

9

Antisemitism
Exposed and Attacked

1945–1950

Antisemitism has plagued Jews since the Colonial era. It waxed especially strong during the years sandwiched by the ends of World Wars I and II, and reached a highpoint between 1945 and 1947.[1] After that date the nation's hostility toward Jews began to decline sharply. Although observers pinpoint different dates for the peak of antisemitism in the United States, all agree that it became increasingly troublesome for Jews in the 1920s and accelerated in the 1930s and early 1940s. Many Jews witnessed the developing intensity of antisemitic feeling after World War I in the United States but for a variety of reasons could not grapple with the problem in any unified fashion. German and East European Jews in this country shied away from one another and frequently saw more differences than similarities among their values. Moreover, many Jewish organizations sought to minimize differences between themselves and their Christian neighbors and did not want to call too much attention to American antisemitism. There were, of course, exceptions. Discriminatory quotas in institutions of higher education came under severe Jewish censure and Henry Ford, who disseminated outright lies with the fabricated "Protocols of the Elders of Zion," which purported to show a Jewish plot to take over the Christian world, had to be made to retract his publication of many falsehoods about Jews and their ideas.

The pollster Elmo Roper noted that antisemitism in the United States reached its zenith as World War II approached, declined somewhat during the conflagration, and rose again immediately after the war ended. Psychologist Gordon Allport found 5 to 10 percent of the American population in 1944 rabidly antisemitic, and another 45 percent mildly so. The following year the British Ambassador in Washington informed his government that "The United States is so strongly anti-Semitic that anti-Semitism at home is an ever present problem for every American Jew." And several professionals who conducted surveys discovered that no matter how it was phrased, more than a third and sometimes more than a half, of the respondents replied "yes" to the question, "Do you think Jews have too much power in the United States?" The percentages replying affirmatively to the inquiry varied as follows:

March 1938	41%
April 1940	43%
February 1941	45%
October 1941	48%
May 1944	56%
June 1945	58%
February 1946	55%

These opinions were shared by all types of people throughout the country.[2]

The nation's best educated men and women both set and reflected the prevailing tone. In an unsigned article in the first issue of the *Journal of Clinical Psychology* (January 1945), the author acknowledged the dearth of trained personnel in his profession but warned against accepting too many graduate students from "one racial group." He went on to explain that

> because of long racial experience with suffering and personality problems, certain groups of students show an unusual interest and propensity for psychological science. . . . While disclaiming racial intolerance, it nevertheless seems unwise to allow any one group to dominate or take over any clinical speciality as has occurred in

several instances. The importance of clinical psychology is so great
for the total population that the profession should not be exploited
in the interests of any one group in such manner that the public
acceptance of the whole program is jeopardized.

The writer's blatant bigotry (and none of his Jewish readers
needed to be informed which "racial group" he was discussing)
was attacked by several correspondents. In the next issue of the
journal the author indicated that "the wording of this paragraph
was admittedly unfortunate," but he did not retract the
sentiment.[3]

That same year other well educated Americans expressed
concern over the "dangers" of accepting unlimited numbers of
dental students from "one racial strain." Dr. Harlan M. Horner,
Secretary of the Council on Dental Education of the American
Dental Association surveyed the students at Columbia and New
York University dental schools and reported that the institutions
should seek more diversity within the student body because too
many of those enrolled seemed to have come from "one racial
strain."[4] Although the President-elect of the American Dental
Association repudiated Dr. Horner's conclusions, his observations
were not totally ignored. In 1946 the dean of one of New York
City's dental schools told a New York City Council investigating
committee that he had been repeatedly "ordered" by the university's president to reduce the number of Jewish students.[5]

Increasingly blunt bigotry alarmed American Jewry and
inspired its leaders to fight back. Efforts had been made earlier to
combat antisemitism but not with any semblance of unity until
World War II. In 1943 every major American Jewish organization
except the American Jewish Committee united under the umbrella
organization of the American Jewish Conference to work for the
Zionist goal—a national Jewish state in Palestine. The American
Jewish Committee opposed the Zionists' demand for a Jewish
Palestine. After the American Jewish Conference endorsed the
Zionist program, an offshoot of the American Jewish Committee,
the American Council for Judaism, began. Composed mostly of
assimilated, Reform, middle and upper class American Jews of
German descent, the American Council for Judaism worked to

undermine Zionism. But despite the aloofness of the American Jewish Committee and the opposition of the American Council for Judaism, the disjointedness and slight differences which had precluded common action in the past now seemed less of a barrier. In just a few short years Adolf Hitler's maniacal scheme to rid Europe of its Jews accomplished what no Jew since Moses had done—practically unified world Jewry in rallying to a common cause.

The first emergence of an almost unanimous American Jewry was remarkable. Once most Jews in the United States joined together under the Zionist umbrella, they tried their hand at other community problems. And in these endeavors the American Jewish Committee willingly cooperated with a host of other groups. Most of the organizational leaders believed that they should attack antisemitism in a multifaceted way. Bigotry affected all Jews and a common approach to the problem was needed. The advent of Hitler in Europe convinced American Jews that they could no longer remain passive about disturbances in the United States. They had to combat them. As a result, several Jewish organizations established the National Community Relations Advisory Council (CRC) in March, 1944, as a coordinating and clearing unit for domestic defense groups. Components of the CRC included national agencies like the American Jewish Committee, the American Jewish Congress, B'nai B'rith, the Jewish Labor Committee, the Jewish War Veterans, the Union of American Hebrew Congregations, and about twenty local community groups. The CRC established committees on legislative information, community consultation, antisemitism, discrimination in educational institutions, intercultural and scientific research projects, and organized its various members to work together for the common good.[6]

Along with the local and national groups, the CRC probed, inquired, and conducted research into the causes of antisemitism and the means of combatting it. To lay the base for a more tolerant society and to reduce prejudice against Jews, the agencies carried on broad educational, social action, and community programs. The Jewish agencies assumed the position that antisemitism, along with other forms of bigotry, threatened American democracy and therefore posed a problem for the entire society, not merely one segment of it. Thus, Jewish leaders decided that they would employ the social sciences to analyze prejudice and develop a cure for it, mobilize public opinion against intolerance, and utilize the courts and legislative bodies to eradicate those discriminatory policies that could be controlled by law. Laws alone would not combat prejudice but they would indicate that the government opposed bigotry and discrimination.[7]

The areas where Jews thought that legal action would lead to significant policy changes included employment, education, and immigration. To a lesser degree attempts were also made to curb discrimination in housing, resorts, and social clubs. One organization usually assumed leadership for each issue. Stephen Wise and the American Jewish Congress took primary responsibility for abolishing educational discrimination. The American Jewish Committee, assisted primarily by Lessing Rosenwald of the American Council for Judaism, stood in the forefront of the movement to alter existing immigration statutes. Other Jewish agencies participated, but to obtain the desired goal, they cooperated without anyone trying to receive too much of the credit; nor did groups split hair on strategy with "losers" going their own way.

One of the first problems addressed was bias in employment. For more than two decades job opportunities for Jews had been narrowing. During the 1920s, when the discriminatory procedures first became obvious, many immigrants and their children accepted the practice as normal—they had known the same thing in Europe. During the Great Depression, when organized antisemitism increased, Jewish defense agencies focused more on the rise of Hitler and the refugee exodus from Germany. In the 1940s, however, after Jews joined together to fight for a homeland in Palestine, and while the United States fought in another world war for "the four freedoms"—freedom from fear, freedom from want, freedom of speech, and freedom of worship—the time seemed ripe for domestic action. Hundreds of thousands of American-born Jews were reaching maturity and, along with those returning home from the war, would need education, jobs, and housing. Resistance to the effects of antisemitism therefore became imperative.

The Jews' initial victories came in the field of employment discrimination. New York State passed the first law, in 1945, prohibiting racial and religious bias in selecting employees. By 1949 fair employment practices legislation existed in several other states including New Jersey, Massachusetts, Connecticut, Rhode Island, Oregon, and Washington. The passage of the laws did not always lead to immediate change—an early 1946 national survey indicated that employment discrimination had increased—but they laid the groundwork for fairer hiring practices.[8]

Jews also made major efforts to reverse educational discrimination. Since the 1920s most of the prestigious American colleges and universities had imposed "Jewish quotas," thereby severely restricting the educational and employment opportunities of many Jews. On the undergraduate level the barrier was humiliating but in the professional schools it was debilitating. Good liberal arts educations were available at a wide variety of colleges. But denial of admission to medical and law schools meant the curtailment of career opportunities. From 1920 to 1940 the percentage of Jews in Columbia University's College of Physicians and Surgeons fell from 46.94 to 6.45; the percentage of City College of New York graduates admitted to any medical school dropped from 58 to 15; and not one graduate of either Hunter or Brooklyn College in New York City entered an American medical school until 1946. In a revealing analysis, an *American Mercury* story on the subject in October 1945, pointed out that although three of every four non-Jewish applicants were admitted to a medical school in the United States, only one of four Jews was successful. A similar decline occurred in law schools. In June 1935, 25.8 percent of all American law school students were Jewish; in 1946 the proportion was 11.1 percent.[9]

Since more than half of America's Jews, and some of the nation's most prestigious law and medical schools—like New York University and Columbia—were in New York State, Jewish organizations, especially the American Jewish Congress, pressured the legislature to pass a law barring nonsectarian colleges and universities from discriminating against student applicants on the basis of race, religion, or national origin. Similar efforts were made on the municipal level in New York City.

The attempts to get legislative action in New York proved successful. The New York City Council investigated the city's private universities and concluded that bias was widespread and that "during the last decade conditions have grown rapidly worse." Within a week of the report's publication, Mayor William O'Dwyer announced that public funds should be withheld from institutions of higher education that discriminate. On March 12, 1946, the Council adopted a resolution endorsing the principle that tax exemptions should be prohibited from nonsectarian colleges and universities that employed racial or religious criteria in selecting students for admission.[10]

On the state level a movement began not only to bar discrimination but for the establishment of a state university. The Jewish groups believed that anti-bias legislation alone would not meet the needs of those seeking entrance to colleges and universities. Veterans were already crowding the state's institutions of higher education and adolescents about to graduate from high school had even keener competition than usual. In 1946, Governor Thomas E. Dewey appointed a committee to explore the possibilities of establishing a state university. Two years later the group recommended that it be done.[11]

The state university committee also recommended legislation prohibiting racial and religious discrimination in the selection process. An antidiscrimination law was defeated in 1947 because of strong opposition from the Catholic Church. The Church allegedly opposed the bill on the grounds that it infringed on the parents' rights of educating their children and was "formed after a Communistic pattern." In 1948, however, a similar measure passed after the governor, who expected the Republican presidential nomination that summer, backed it strongly. Within a year similar legislation was approved in Massachusetts and New Jersey.[12]

A third area of significant change occurred in national

immigration legislation. Before World War II attempts to alter the quota system to aid European refugees failed. Neither the President, the Congress, nor the nation cared to make an all-out fight to bring more of Hitler's victims to the United States. After the war that sentiment had not diminished. Not even the leaders of organized Jewry made any public pronouncements about the necessity of bringing some of the war's survivors to the United States. Many gentiles opposed changing the laws because they feared the admission of more Jews to this country. Congressional mail explicitly stated widespread attitudes. "The word 'refugee,' " a New York woman wrote, "is synonymous with *Jew*, and the *latter* is synonymous with Red!" A Texan informed his Senator that lowering the barriers would result "in a flood of Jews coming to the United States. We have too many Jews." "If it was left to me," another New Yorker observed in 1950, "I'd admit all of the D[isplaced] P[ersons] except the Jewish D.P.'s. I'd let in the Catholics, the Protestants, and those in between—but no more Jewish boys."[13]

With attitudes like these, and with the Zionists clamoring for a Jewish homeland, it is understandable why Jews and other Americans supported a move to get Great Britian to open the gates of Palestine to the Jewish survivors of the Holocaust. The British government, however, would not act quickly. Prime Minister Clement Attlee in 1945 proposed to President Harry S. Truman that their two nations jointly examine the possibilities of resettlement in the Middle East and elsewhere. An Anglo-American Committee of Inquiry was established, surveyed conditions, and recommended that 100,000 Jews be permitted to emigrate to the Holy Land. Attlee then stipulated that before he would sanction such a plan the Haganah, the Jewish people's army in Palestine, must disband and the American government must send troops to help maintain order in Palestine—two impossible conditions. Further efforts to reach an American-British accord on admitting 100,000 Jews to Palestine in the summer of 1946 failed. At that point Truman announced that he would recommend to the Congress that it make special provisions for accepting some of Europe's refugees.[14]

The President's announcement was greeted cooly in Congress but it stimulated leaders of the American Jewish Committee and American Council for Judaism to act. It also propelled some, but not all, of the American Zionists. The non-Zionist American Jewish Committee and the anti-Zionist American Council for Judaism, both to lessen the pressure on getting displaced persons into Palestine, as well as genuine humanitarian concerns, helped organize a nonsectarian Citizens Committee on Displaced Persons to mobilize the nation, and consequently the Congress, behind ameliorative legislation. The Citizens Committee correctly emphasized that about 80 percent of the 850,000 or so DP's in Europe were Christians, and that the legislation would obviously help them the most. It took less than two years of concerted lobbying before Congress passed the Displaced Persons Act of 1948.[15]

Although the law called for the admission of 205,000 DP's, its provisions minimized the number of Jews who might qualify for entry to the United States. The bill's main clauses gave preference to Balts and agricultural workers and restricted admission to those DP's who had arrived in Germany, Austria, or Italy no later than December 22, 1945. But not until the Spring of 1946 did Russia release the Polish Jews who had stayed in the Soviet Union during the war, and a massive pogrom in Poland that summer led to the exodus of more than 100,000 Jews to the West. None of these people, who in 1948 constituted about 90 percent of the Jewish DP's in Europe (most of those Jews who had arrived in the DP camps in 1945 had already left for Palestine or other countries), could qualify for an American visa. The antisemitic aspects of the 1948 law were further underscored by the fact that most of the Jews came from Poland, not the Baltic states, and were not agricultural workers. Finally, the *Volksdeutsche*, Eastern and Central Europeans of German ancestry who were expelled from their native lands after the war, could qualify for admission to the United States if they arrived in Germany or Austria by July 1, 1948, the effective date of the act.

The passage of this bill not only marked the last legislative victory for American antisemites but opened new doors as well. The principle of aiding refugees was written into American law as a way of getting around fixed immigration quotas. Two years later, in 1950, Congress beat back those who wanted to retain the discriminatory provisions of the 1948 DP act, and produced a new piece of legislation which eliminated all of the real and implied antisemitic barriers written into the previous bill.[16] In subsequent years legislation of this type would be passed again to help a variety of people including anti-Communist Cubans, Vietnamese, and Russian Jews.

Tribute for the turnabout in American antisemitic feelings must be given to both Jews and Gentiles. Antisemitism had not disappeared by 1950 but a larger segment of the American public realized that bigotry and discrimination were not in the national interest. Hence many American Gentiles joined organized Jewry's attempts to blot out manifestations of intolerance.

The most pointed example came from the White House. Truman selected blue ribbon panels to investigate fair employment practices, higher education, and civil rights in the United States. These groups invariably discovered widespread prejudice in this country. The President's Commission on Higher Education specifically recommended that college and university applications remove all questions pertaining to religion, color, race, and national origin, while the Committee on Civil Rights reported that in many Northern institutions "enrollment of Jewish students seems never to exceed certain fixed points." The President proposed a major civil rights bill in 1948 and a year later told the National Conference of Christians and Jews:

> I have called for legislation to protect the rights of all . . . [United States] citizens and to assure their equal participation in American life, and to reduce discrimination based on prejudice.
>
> My friends, I am doing everything of which I am capable to organize the moral forces of the world.[17]

Even before Truman lent his moral suasion for change, others attacked prejudice. Popular "crooner" Frank Sinatra starred in *The House I Live In* in 1945, a subsequent winner of a special Academy Award, which made a special plea for racial and religious tolerance. Not since D. W. Griffith's *Intolerance* (1913) had Hollywood producers directly acknowledged and criticized the intense bigotry that existed in the United States.[18]

In 1947 Hollywood more specifically exposed American antisemitism in two outstanding films. RKO's *Crossfire*, based on Richard Brooks' novel *The Brick Foxhole*, sharply condemned the previously unmentioned subject and the film's producer, Dore Schary, received commendation for his pioneering efforts in public education. Darryl F. Zanuck of 20th Century-Fox also came out with his dramatic and widely hailed movie on the existence and consequences of antisemitism—*Gentleman's Agreement*. Based on a popular, though pedestrian, novel by Laura Z. Hobson, it became the best known movie about American antisemitism ever produced in Hollywood. Unlike *Crossfire*, whose villian was a despicable and demented ruffian, *Gentleman's Agreement* dealt with genteel Protestants who never threw stones, uttered vile remarks, or broke laws. They merely preferred to live and work apart from Jews. It was these basically "decent" gentiles who discriminated in employment, refused to rent housing to Jews, and who provided the major support for antisemitic covenants and agreements that existed in the United States. *Saturday Review of Literature* critic John Mason Brown observed that "perhaps what is more exciting about both films is that they dare to speak publicly for the first time on a subject which moviegoers have long spoken privately."[19]

Of the two works, *Gentleman's Agreement* made the greater impact. The book and movie exposed those who tried to hide their bigotry under the guise of gentility and conformity. The picture reached millions in a day when adult Americans regarded the movies as more important than TV, and the novel remained a best seller throughout most of 1947. Elliot Cohen, of *Commentary*, did not like the book but called the movie, "a moving, thought-provoking film, which dramatically brings home the question of antisemitism to precisely those people whose insight is most needed—decent, average Americans." *Crossfire* and *Gentleman's Agreement* were both nominated by the Motion Picture Academy for the year's best picture. *Gentleman's Agreement* won the Oscar.[20]

Attacks on antisemitism also came from popular and erudite periodicals as well as respected authors. Editorials, articles, and cartoons appeared in magazines like *America, Collier's, Life, Look,* and *Seventeen.* Bruce Bliven wrote an eight-part series in *The New Republic* detailing almost every facet of antisemitism in America. Carey McWilliams argued in *A Mask For Privilege* that antisemitism continued because the elite in society needed it to buttress their positions. Two years later the first two volumes of the highly regarded *Studies in Prejudice,* sponsored by the American Jewish Committee, were published and three more volumes followed in 1950. The most well-known, *The Authoritarian Personality* by Theodore W. Adorno, examined the personality traits of more than 2,000 subjects and concluded that antisemitism is most likely to occur among rigid and repressed individuals who were most susceptible to fascist teachings.[21]

The various movies, studies, and critical assessments of antisemitism reached an American populace relatively free of economic problems and somewhat receptive to pleas for tolerance. The managing editor of *Yank,* a World War II Army publication, indicated one of the possible reasons for this hospitable atmosphere in 1945 when he wrote

> Many of the soldiers I have known in the four years I have been in the Army, especially the ones who have been or are overseas, are, if anything, more conscious of the need for certain post-war changes in America than most of the civilians I have known during the same time.

To a question, "What changes would you like to see made in postwar America," the editor found that a majority of the GIs responded, "above everything else, the need for wiping out racial and religious discrimination."[22] After the war these young men provided one of the cores particularly receptive to the movement for change.

With some people ready to assimilate the message calling for greater tolerance, the concerted Jewish activities, the new legislation, and the numerous critiques of antisemitism combined to help the nation start turning around. The extensive efforts made by Jewish agencies resulted in new legislation, judicial decisions, and administrative regulations which were intended to extend equal rights for all Americans. Furthermore, antisemitism and bigotry, in general, began to arouse national concern. From the President on down, groups and organizations hitherto uninvolved took up the cudgels. The United States Supreme Court had already begun to chip away at the barriers against equality in previous decades and in 1948 a majority voted to outlaw restrictive covenants that barred the sale or rental of housing to members of minority groups. Labor, educational, and women's groups inaugurated programs for the eradication of antisemitism and other aspects of intolerance while many individuals of all faiths worked diligently to promote racial and religious harmony. In the campaign for displaced persons legislation, for example, many Jews and gentiles worked well together. For most of these Jews it was the first time that they had engaged in common cause with non-Jews—and they liked it.[23]

The intensity and effect of antisemitism in the United States diminished in the late 1940s. One of the most obvious signs of decreased hostility was that the *New York Times* devoted considerably less space to the subject in 1949 and 1950 than it had in 1945 and 1946. Jewish organizations also noted declines in antisemitic activity. The Anti-Defamation League of B'nai B'rith found a marked decrease in antisemitism in the 1948 political campaigns as compared to those in 1940 and 1944. It attributed "the comparative absence of antisemitic activity in the . . . [1948] campaigns . . . to the fact that there is economic prosperity and no national or international problems which are sharply and deeply dividing Americans."[24]

Isolated examples of change dotted the American map. In Minneapolis, characterized by Carey McWilliams in 1946 as the nation's most antisemitic city, the Jewish Community Relations Council recorded fewer complaints about literature, rumors, and verbal attacks hostile to Jews. In Los Angeles, Screen Actors Guild President Ronald Reagan resigned from the Lakeside Country Club when it refused to accept a Jewish member. Michigan eliminated objectionable material from the brochures distributed by the state sponsored Tourist Council and, in 1950, forty travel agents in New York City, whose agencies handled more than half of the city's travel bookings, pledged to avoid recommending exclusionist resorts and hotels. Furthermore, several states and cities established interracial commissions or councils to combat bigotry in their midst.[25]

Institutions of higher learning also began to manifest a growing tolerance as enrollments of Jewish students in private universities increased. Medical school admissions showed the sharpest rise with some New York state institutions choosing approximately 25 to 30 percent of their 1945 and 1946 entering classes from Jewish applicants. (This was before the passage of state antidiscrimination legislation but during the public campaign exposing those institutions that discriminated against Jews.) By the end of 1949 the Chancellor of the New York State Board of Regents declared that virtually every one of the state's nondenominational colleges and universities had eliminated questions from their applications for student admissions that dealt with race, color, or religion. The following year a national conference on higher education, cosponsored by the Anti-Defamation League of B'nai B'rith and the American Council of Education, adopted a resolution branding the quota system "undesirable and undemocratic."[26]

Also in 1949 college fraternities displayed evidence that their discriminatory policies needed reevaluation. In November of that year the Dartmouth College Interfraternity Council urged similar groups in twelve northeastern states to support "a real step" to eliminate restrictive clauses in fraternity charters which barred members because of race or religion. Two weeks later the National Interfraternity Conference, meeting in Washington, voted 36-3 to recommend that view to all of its constituents. Within the next two years changes in fraternity rules regarding minority members were apparent in places like Amherst, Brown, Harvard, the Massachusetts Institute of Technology, New York University, Ohio State, Rutgers, Swarthmore, and the Universities of Chicago, Colorado, Connecticut, Massachusetts, Michigan, Minnesota, and Washington. The editors of *Christian Century* observed, however,

> a fact worth noting is that most of the agitation for this lowering of racial and religious bars has come from the student members of the fraternities, and that the changes have been brought about in

the face of determined opposition from older alumni. Most of the
older alumni, we expect, are 'pillars' in their local churches.[27]

The caustic remark about the "pillars" of the church had a
good deal of truth. Although many individual Christians devoted
themselves to promoting the cause of tolerance, there was less
evidence of institutional concern. In 1949 a former editor of the
Catholic Worker, a liberal publication, wrote that he had "never
heard a single sermon on the evil of antisemitism, before, during
or since the war. And an experienced priest tells me that he can
recall no instance of hearing the sin mentioned in the confes-
sional." Thus, the writer continued, "when one considers the
enormity of the Nazi blood-carnival, it never ceases to be amazing
that the Christian conscience has been so slightly disturbed." A
similar indifference must have existed among many Protestant
denominations as well. In a 1978 scholarly examination of the
Protestant press in the United States between 1933 and 1946,
Robert W. Ross of the University of Minnesota's Department of
Religious Studies, lamented, "Thirty-three years . . . after the Holocaust the 'general stillness' of American Protestantism still hangs
like a pall over all Holocaust studies." Ross found that not only
did the Protestant newspapers display an extremely limited sympathy to the plight of the Jews but that somehow they believed
that the "Jewish misfortunes" were "God's chastisement against
his people for rejecting Jesus."[28]

But despite the general indifference of organized Christian
groups by 1950 changes in attitudes toward Jews in the United
States had occurred. An Anti-Defamation League survey of American antisemitism in 1949 indicated that the greatest progress
made against discrimination came about as a result of state fair
practices acts in the areas of employment, education, and housing.
For these accomplishments one must credit the significant lobbying efforts of Jewish organizations and their allies. A college president also acknowledged the importance of public pressure when
he remarked

For the most part, whenever colleges have become more liberal
and wise in their selection of students other than those who are

white and Gentile, they have done so, not because of a zeal for fair play and democracy, but because they were forced to by the pressure of organized and unorganized opinion upon their public-relations policy.[29]

The weight of the federal government's efforts, symbolized by President Truman's stands, no doubt played a role in bringing about some alteration of public attitudes. So, too, did the movies. Finally, and this is the most difficult aspect to measure or quantify, the establishment of the State of Israel in 1948 gave many Jews renewed pride. Perhaps their self-confidence, and consequently their bearing, may have in some intangible ways changed their behavior and the reaction of non-Jews toward them.

Nevertheless, no matter what the causes or reasons, public opinion polls began reflecting altered feelings of gentiles toward Jews. In 1952 marked declines in antisemitic responses were measured and ten years later prejudices had waned still further. By the early 1970's antisemitism in the United States seemed almost a thing of the past—except among blacks. Careful monitoring by Jewish agencies, however, indicated, as one executive of a national Jewish agency told me, that tolerance of Jews was "a mile wide but only an inch deep." And at this writing, in March 1981, evidence of hostility toward Jews in the United States is not difficult to find despite the small percentages of "antisemites" who turn up in public opinion polls.[30] But there is no question that in our own day Americans are much more accepting of Jews and far less intolerant than they were at the end of World War II.[31]

During the years 1945-1950 a wide variety of forces worked in concert to make Jews more assertive and non-Jews in the United States more tolerant. The growing fears of Communism as the Cold War developed in the late 1940s, improved economic conditions, the lessening of personal anxieties as the war ended and a depression did not come, the Jews' willingness to fight more actively than ever before for equal rights, the impact of Zionism, and perhaps the sinking in of the knowledge that six million Jews had perished in the Holocaust, contributed to the changed atmosphere by 1950. At the very same time that Americans were focusing on the need to become more accepting of people of different racial and religious backgrounds, however, they were also becoming much more intolerant of ideological differences. The paradox is perplexing and impossible for me to explain. Therefore future scholarly studies should probe, in depth, the nature of American society as well as the activities of the American Jewish organizations in the immediate post World War II era to unravel some of the problems posed by the comments made in this essay.

Notes

1. Charles Herbert Stember et al., *Jews in the Mind of America* (New York, 1966), p. 144; *American Jewish Yearbook* (1950) 51:110. Hereafter *AJYB*. *New Republic* April 12, 1948. p. 18.

2. Samuel H. Flowerman and Marie Jahoda, "Polls on Anti-Semitism," *Commentary* (April 1946) 1:83; British Public Record Office, Kew, England, Foreign Office MSS, FO 371 44538/AN3069; Bruce Bliven, "U.S. Anti-Semitism Today," *New Republic* (November 3, 1947) 117:19; *The New York Times*, October 22, 1946, p. 17 (hereafter *NYT*); Melvin I. Urofsky, *We Are One! American Jewry and Israel* (Garden City, N.Y., 1978), p. 126; Harold U. Ribalow, "The Maturity of Hollywood," *Chicago Jewish Forum* (Spring 1948) 6:165; Stember, *Jews in the Mind of America*, pp. 121–22.

3. "The Field of Clinical Psychology: Past, Present and Future," *Journal of Clinical Psychology* (1945) 1:12–13, 166.

4. *NYT*, February 7, 1945, p. 19; February 9, 1945, p. 32; February 10, 1945, p. 20.

5. Ibid., January 23, 1946, p. 20.

6. *AJYB* (1945–46) 47:282–82; (1946–47) 48:189–90; (1947–48) 49:211.

7. Ibid., (1947–48) 49:200–201, 207; *NYT*, January 5, 1948, p. 2; January 22, 1949, p. 5.

8. Milton R. Knovitz, *A Century of Civil Rights, whith a Study of State Law Against Discrimination, by Theodore Leskes* (New York, 1961), pp. 199, 201; *AJYB* (1945–46) 47:285; (1946–47) 48:191; (1950) 51:103; *NYT*, April 19, 1946, p. 3.

9. Frank Kingdom, "Discrimination in Medical Colleges," *American Mercury* (October 1945) 56:394; Walter R. Hart, "Anti-Semitism in N.Y. Medicals Schools," ibid. (July 1947) 65: 56; Edward N. Saveth, "Discrimination in the Colleges Dies Hard," *Commentary* (February 1950) 9:199–20; *NYT*, January 23, 1946, p. 20; December 24, 1946, p. 1; September 29, 1947, p. 8. For an extensive discussion of twentieth-century antisemitism in the American legal profession see Jerold S. Auerbach, *Unequal Justice* (New York, 1976).

10. Hart, "Anti-Semitism in N.Y. Medical Schools," p. 56; *NYT*, January 23, 1946, p. 1; January 28, 1946, p. 10; January 31, 1946, p. 23; March 13, 1946, p. 48.

11. *NYT*, January 13, 1948, p. 1; February 17, 1948, p. 1; February 22, 1948, section 4, p. 9.

12. *NYT,* December 27, 1947, p. 13; March 3, 1947, p. 3; January 4, 1948, p. 1; January 13, 1948, p. 1; January 17, 1948, p. 1; April 6, 1948, pp. 1, 15; Saveth, "Discrimination Dies Hard," p. 121; Konvitz, *Century of Civil Rights,* pp. 201–202, 225, 227–29.

13. Camilla G. Booth to William G. Stratton, May 26, 1947, box 23, Stratton MSS., Illinois State Historical Society, Springfield; G. D. Minick to Tom Connally, May 26, 1946, box 185, Connally MSS., Library of Congress; Henry G. Fuller to Pat McCarran, January 6, 1950, S/MC/9/1, itemized file, McCarran MSS., Nevada State Archives, Carson City.

14. For a discussion of the joint efforts made by the United States and Great Britain to get 100,000 Jews into Palestine after the war, see Leonard Dinnerstein, "America, Britain, and Palestine: The Anglo-American Committee of Inquiry and the Displaced Persons, 1945–46," *Diplomatic History* (Summer 1980) 4:283–302.

15. Dinnerstein, *America and the Survivors of the Holocaust* (New York: Columbia University Press, 1982), chs. 5–7.

16. Ibid, chs. 7, 9.

17. *AJYB* (1947–48) 49:196; *NYT,* September 5, 1946, p. 25; December 6, 1946, p. 26; October 30, 1947, p. 1; November 12, 1949, p. 4.

18. Dore Schary, "Letter from a Movie-Maker," *Commentary* (October 1947) 4:344.

19. Elliot E. Cohen, "Letter to the Movie-Maker," ibid, p. 111; John Mason Brown, "If You Prick Us," *Saturday Review* (December 6, 1947) 30:60.

20. Elliot E. Cohen, "Mr. Zanuck's 'Gentleman's Agreement,' " *Commentary* (January 1948) 5:51; *NYT,* January 11, 1948, section 2, p. 4.

21. *AJYB* (1947–48) 49:201; (1948–49) 50:220; "Anti-Semitism," *Life,* December 1, 1947, p. 44; Bruce Bliven, "U.S. Anti-Semitism Today," *New Republic,* November 3, 1947, pp. 16–19; November 17, pp. 20–23; November 24, pp. 21–24; December 8, pp. 18–21; December 15, pp. 22–24; December 22, pp. 16–18; December 29, pp. 22–25; Naomi Wiener Cohen, *Not Free To Desist: The American Jewish Committee, 1906–1966* (Philadelphia: The Jewish Publication Society of America, 1972), p. 334; *NYT,* December 27, 1949, p. 12; Theodore A. Adorno, *The Authoritarian Personality* (New York, 1950).

22. Joe McCarthy, "GI Vision of a Better America," *NYT Magazine,* August 5, 1945, p. 10.

23. See *Shelley v. Kramer,* 334 U.S. 1 (1948); *AJYB* (1945–46) 47:279; (1948–49) 50:210; Interview with Abraham G. Duker, August 1, 1978, New York City.

24. *NYT,* October 27, 1948, p. 31.

25. *NYT,* January 8, 1948, p. 40; October 27, 1948, p. 31; April 12, 1950, p. 22; *AJYB* (1946–47) 48:190, 193; (1947–48) 49: 188, 196; (1950) 51:116; Carey McWilliams, "Minneapolis: The Curious Twin," *Common Ground* (Autumn 1946) 7:61; Michael G. Rapp, "An Historical Overview of Anti-Semitism in Minnesota, 1940–1960" (Ph.D. diss., University of Minnesota, 1977), p. 178; Aaron Rosenbaum, "Woo and Woe on the Campaign Trail," *Moment* (January–February 1981) 6:52.

26. *NYT,* December 24, 1946, p. 1; "Discrimination in College Admissions." *School Review* (February 1950) 58:68; Marcia Graham Synnott, *The Half-Opened Door: Discrimination and Admissions at Harvard, Yale, and Princeton, 1900–1970* (Westport, Conn.:, 1979), pp. 201–2; Harold Taylor, "Education and Human Relations," *School and Society* (March 14, 1949) 69:346; Frank K. Shuttleworth, "Discrimination in College Opportunities and Admissions," ibid. (December 22, 1951) 74:398–402.

27. *NYT,* November 16, 1949, p. 34; November 27, 1949, p. 1; "College Fraternities Are Lowering Race Bars," *Christian Century* (July 11, 1951) 68:812; Harold Whitman, "The College Fraternity Crisis," *Collier's,* January 8, 1949, pp. 9, 65; January 15, 1949, pp. 34–35.

28. John Cogley, "A Program for Tolerance," *Commonweal* (June 10, 1949) 50:217; Robert W. Ross, *So It Was True: The American Protestant Press and the Nazi Persecution of the Jews* (Minneapolis, 1980), pp. xiii, xv–xvi.

29. *NYT,* April 10, 1950; Taylor, "Education and Human Relations," p. 345.

30. Stember, *Jews in the Mind of America,* pp. 151–209; interview with an executive of the American Jewish Committee, July 1977.

31. William G. Blair, "Survey Finds Anti-Semitism in U.S Has Declined Since 1964," *NYT,* July 29, 1981.

10

Antisemitism in the Eightieth Congress:

The Displaced Persons Act of 1948

The Displaced Persons Act of 1948, a supposedly humanitarian effort on the part of the American Congress to aid the hapless victims of World War II who would not, or could not, return to their former homes, discriminated against Jews and favored the *Volksdeutsche,* or ethnic Germans, who either had fled, or had been expelled, from eastern Europe after the war. Many Jewish observers were shocked by this legislation, which they had spent the previous two years trying to obtain. Will Maslow of the American Jewish Congress concluded that the "law might appropriately be entitled a bill to exclude DPs, particularly Jews, and to admit Hitler's collaborators."[1]

In *American Immigration Policy* Robert Divine wrote: "In the welter of confusion that characterized the months that followed the close of the second World War, the problem of displaced persons went virtually unnoticed in the United States."[2] While this statement is certainly correct so far as the mass of the population was concerned, it is incorrect in reference to American Jews. In June 1945, President Harry S Truman dispatched Earl G. Harrison, the American Representative to the Intergovernmental

Committee on Refugees and formerly United States Commissioner of Immigration, to examine conditions, particularly of Jews, in the European displaced persons camps.[3] Harrison toured the camps, found the situation deplorable, and reported to the president:

> As matters now stand, we appear to be treating the Jews as the Nazis treated them except that we do not exterminate them. They are in concentration camps in large numbers under our military guard instead of S.S. troops. One is led to wonder whether the German people, seeing this, are not supposing that we are following or at least condoning Nazi policy.[4]

As a partial solution to this situation, Harrison urged that 100,000 Jewish DPs be allowed to go to Palestine.[5] Truman accepted the suggestion and wrote to Prime Minister Clement Attlee of Great Britain making the request.[6] Attlee countered with a proposal that an Anglo-American committee of inquiry be established to examine the problem of Jewish DPs, determine opportunities for them in Palestine, and recommend a course of action which both governments might follow.[7] Truman agreed. The committee, appointed in December 1945, completed its report in April 1946. Its members unanimously recommended that Great Britain allow 100,000 Jews into Palestine, but Attlee refused to accept the decision.[8] In an effort to get the British to change their position, Truman sent a sub-cabinet level committee to London to negotiate another plan. Their proposal—a federalization of Palestine with the Jews receiving a small area—was almost universally condemned.[9]

More than a year after the end of the war, the DP problem remained unresolved. Jews who had returned to their homes in Poland, Rumania, and other areas of Eastern Europe were uprooted again in late 1945 and 1946 as a result of increased antisemitic outbursts and progroms.[10] American Jews, realizing that the United States would have to receive some of these people, began mobilizing to change the immigration policies of the United States.

In October 1946, the leaders of the American Jewish Committee (AJC), the foremost Jewish defense organization in the United States, decided to take the lead.[11] Until that point, Jewish organizations had hesitated to do anything about changing the immigration laws for two reasons. In the first place. Zionists wanted to concentrate on getting Jewish DPs into Palestine, and did not want to dilute these efforts. Non-Zionist Jewish groups, and gentile organizations, therefore, "faced with the outcry of the Zionists for immigration exclusively into Palestine, hesitated to act for fear of being denounced as antisemites and for fear of actual sabotage by the Zioinists of any movement they might start."[12]

The second factor revolved around American attitudes toward immigrants and Jews. During and after World War II, congress had made several attempts to curtail immigration to the United States, and major patriotic and veterans groups had called for a total ban on immigration for periods of from five to ten years.[13] The national commander of the American Legion, Colonel Paul H. Griffiths, explained his position: "The admission of displaced persons would lead to a drive to relax immigration laws to permit their relatives and others to enter the country. There will be no end to it."[14]

Most opponents of increased immigration probably feared that more Jews would enter the United States if the laws were changed. Several letters to the War Refugee Board and members of Congress communicated these apprehensions. One clearly articulated conventional beliefs: "The word 'refugee' is synonymous with *Jew*, and the *latter* is synonymous with Red!" Another opposed "Communistic Hebes, new dealers of the rankest kind." A third claimed that DP legislation would result "in a flood of Jews coming to the United States. We have too many Jews . . . '"[15] *Newsweek* reported that many Americans asked, "Weren't the DP's Jews? Didn't they come from Eastern Europe? And didn't that mean that most of them were probably Communists?"[16] Competent pollsters and psychologists wrote about the intensity of American antisemitism; 5 to 10 percent of Americans were rabidly antisemitic, another 45 percent were mildly so.[17]

By fall 1946, *AJC* President Joseph M. Proskauer explained why his organization felt that new efforts had to be made to help displaced Jews enter the United States:

> The problem of migration is by far the most serious problem confronting the Jews today. A few months ago, it was still possible to hope that early admission of 100,000 Jews into Palestine would go far toward solving it. Today, with the doors of Palestine still closed, the number of Jewish displaced persons in the occupation zones of the Western allies in Germany and Austria has already grown to 200,000, and with continuing infiltration of refugees from Poland, is expected to reach a quarter of a million by the end of the year. In Hungary, Rumania, and other Eastern European countries, there are additional hundreds of thousands of Jews on whom the pressure to emigrate is, and will probably continue, strong. Even with an early and favorable solution of the Palestinian impasse, homes in countries other than Palestine will have to be found for a far larger number of European Jews than was anticipated.
>
> Appeals to the nations of the world have fallen on deaf ears, and it is now clear that unless the United States sets an example, no change in their attitude can be expected.[18]

The American Jewish Committee, founded in 1906 to protect the civil rights of Jews throughout the world, had had four decades of experience tackling difficult problems. Its leaders were prominent lawyers and businessmen whose accomplishments and talents provided them entry to the highest levels of government. Moreover, the AJC was extremely well organized and staffed by individuals with expertise in community and public relations, research, finance, and political analysis. For forty years it had exerted influence by quiet and direct contacts with powerful individuals. The AJC did not always win campaigns or change public policies, nor did it exert itself strenuously in hopeless battles. Nevertheless, it did speak up on issues of concern to Jews and had established a reputation for professional competence.

Once the AJC committed itself to work for DP legislation, it mobilized its considerable resources. Its Administrative Committee established an Immigration Subcommittee. The National Committee on Post-War Immigration Policy (NCPWI), which

Jewish organizations had established with the American Council for Nationalities Services in 1944 to help prepare Americans to accept immigrants after the war, had been studying the problems of the DPs for more than two years. It was approached for advice and assistance.[19] The NCPWI, chaired by Earl Harrison, had started in 1944 with three specific goals: (1) to study and recommend policies for United States postwar immigration, (2) to conduct a nation-wide education campaign to educate the public about postwar immigration problems, and (3) to follow and report on legislation in the committee's field of interest and to place its information and experience at the disposal of public officials to help reach constructive solutions.[20]

The NCPWI had little political power, but had gathered a considerable amount of information. The AJC had political expertise, access to huge amounts of money, and an intense desire to do something to help the displaced persons. To utilize the talents of both groups, the head of the AJC's Immigration Committee, Irving M. Engel, approached the American Council For Nationalities Services about the establishment of a Citizens Committee on Displaced Persons (CCDP). Engel recognized that prejudice was so deeply embedded in the United States that no bill designed to assist Jewish DPs, or sponsored solely by Jewish organizations, would have a chance of passage.[21] Hence, a broad based coalition of prominent Christian, and perhaps a few Jewish, leaders from the ranks of the ministry, business, labor, education, and social welfare was needed. In the classic tradition of lobbying, a narrow humanitarian interest (aiding Jewish DPs) would take on a broader focus (helping all DPs) to achieve widespread support. Once the AJC immigration committee members had decided on this goal, Earl Harrison was asked to accept leadership of the CCDP. He agreed, and over his signature, but with a great deal of assistance from the AJC, letters went out to prominent national figures inviting them to participate. In response, individuals like Eleanor Roosevelt, Fiorello LaGuardia, William Green of the American Federation of Labor, former Secretary of State Edward R. Stettinius, and Charles P. Taft, brother of the Ohio Senator, lent their names as vice chairmen to the CCDP.

The CCDP functioned as a lobby to inform the public and the Congress of the plight of the DPs, and it urged appropriate legislation. At the outset, its leaders emphasized that 80 percent of the approximately 1,000,000 DPs in Europe were Christian, which was not widely known at that time. The lobby pointed out that, at the end of World War II, there were several million up-rooted people in Europe, but most had been resettled. There remained about a million "hard core" DPs, mainly from Eastern Europe, who did not return home either because they feared persecution, or because their families and former lives had so completely disintegrated that they had no reason to return. According to CCDP literature, there remained only four possibilities for dealing with DPs: (1) they could be repatriated against their will, (2) they could remain in DP camps indefinitely, (3) they could be dumped into the shattered European economies and left to fend for themselves, or (4) they could be resettled elsewhere. "Obviously," leaders of the CCDP concluded, "the last was the only humanitarian as well as realistic solution."[22]

The CCDP and the AJC worked closely with one another. Over 90 percent of the financing of the new group came from individual Jews, Jewish groups, and their friends. Lessing Rosenwald, heir to the Sears, Roebuck fortune, a member of the executive committee of the AJC, and head of the anti-Zionist American Council for Judaism, along with members of his family, contributed over $400,000 of the CCDP's $650,000 budget.[23] Prominent Jews like Joseph M. Proskauer, Herbert Lehman, formerly Governor of New York, and Ben Lazarus, founder of Benrus Watches, continually solicited funds from friends.[24] Furthermore, the AJC and other Jewish organizations recruited members for the CCDP and provided it with contacts, speakers, ideas, etc.

The CCDP tried to alert an apathetic nation to the fact that most DPs were Christians, that they had no place to go, and that humanitarian concerns dictated that the United States take its "fair share" of these people. To this end, CCDP representatives went to conventions, spoke with key leaders, inspired letter writing campaigns, organized local groups, analyzed the nature of various communities, decided which individuals to isolate for special attention, sent out mailings, and wrote area reports and sent them back to the home office. Thousands of pieces of paper went out to citizens and newspapers, radio scripts were prepared, magazine articles were suggested, posters were drawn and, according to one authority, "almost all editorials on the displaced persons problems appearing in the press of the nation were inspired, if not written, by the Committee." Almost every prominent American organization, except for the Daughters of the American Revolution and the Junior Order of American Mechanics, eventually endorsed the goals of the CCDP. The strongest newspaper supporters included *The New York Times*, the *New York Herald-Tribune*, the Louisville *Courier-Journal*, the St. Louis *Post-Dispatch*, and *The Evening Star* (Washington, D.C.).[25]

The publicity helped develop a climate of favorable opinion for concrete legislation. To this end, the CCDP prepared a bill, based on AJC recommendations, for the United States to accept its "fair share" of DPs. CCDP leaders earlier decided that, to receive the widest possible support, their legislation should be put forth by a member of the majority party from the isolationist Midwest. Hence they approached, in turn, Republican Senators Homer Ferguson and Arthur H. Vandenburg of Michigan, and Robert Taft of Ohio, but each refused to sponsor the measure.[26] They then turned to the House of Representatives, where freshman William G. Stratton, congressman-at-large from Illinois, who not only sympathized with CCDP objectives but who also saw an opportunity to develop a national reputation, agreed to sponsor the measure.[27] On April 1, 1947, Congressman Stratton introduced a bill which would allow 400,000 DPs, in addition to immigration quotas, to enter the United States during the next four years.

Most congressmen knew little about the DPs, could not understand why they had not gone home after the war, and feared depression or scarcities if a large number of immigrants started coming to the United States. Many also shared constituents' anti-immigrant and antisemitic feelings. In the 1930s, several proposals to increase refugee quotas as a means of helping German Jews escape from Nazi persecutions were roundly condemned in Congress. Excuses were given that the United States economy could not support any additional refugees. In 1940, however, a bill to help English refugees sailed through Congress without difficulty or vocal opposition. Hostility to Jews increased in the United States during the 1940s, and after World War II mail to the White House ran seven to one against allowing DPs into the United States. Congressional soundings in 1947 confirmed the public sentiment. In February 1947, Eleanor Roosevelt revealed that "every representative in Congress with whom I have talked has told me that the general feeling is that they wish to stop all immigration."[28]

Hearings on the Stratton measure were held in the summer of 1947, but no bill was reported on the floor of the House of Representatives. President Truman, first in January 1947, and again in July, called upon Congress to produce suitable legislation to aid DPs but did not endorse the Stratton bill. In the middle of July, *The New York Times* reported that "canvasses indicated the proposed mass-entry of DP's faced determined, possibly majority opposition."[29]

The key to passage of displaced persons legislation lay in the Senate. The House of Representatives was not prepared to pass any bill unless favorable action seemed likely in the upper chamber. As one of Senator Pat McCarran's (D. Nev.) assistants telegraphed to him, "STRATTON BILL IS BEING HELD ON ICE UNTIL HOUSE COMMITTEE SEES WHAT SENATE WILL DO IN MATTER."[30] After an initial period of hesitation, in which it appeared that no bill would be passed, propaganda of the CCDP, subsequent letters to representatives and senators, and newspaper editorials urging action began to take effect. Congress received more mail, most of which was favorable, on aiding the displaced persons than on any subject since prohibition.[31] Senator Alexander Wiley (R. Wis.) complained "that he could not walk down the streets of his home town without someone like his banker, butcher or former Sunday School teacher stopping him and saying 'Senator, why aren't you a good Christian? Why are you against DPs?' "[32]

Unfortunately for the displaced persons, Senator Chapman Revercomb (R. W. Va.) chaired the Immigration Subcommittee of the Senate Judiciary Committee, and his views were anything but favorable toward helping them. He had done a study of the displaced persons for the Republican Steering Committee in November-December 1946. In the conclusion to his report he observed:

> Many of those who seek entrance into this country have little concept of our form of government. Many of them come from lands where communism has had its first growth and dominates the political thought and philosophy of the people. Certainly it would be a tragic blunder to bring into our midst those imbued with a communistic line of thought when one of the most important tasks of this Government today is to combat and eradicate communism from this country.[33]

When the Senate appeared ready to consider DP legislation in the summer of 1947, Revercomb urged his colleagues to schedule a Senate inspection tour of the Displaced Persons camps in Europe before taking action. After lengthy debate the Senate agreed to this proposal and Revercomb was appointed to head the tour.[34]

In the fall of 1947, both the House of Representatives and the Senate sent committees to investigate the DP camps. The CCDP sponsored an inspection tour of the camps by Commander Paul Griffiths of the American Legion, who thereafter changed his position and endorsed emergency legislation to aid DPs. Both the House and Senate committees also reached the conclusion that something should be done for the people there. The House report noted: "If the Jewish facet of the problem could be cleared up, the solution of the remainder of the problem would be facilitated. The opening up of Palestine to the resettlement of Jewish displaced persons would break the log jam." Around the same time, the governors of several midwestern states established local commissions to study the possibilities of resettling DPs in their midst. Finally, and perhaps most important for the future passage of legislation, Robert A. Taft, a Republican leader in the Senate, called for "immediate action" to help the DPs.[35] As winter began, it seemed likely that Congress would act.

In the second session of the Eightieth Congress, Frank Fellows (R. Me.), chairman of the Subcommittee on Immigration of the House Judiciary Committee, proposed a measure which called for the admission of 200,000 DPs from among those who had registered by April 21, 1947 with the DP camps. Those admitted were to be charged against future immigration quotas for their countries of origin.[36] In the Senate, Revercomb's committee proposed legislation that would admit 100,000 DPs over a two-year period, confine eligibility to those who had been in the DP camps by December 22, 1945, and reserve 50 percent of the visas for agricultural workers. It also suggested that 50 percent of those admitted come from the Baltic states of Europe, which had been annexed by Russia after the war.[37]

An interoffice memo, circulated in the AJC, pointed out the discriminatory aspects of the proposal: "The effect of these restrictions would be to bar the entry of virtually every Jewish DP, since: (a) very few Jewish DP's come from the Baltic countries, (b) very few Jewish DP's acquired such status before December 22, 1945, and (c) very few Jewish DP's are agriculturists."[38]

Adherents of a generous immigration bill considered the Revercomb proposal a disaster. *The New York Times* wondered "whether its sponsors sat up nights to be certain of producing the worst possible offer for DP's."[39] The measure was everything the Jews had feared from Revercomb. They knew that he had spoken of his dislike of Jews to social acquaintances.[40] As early as the summer of 1947 Irving Engel, of the AJC's Immigration Committee, had warned other members of the AJC:

> Both in the country and in Congress there is a stubborn opposition reflecting distrust of foreigners in general and, to a shocking extent, of Jews in particular. It is to be feared that, if the legislation cannot be sidetracked entirely, an attempt may be made so to shape its terms as to reduce the number of Jewish DPs who could benefit by it.[41]

Rumors of antisemitism in Washington abounded. Many representatives and senators expressed antagonism toward Jews only in private, but knowledgeable individuals knew their sentiments. A consultant to Secretary of State George Marshall, Goldthwaite H. Dorr, wrote to presidential advisor John Steelman in the summer of 1947, "we find there is a strong tendency among the opponents of a [DP] bill to ascribe the whole pressure for DP admission to Jewish interest in it."[42]

Another letter writer observed in 1947:

> What the Departments of State, Justice and Interior really want is a hidden formula for discrimination. What I mean can be illustrated by the choice of 1920 as the base year for computing quotas, and the inclusion of the whole ethnic stock rather than merely the foreign born. Thru these means, the people of South and East Europe are kept out, but not discriminated against![43]

And a scholarly essay, written by one who had intimate contact with DPs in Europe and who testified frequently before congressional committees, included the observation: "It has been stated by people close to the problem, though this cannot be documented, that various Congressmen said if there were no Jews in the displaced persons camps, the problems would be solved in no time."[44]

Analysis of the Wiley-Revercomb bill (Alexander Wiley, the chairman of the Judiciary Committee added his name to the measure reported by the Revercomb committee) shows how ingenious a device it really was. President Truman, on December 22, 1945, had issued an executive order mandating favorable treatment for DPs under the existing immigration laws.[45] It was a temporary measure designed to aid those most in need. Then, in 1946, over 100,000 Jews from Poland and other areas of Eastern Europe fled discriminatory treatment and pogroms and headed either for the DP camps in Germany, or directly for Palestine. The Jews escaping Eastern Europe and the DP camps received far more attention and publicity than all of the Christian DPs. These were the Jews that Revercomb wanted to keep out of the United States. Furthermore, when Revercomb sought an assessment of his proposed bill from the Department of State, Robert A. Lovett, the under-secretary, advised him that the department found it unacceptable. Not only would the December 22, 1945 cutoff date "be extremely difficult to administer," Lovett wrote, but it "would apparently result in discrimination against most of the Jewish displaced persons."[46] Revercomb chose not to share this information with other members of the Judiciary Committee who favored the State Department's position but were unaware of Lovett's communication.[47]

The Wiley-Revercomb bill was discussed on the Senate floor in May and June 1948. Its sponsors defended it as nondiscriminatory although Wiley did urge his colleagues "to be careful about letting displaced persons into this country. He said he want[ed] 'good blood' to come here and added: 'We don't want any rats. We've got enough of them already.'"[48] Every amendment to curb the discriminatory features was beaten down. Several senators, including Leverett Satonstall (R. Mass.), H. Alexander Smith (R. N.J.), J. Howard McGrath (D. R.I.), and Claude Pepper (D. Fla.), commented about how the proposed legislation affected Jews. Senators Pepper and McGrath were perhaps the most eloquent. Pepper spoke of the "appalling inadequacy of the bill," which gave a majority of places to a minority of the DPs, yet limited, "if not by design at least by effect" the slots available for Jews. McGrath lamented:

> We come to this sad moment in the Senate of the United States when we probably shall have to write into the law of this country the principles of narrowness, intolerance, and bigotry. The date of December 22, 1945 was deliberately written into this bill because that date prohibited Jews from taking part in this program.[49]

Two significant amendments to the Wiley-Revercomb bill passed. One increased the total number of DPs to be admitted to the United States to 100,000 per year for two years while the other, proposed by Senator William Langer (R. N.D.), gave preference to the *Volksdeutsche*. Langer, the only member of the Senate Judiciary Committee to oppose even the Revercomb bill in a committee vote, believed that the *Volksdeutsche* were "much worse off than the so-called displaced persons," most of whom he assumed "are related to residents [i.e. Jews] of New York City."[50]

The Wiley-Revercomb bill passed the Senate by a vote of 63 to 13. Twelve southern democrats, whose constituents were quite strong in their opposition to increased immigration quotas, and Republican Albert W. Hawkes of New Jersey constituted the minority.[51] The Senate action led to a vitriolic response from Earl Harrison. He called the measure a "booby trap" and urged the House of Representatives, which had not yet passed the Fellows bill, to undo the "monstrosity of Senate action," which not only discriminated on religious, national, and occupational grounds, but which contained "a special provision to admit *Volksdeutsche*, the notorious Nazi Fifth Column. The bill's racist character makes all decent Americans hang their heads in shame." He then spelled out his opposition in greater detail. That the *Volksdeutsche* "should be handed special privileges over the victims of Nazi oppression, is a mockery of American justice. For the first time in American history, immigrants can now be classified not by nationality, but by 'race.' Thus, do we not only admit our former enemies, but we accept Hitler's twisted philosophy of blood."[52]

Harrison's statement expressed the views of several anguished individuals, but did not affect the outcome in the House of Representatives, where some of the members did not mince words in voicing their opposition to helping the DPs. Georgia's Eugene Cox (D.) called them "the scum of Europe," while Ed Gossett (D. Tex.), a well known opponent of expanded immigration, characterized many of the DPs as "bums, criminals, subversives, revolutionists, crackpots and human wreckage."[53] Despite the expressed sentiments of a minority, however, the Fellows bill passed essentially as presented, and the two houses of Congress prepared for the conference committee to reconcile the bills. Of the seven House conferees, six supported a liberal DP measure.[54] Senator Wiley had originally chosen Senators Revercomb, Ferguson, and Harley M. Kilgore (D. W. Va.), to represent the upper chamber. Since Revercomb was the only "fanatic bigot" among the three, Ferguson and Kilgore both having lined up for a more generous proposal, chances for a bill satisfactory to the CCDP and the Jews appeared good.[55] However, Senator Wiley, realizing what the conference result was likely to be, asked unanimous consent of the Senate to add two restrictionists, Senators James Eastland (D. Miss.), and Forrest Donnell (R. Mo.), to the conference committee. An AJC observer, George Hexter, later explained that Wiley's ploy "was intended to and did load the dice against us." It succeeded because "no active supporters of fair legislation were on hand to block this move." Hexter also expressed the opinion that Wiley would not have done what he did had he not also had the approval of the leaders of the Republican party in the Senate, Robert A. Taft and Arthur Vandenburg.[56]

In the conference, the Senate group remained adamant against accepting provisions which might help Jewish DPs. They gave the House members an ultimatum: either the Senate measure or nothing. One of the House conferees, Frank L. Chelf (D. Ky.), claimed "they had a gun barrel at our heads and that the gun was the legislative rush." As a result, the conferees went along with modified aspects of the worst features of both the House and Senate bills: the mortgaging provision of the Fellows measure was retained, the 50 percent Senate provision for DPs from the Baltic countries was cut to 40 percent, and the 50 percent preference for farmers was cut to 30 percent. The cut-off date was allowed to remain at December 22, 1945, and the *Volksdeutsche* received a 50 percent preference within the regular German and Austrian quotas. Unlike the DPs, however, the *Volksdeutsche* qualified for admission to the United States if they had entered Germany by July 1, 1948, the effective date of the bill. Other provisions called for the admission of 3,000 orphans and 2,000 Czechs who had fled their native land after the communist coup in early 1948. And 15,000 DPs temporarily in this country were allowed to apply for resident status. In addition, the DPs, but not the *Volksdeutsche*, would have to have guarantees of jobs and housing in the United States before receiving their visas. Finally, a displaced persons commission was established to administer this law which would allow 205,000 immigrants into the country.[57] The report so displeased some of the conferees that four refused to sign it.[58] Congressman Celler later wrote about the compromise, "it wasn't 'half a loaf'; it wasn't even half a slice."[59] Although many members of both houses of Congress believed that the bill was deliberately intended to exclude Jews, President Truman reluctantly signed it while denouncing the measure as antisemitic and anti-Catholic.[60]

It was the former, but not the latter; Catholics predominated among both the displaced persons and the *Volksdeutsche*.

Jews and Jewish groups were incensed. One periodical labeled the bill, "the most glaring expression of nativist Protestant exclusionism by any Congress since the Immigration Act of 1924," and added, "it will stand as one of the blackest marks in the record of one of our most misguided Congresses." An individual deplored the fact that "many, if not most, of the non-Jewish DP's are former German collaborationists, past killers, present fascists and anti-Semites. . . ." The executive director of the AJC, John Slawson, lamented: "It was the persistent, bigoted attitudes of persons like Senator Revercomb of West Virginia and Senator Wiley of Wisconsin that finally resulted in this inhumane act. The implications for the Jews of the United States are great."[61] Several individuals thought that the CCDP had failed in its endeavors. "All it has to show for its vast expenditures," wrote Will Maslow, a member of the CCDP executive committee, is a law which many of its members will agree is worse than no law at all." One AJC staff member thought that a study should be made to see where the Jews had gone wrong. "One of the questions I should like to see the study address itself to," this member wrote, "is the aspect of the strategy of always setting up a non-Jewish front to press for Jewish causes."[62]

Many Jewish groups, including B'nai B'rith's Anti-Defamation League and the American Jewish Congress, wanted the bill vetoed, but on this point there was no unity. Despite the obvious antisemitic drawbacks, the odious law did provide some help. Moreover, some argued that it would be easier to amend a bad bill than to start from scratch the following year. Finally, after having supported the goals of the CCDP, which had emphasized that 80 percent of the DPs were Christian, it would have been politically unwise for Jewish groups to demand that no one receive any assistance because Jews were discriminated against. The bill also was condemned by spokesmen for the Federal Council of Churches and the National Catholic Resettlement Conference, but the latter two groups wanted the measure amended, not vetoed.[63]

Knowledgeable Jews realized that had it not been for their efforts, contacts, and especially finances, there would have been no Displaced Persons Act. Hence the legislation passed was ironic: Those who had done the most, because they wanted to help Jewish DPs, ultimately wound up supporting a bill which discriminated against Jews.

In the summer of 1948, during the brief session of the recalled Eightieth Congress, both President Truman and the Republican presidential nominee, Thomas E. Dewey, urged the Revercomb committee to change the cut-off date to April 21, 1947, but the West Virginia senator would not budge. Although several Republican senators also pressed Revercomb to alter the date, he had the support of two members of his immigration subcommittee, Donnell and McCarran, and they constituted a majority.[64] During the Eighty-first Congress the Senate amended the DP act, but by that time most of the Jews in the DP camps had gone to Israel, which became an independent nation in May 1948.

The Displaced Persons Act of 1948, despite its restrictive flaws, stands as a landmark in the history of American immigration. The bill not only broke precedent with existing legislation by mortgaging future quotas, but also laid the groundwork for granting asylum to escapees from repressive governments. It was the principle of helping the politically dispossessed that eventually allowed the United States to assist Hungarian, Cuban, and Vietnamese refugees in the 1950s, 1960s, and 1970s. It also provided, for the first time, a specific agency, the Displaced Persons Commission, to facilitate immigrant entry into the United States.

In his assessment of the displaced persons legislation, Robert Divine credited congressional beliefs "that the resettlement of the displaced persons was essential for the proper conduct of American foreign policy in western Europe." Although he acknowledged that the original December 22, 1945 cut-off date and the Baltic priority "tended to exclude Jewish persons," he seemed to think that there was "little basis for concluding that the framers of the bill drew up these provisions to discriminate against people of the Jewish faith."[65] Divine is wrong on both counts. The outstanding lobbying efforts of the CCDP certainly had more to do with the preparation of ameliorative legislation than did feelings about foreign policy in Western Europe. In less than two years, the CCDP reversed the negative attitudes of a majority of both the public and the Congress toward liberalization of the immigration laws. It is possible that without the intensive efforts of the CCDP, Congress might have further restricted, rather than broadened, opportunities for entry into the United States. When displaced persons legislation was first urged upon the Congress, in late 1946, there was "hardly a single man in favor" of it.[66] "Apathy, not to say hostility," the president of the AJC reminded its members, "was rife in both the country and in the Congress. Only a vigorous and extensive program of public education made possible the passage of any such legislation at all."[67] President Truman did not help much. Although he supported the idea of admitting DPs into the United States, he never exerted the full influence of his office toward obtaining that goal. Certainly his efforts to obtain legislation to implement the Truman Doctrine and the Marshall Plan were much greater. Therefore, had it not been for the CCDP and its ability to galvanize both public and congressional opinion, the displaced persons might have languished in Europe indefinitely.

As to antisemitism, the evidence belies Divine's assertion. Senator Revercomb and his allies knew exactly what they were doing when they prepared the legislation, and contemporaries criticized them for it. Although Revercomb bore the brunt of the criticism for those aspects of the Displaced Persons Act which discriminated against Jews, it is possible, if not probable, that he represented the views of a significant number of senators who were glad not to be publicly identified with discriminatory provisions they wholeheartedly endorsed. Therefore, Will Maslow's assessment, that the "law might appropriately be entitled a bill to exclude DP's, particularly Jews, and to admit Hitler's collaborators" is most apt.

1. Will Maslow and George J. Hexter, "Immigration—or Frustration? *The Jewish Community* (September 1948), p. 17.

2. Robert A. Divine, *American Immigration Policy, 1924–1952* (New Haven, 1957), p. 112.

3. Joseph C. Grew, "Memorandum for the President: *Mr. Earl G. Harrison's Mission to Europe on Refugee Matters*," June 21, 1945, Independence, Mo., Harry S Truman Library, Papers of Harry S Truman, Official File 127–A, Box 555.

4. *The New York Times*, September 30, 1945 (hereafter *NYT*).

5. Ibid.

6. U.S. President, *Public Papers of the Presidents of the United States* (Washington, D.C., 1945–1953), Harry S Truman (1945), pp. 469–70.

7. Ibid., p. 468.

8. The members of the Anglo-American Committee were, American: Judge Joseph C. Hutcheson (chairman), Frank Aydelotte, Frank W. Buxton, Bartley Crum, James G. McDonald, William G. Phillips; English: Sir John E. Singleton (chairman), Wilfred Crick, Richard S. Crossman, Sir Frederick Leggett, Lord Robert Morrison, Major Reginald E. Manningham-Buller. Ibid. (1946), pp. 218–219.

9. *NYT*, August 8, 1946; Files of the American Jewish Committee (AJC), New York, folder, "Federalization Plan, Anglo-American Committee of Inquiry, AJC Israel, Palestine, 1945–47."

10. Samuel Lubell, "The Second Exodus of the Jews," *The Saturday Evening Post* (October 5, 1946) 219:17; *NYT*, July 6, 15, 1946.

11. Joseph M. Proskauer, "Memorandum on Immigration," AJC folder, "Immigration, Displaced Persons, 1950."

12. "A Campaign Starts," *Commentary* (December 1946), p. 553.

13. Clipping from Independent Jewish Press Service, Inc., June 28, 1943, in New York Public Library, Vito Marcantonio Papers, Box 2, folder, "Civil Liberties, Discrimination Against Negroes and Jews in the Army, 1935–1944," *NYT*, March 6, 19: April 6, 13; October 13, 1944; *Newsweek* (December 30, 1946) 28:23.

14. *NYT*, November 1, 1947.

15. Camilla G. Booth to William G. Stratton, May 26, 1947 and Robert Zachary to Stratton, June 4, 1947, Springfield Illinois State Historical Society, Stratton Papers, Box 23, folder "Out of State Corr against 2910," and Box 22, folder, ' "Displaced Persons, April thru June, 1947' "; G. D. Minick to Senator Tom Connally May 26, 1946, Library of Congress, Tom Connally Manuscripts, Box 185.

16. *Newsweek* (May 10, 1948) 31:23.

17. Samuel H. Flowerman and Marie Jahoda, "Polls on Anti-Semitism," *Commentary* (April 1946) 1:83.

18. Proskauer, "Memorandum on Immigration."

19. Meeting of the American Jewish Committee's Immigration Committee, November 25, 1946, AJC folder, "AJC Committee Minutes, Immigration."

20. St. Paul American Council for Nationalities Services Papers, Immigration History Archives, Shipment 3, box 23, "Joint Conference on Alien Legislation. National Committee on Post-War Immigration Policy."

21. Minutes of the Immigration Committee, December 17, 1946, AJC.

22. William S. Bernard, "Refugee Asylum in the United States: How the Law Was Changed To Admit Displaced Persons," *International Immigration* (1975) 13(1–2):3–4.

23. Citizens Committee on Displaced Persons, Manuscripts, Immigration History Archives, box 1, folder, "1950–53: Citizens Comm. on Displaced Persons. Correspondence, General."

24. Joseph M. Proskauer to Jesse Steinhardt and 15 others, May 9, 1947, AJC, CCDP files, folder, "March–May '47"; Lessing Rosenwald to Irving M. Engel, December 29, 1947, ibid., folder, "Fund Raising, 47–48"; Rosenwald to Engel, March 4, 1947, ibid., folder, "June–Dec., '47." The situation was most clearly stated in a letter from Ely M. Aaron to Proskauer: "We are getting practically no help from the non-Jewish groups in raising funds. . . ." May 21, 1947, ibid., "Fund Raising." Of the first $47,000 collected for the CCDP, the Rosenwald family contributed $36,000 and non-Jews, $4400, George Hexter to Proskauer, February 27, 1947, ibid., folder, "Nov. 46–Feb. 47."

25. Sister M. Madeline Lorimer, "America's Response to Europe's Displaced Persons, 1948–1952: A Preliminary Report" (Ph.D. diss., St. Louis University, 1964), p. 110; U.S. Congress, House, Hearings Before the Subcommittee on Immigration and Naturalization of the House Committee on the Judiciary, 80th Congress, 1st session, H.R. 2910, July 1947, pp. 40–44.

26. Minutes of the CCDP Executive Committee, February 21, 1947, AJC, CCDP files, folder, "Nov. 46–Feb. 47."

27. Interview with William Bernard in New York City, June 30, 1977.

28. *NYT*, January 20, February 20, and April 6, 1947; *Newsweek* (December 30, 1946) 28:23; memo to chapter chairmen from Nathan Weisman of the AJC, March 20, 1947, AJC, CCDP files, folder, "March–May '47." Polls taken for the AJC showed a strong anti-immigrant sentiment in the United States. See Proskauer, "Memorandum on Immigration." The CCDP representative was told in Washington, ca. March 26, 1947, that a bill to aid Displaced Persons did not have "a chance of seeing the light of day this session." American Council for Nationalities Services Papers, Shipment 6, Box 8, folder, "F-Misc." For discussions of the difficulties of Jewish refugees between 1938 and 1945 see David S. Wyman, *Paper Walls: America and the Refugee Crisis, 1938–1945* (Amherst, Mass., 1968), and Henry L. Feingold, *The Politics of Rescue* (New Brunswick: Rutgers University Press, 1970).

29. *Public Papers of the Presidents* (1947):327–29; *NYT*, July 15, 1947.

30. Eve Adams to Senator McCarran February 15, 1948, in National Archives, Files of Senator McCarran, Immigration Subcommittee, Displaced Persons, S 1563, Docket 668.

31. Emanuel Celler, *You Never Leave Brooklyn* (New York, 1953), p. 94; *NYT*, May 18, 1947.

32. William Bernard to Leonard Dinnerstein, October 13, 1976 and October 5, 1977.

33. U.S. Congress, Senate, *Congressional Record*, 80th Cong. 1st sess. 93 (part 2):2520.

34. Ibid., part 1, pp., 10, 324–32, 3500–53.

35. Divine, *American Immigration Policy*, p. 118–19; *NYT*, November 1, 16, 19, 21, 1947.

36. Divine, *American Immigration Policy*, p. 125.

37. U.S. Cong., Senate, *Displaced Persons in Europe*, S. Rept. 950, 80th Cong., 2nd sess., March 2, 1948, pp. 50–52.

38. Memo from Sidney Liskofsky to Dr. Simon Segal, April 20, 1948, AJC folder, "Immigration Displaced Persons, 1951."

39. *NYT,* May 27, 1948.

40. Samuel Herman to John Slawson, April 11, 1947, AJC Administrative Committee folder, "DPs, Immigration, 1946–1950"; American Council for Nationalities Service, Shipment 6, box 7, folder "Congressional Attitudes Towards Displaced Persons Legislation."

41. Irving M. Engel to members of AJC August 26, 1947, AJC folder, "Immigration Displaced Persons, 1950."

42. Dorr to Steelman July 11, 1947, Truman Papers, Official File 127, box 552.

43. Robert M. Cullom to Richard J. Walsh Sr. August 13, 1947, American Council for Nationalities Services, shipment 3, box 7, folder 40, "CM for Equality in Naturalization."

44. Jerry M. Sage, "The Evolution of U.S. Policy Toward Europe's Displaced Persons: World War II to June 25, 1948" (M.A. thesis, Columbia University, 1952), p. 41.

45. *Public Papers of the Presidents* (1946):572–78.

46. Robert A. Lovett to Senator Revercomb, April 15, 1948, National Archives, Record Group 51, Budget, HR 2910, K8–11/47.1.

47. Senator Harley M. Kilgore (D. W. Va.) resented the fact that Revercomb had not told Judiciary Committee opponents of his bill about Lovett's letter. Sidney Liskofsky to Morton Thalhimer, August 19, 1948, AJC folder, "Immigration Displaced Persons 1945–47."

48. Associated Press clipping, May 26, 1948, in The State Historical Society of Wisconsin, Madison, Alexander Wiley Papers, series 14, box 24, "Scrapbooks, September 1947–March 1949."

49. U.S. Cong., Senate, *Congressional Record,* 80th Cong., 2nd sess. 94 (pt 5):6403–4, 6585, 6856–59, 6900, 6913–14. For a good summary of the Senate debate, see Divine, *American Immigration Policy,* pp. 121–24, 127–28.

50. *NYT,* March 2, 1948; *Congressional Record,* ibid., pp. 6583, 6584.

51. Both Senators from Georgia (Walter F. George and Richard B. Russell), Louisiana (Allen J. Ellender and William C. Feazel), Mississippi (James O. Eastland and John L. Stennis), and Texas (Tom Connally and W. Lee O'Daniel), as well as Arkansas's John L. McClellan, Oklahoma's Elmer Thomas, South Carolina's Olin D. Johnston, and Virginia's Harry F. Byrd opposed the bill.

52. Press statement released by the CCDP, June 7, 1948, AJC folder, "DPs, Immigration, 1946–1950."

53. Quoted in *NYT,* June 11, 1948.

54. Frank Fellows, Louis E. Graham (R. Pa.) Emanuel Celler (D., N.Y.), Frank Chelf (D. Ky.), J. Caleb Boggs (R. Del.), Ed Gossett, and E. Wallace Chadwick (R. Pa.) were the members. Only Gossett opposed allowing the displaced persons into the United States.

55. Irving M. Engel to Herbert Bayard Swope, December 28, 1948, AJC, CCDP files, folder, "48–60."

56. Memo to CRC (National Community Relations Advisory Council), from George Hexter, June 25, 1948, AJC folder, "DPs Immigration," 1946–1950."

57. Minutes of the CCDP Executive Committee June 17, 1948, AJC, CCDP files, folder, "48–50"; *NYT,* June 20, 1948.

58. The four were Senators Ferguson and Kilgore and Representatives Celler and Boggs.

59. Celler, *You Never Leave Brooklyn,* p. 96.

60. *Public Papers of the President* (1948):382–84.

61. "Congress 'Helps' the D.P.s," Jewish Frontier (July 1948) 15:4; Abraham G. Duker, "Admitting Pogromists and Excluding Their Victims," The Reconstructionist (October 1, 1948) 14:21; John Slawson to Bill Haber, June 21, 1948, AJC folder "DPs, Immigration, 1946–1950."

62. Interview with Selma G. Hirsch of the AJC in New York City, July 26, 1977; Maslow and Hexter, "Immigration—or Frustration," p. 17; memo from "Marc" [Vosk] to "Sandy" [Flowerman] re DP Legislation," July 9, 1948, AJC folder "DPs Legislation, Immigration."

63. See Maslow and Hexter, ibid., pp. 17–20; Minutes of the CCDP Executive Committee, June 17, 1948, AJC, CCDP, folder, "48–50"; E. E. Swanstrom to Frank Fellows, July 27, 1948, Congressional Record (June 2, 1949) 95:7170; NYT, July 15, 1948, p. 15.

64. Memo from George Hexter to CRC members, August 9, 1948, AJC folder, "Immigration DPs, 1945–47"; Sidney Liskofsky to Morton G. Thalhimer, August 19, 1948, ibid.; Harley Kilgore to Louis Treadway, February 1, 1950, Hyde Park, N.Y., Franklin D. Roosevelt Library, Harley Kilgore papers, box 30.

65. Divine, American Immigration Policy, p. 143.

66. Speech of Rep. Sam Hobbs (D. Ala.) June 11, 1948, cited in American Council for Nationalities Services, shipment 6, box 7, folder, "Debate Before the House on HR 6393."

67. American Jewish Committee, 42nd Annual Report (New York, 1948), p. 112.

11

Black
Antisemitism

The conflict between Jews and blacks features all the characteristics
we are familiar with as forming part of the antisemitic syndrome;
it has an element of intergroup conflict but also a peculiar fixation
upon the Jews; it has borrowed images and rhetoric from abroad
especially the so-called 'Third World'; it has an element of religious
tension which stems from the presence of religious exotica among
blacks; it has envy of the Jewish position and an exaggerated notion
of their power which is standard in the antisemitic imagination.
Above all, it is inchoate and lacks ideological coherence which is
also typical of the American scene. An understanding of the dynamics of American antisemitism might well be found in studying
its presence among American blacks.''

Henry Feingold[1]

Manifestations of black antisemitism erupted in the United
States in the 1930s and tensions in black-Jewish relations have
surfaced in every succeeding decade. Poll data since the 1960s
suggest that among young black adults the intensity of feelings
has increased, and Black Muslim and Black Power advocates'
attacks upon Israel indicate that anti-Zionism has been added to
the traditional prejudices. Conventional wisdom holds that this
hostility began when Jews and blacks met in the urban ghettos of
the North where Jews were first perceived as the seemingly powerful or exploitative landlords, shopkeepers, employers, teachers,
or welfare workers. Yet it is quite clear from the historical records

that negative black perceptions of Jews had been firmly implanted long before significant numbers of the two groups interacted on a regular basis. Although later commentators would point to real problems between the two groups as rationales for existing animosities, black antisemitism originated and continued quite apart from encounters with Jews. But the subject itself did not capture the imagination of scholars before the 1940s and "discussions of black anti-Semitism," as Hasia Diner noted, "remained muted and hushed in both Jewish and black circles until the late 1960s."[2]

Then, in April 1967, *The New York Times Magazine* published two provocative articles on black antisemitism. In the first, James Baldwin argued that "Negroes are Anti-Semitic Because They're Anti-White"; in the second, Robert Gordis responded, "Negroes are Anti-Semitic Because They Want a Scapegoat."[3] Never before had black animosity toward Jews been proclaimed so dramatically by a major American publication. The reasons for this were that before the 1960s the beliefs that most white Christian Americans held about Jews were basically the same as those articulated by blacks. Both groups pictured the Jew as usurer, infidel, and Christ-killer. This mythology has existed since colonial times and for many centuries before that in Europe. No matter that such fantasies were firmly implanted before most Americans—white or black—had ever seen a Jew and were perpetuated in folk culture independently of any personal experience.[4] As Richard Wright wrote about his youth in Mississippi and Tennessee before World War I: "All of us black people who lived in the neighborhood hated Jews, not because they exploited us but because we had been taught at home and in Sunday School that Jews were 'Christ-killers.' " "To hold an attitude of antagonism or distrust toward Jews," he continued, "was bred in us from childhood; it was not merely racial prejudice, it was part of our cultural heritage."[5]

The earliest roots of black antisemitism can be traced back to the religious teachings the slaves imbibed from Protestant fundamentalist ministers.[6] Black slaves knew the stories of the Old Testament concerning Moses, Joshua, Daniel, and other biblical heroes, but the messages conflicted with one another. Thus they identified with the Children of Israel whom Moses led out of

slavery and into freedom,[7] but they also believed that the Jews
had killed their Saviour, rejected his teachings, and were outcasts
in Christian society.[8] Blacks sang spirituals with lines like, "The
Jews killed poor Jesus," "Were you there when the Jews crucified
my Lord," and "De Jews done killed poor Jesus. . . ."[9] Black
jingles and folk ditties also included rhymes like

> Virgin Mary had one son
> The cruel Jews had him hung[10]

and

> Bloody Christ Killer
> Never Trust a Jew
> Bloody Christ Killer
> What won't a Jew do?[11]

Throughout the nineteenth and twentieth centuries the
negative references to Jews as Christ-killers kept cropping up
among blacks in a wide variety of circumstances. In 1859 a female
slave disappeared on the day she was to be transferred to a new
owner. When found and asked why she did not want to go to her
new mistress the following dialogue ensued:

> "I don't want to go to live with Miss Isaacs."
> "Why don't you want to live with her? She is a good lady and will
> make you a kind mistress, and besides, you won't have any hard
> work to do."
> "Ah! but Mass F—, they tell me Miss Isaacs is a Jew; and if the
> Jews kill the Lord and Master, what won't they do to a poor little
> nigger like me!"[12]

In the middle of the twentieth century educator Horace
Mann Bond recalled responding in 1915 to a twelve-year-old boy
who taunted him by shouting, "Nigger, Nigger, Nigger, Nigger,"
with the expression "You Christ killer!" Bond at first claimed that
he had no idea why that phrase came into his mouth but after
reflection he conceded that he grew up in a house where the
family prayed before each meal, read scripture every morning and
evening, attended daily chapel and three services on Sundays. "Of

course," he added "the thought that Christ had been killed and by the Jews, and that this little boy was such a one, may have had a more ancient basis in my twelve-year old mind than I can now bring myself to admit."[13] Novelist James Baldwin, on the other hand, quite candidly acknowledged that

> the traditional Christian accusation that the Jews killed Christ is neither questioned nor doubted, the term "Jew," actually operates in this initial context to include all infidels of white skin who had failed to accept the Savior. No real distinction is made: the preacher begins by accusing the Jews of having refused the light and precedes from there to a catalog of their subsequent sins and the sufferings visited on them by a wrathful God.[14]

And in the 1930s, when Hortense Powdermaker did her study of people in Bible Belt communities, two sociologists, Charles Johnson and E. Franklin Frazier, cautioned her not to reveal her Jewish background because the people she would be dealing with, blacks and whites, still regarded the Jew as "Christ-killer."[15]

Secular stereotypes of the Jew absorbed from the white Christian culture reinforced black religious antisemitism. The view of the Jew as economic predator seems to have developed during the Middle Ages when Jews were banned from owning land in most of Western Europe and were allowed to engage in the practices of borrowing and lending money. From this activity, a variety of myths developed among Christians about Jewish behavior which Shakespeare infamously immortalized in his classic play, *The Merchant of Venice*. In an extraordinarily perceptive essay in 1913 the black newspaper, *The New York Age*, observed:

> Perhaps no work of a dramatist ever did a whole people more serious and lasting damage than Shakespeare's "Shylock" which for centuries in Europe fixed in popular opinion the Jewish character as uncouth, greedy and soulless, demanding always his "pound of flesh," for the forfeited debt. . . .[16]

These ideas were accepted uncritically by whites and passed along to blacks who have, in turn, expressed some of the harshest condemnations of Jewish activities.

The image of Jews as pecuniary predators, "loyal only to

wealth and each other," characterized black attitudes in the nineteenth and twentieth centuries and constituted a regular feature of black newspapers. The expressions, once again, reflected views generally held by whites and were probably similar in intensity. The New Orleans *Louisianan*, which "regularly portrayed Jews in an unfavorable light," wrote, in 1879, that the Jews had lent money at usurious rates to nobles and warriors in England after 1066 and thereby acquired great wealth. The Indianapolis *Freeman* informed readers in 1895 about the "immense wealth" of the Jews who "are today a power in the money market." The Washington *Bee*, just a few years later, opined that "the time is fast coming when the Jews will be the financial rulers of the world." A writer for *The Colored American*, in 1903, stated "in an incredibly short time after the arrival of a Jew in any community he has nearly every family in his debt or under obligations to him. . . ." In 1905 Jessie Fortune, writing about the immigrant Jews on New York City's Lower East Side used phrases like "Jews will make money," "few of them are really destitute," and the Jew's "sole aim seems to be earning money." Then in another *New York Age* article, a few weeks later, the Jewish "race" is described as

> tribalistic rather than national in character, and parasitical and predatory rather than conservatory and constructive in tendencies—preying upon and devouring the substance of others, rather than creating and devouring the substance of itself.
>
> As a salesman, as a money-lender, the disposition of the Jew is to take the long end and let the other man take and hold the short end of every proposition . . . as a moneylender he holds the purse strings of the world and exacts his own terms of those, whether states or individuals, who need and must have money to finance their necessities. . . .

A southern black writer commented in 1910 that "the Jews have always been tradesmen, clothiers, pawnbrokers, and money-lenders with enormous extorted gains from which they have cornered our markets, squeezed our trade, and exacted the 'pound of flesh.' . . ." Half a century later two white scholars reported that in the black ghettos, "frequently Jews are associated, almost reflexively, with money, parasitism, and oppression." Ralph Bunche had already underscored the transference in 1942 when he wrote, "The Negro is not very original in his anti-Jewish stereotypes. He simply takes over, with slight refinement, the attitude of white anti-Semites."[17] At the time that Bunche wrote, his observations were generally accurate, but the nature of the manifestations of black antisemitism had already begun to be somewhat different than those of whites in the 1930s and would move wider apart thereafter.

There was one major area, however, where Bunche's analysis does not fit. Beginning in the 1890s, and continuing into the twentieth century, blacks, unlike most whites, were often encouraged by the same journals and leaders that criticized Jews to emulate their group cohesiveness and economic accomplishment. In 1899 Booker T. Washington wrote

> these people have clung together. They have a certain amount of unity, pride, and love of race; and as the years go on, they will be more and more influential in this country,—a country where they were once despised, and looked upon with scorn and derision. It is largely because the Jewish race has had faith in itself. Unless the Negro learns more and more to imitate the Jew in these matters, to have faith in himself, he cannot expect to have any high degree of success.[18]

The next year, a black attorney, practically echoing Washington, admonished his brethren, "If blacks were to be accepted, they had to become like the 'despised Jew, the representative of business and money.' "[19] A *New York Age* editorial in 1905 acknowledged that

> Prejudice against Jews is almost as general and persistent as it is against the Afro-American people; but it is displayed less, because the Jews are among the wealthy people of the country and know how to advance themselves by properly directing their wealth against those who offended them.[20]

James Weldon Johnson, one of the early leaders of the NAACP, also wrote of "the two million Jews [who] have a controlling interest in the finances of the nation," and he urged fellow blacks to "draw encouragement and hope from the experiences of modern Jews."[21] Repeating in 1927, this sentiment that blacks should emulate the Jews in standing together and making money, *The Norfolk Journal and Guide* also noted that "in many ways [the Jew] sympathizes with and helps us. He gets his pound of flesh for doing it. . . ."[22] That this theme of Jewish wealth, and what it could purchase, remained constant throughout the twentieth century was attested to by Martin Luther King, Jr., when he wrote, shortly before his death in 1968, "Negroes nurture a persisting myth that the Jews of America attained social mobility and status solely because they had money."[23] (Although King used the word "myth," most of his black contemporaries who spoke on the subject indicated that they believed what they said to be true.)

Folklore is another area in which cultural mores expressed black ambivalence toward Jews. "The persistence of folkloristic expressions of hostility and prejudice that have their origins in social conditions much different from those that presently prevail," folklorist Nathan Hurvitz suggested a little more than a decade ago, "indicates that they serve a purpose in our society. This purpose is to maintain and create cleavages between groups," and thus promote intragroup solidarity. And in the case of black folklore, that point is certainly true. "The traditional stereotype of the Jew as a money-grubbing materialist," historian Lawrence W. Levine tells us, "was prominent in Negro humor." And folklorist Daryl Dance reported that the black jokes and stories she collected "usually depict the Jew as a dishonest, unscrupulous, but successful businessman." There are several humorous tales about a "Colored Man, a Jew, and a White Man" in which the Jew is distinguished from other Caucasians. The main thrust of almost all of these jokes is the compulsive Jewish concern for wealth. There are many variations of black folk humor concerning Jews exchanging checks for cash in the coffins of deceased friends. One frequently told southern tale instructed other blacks in how to distinguish a "cracker" from a "Jew." "Some white people is crackers and some is all mean and stingy," the narrator relates to his listener. "If one of dem is more stingy than he is mean, he's a

Jew; and if he's more mean than stingy, he's a cracker." A tale from Brooklyn in the 1930s also reflects black impressions of Jews. The folklorist, Richard Dorson, included it in one of his collections:

> The local Christian church had burned down and the Jewish congregation in the neighborhood, very interested in furthering relations between the groups, agreed to let them use their synagogue for their Sunday prayers. And so they had their service in there. And as they were walking out, the two Negroes were walking by after this service and they looked down to see these people coming out of this synagogue. And the one says to the other, "You know, dat dere's the poorest bunch of Jews I ever did see."[24]

The great black leaders at the turn of the century, Booker T. Washington and W. E. DuBois, had the same kind of ambivalent feelings toward Jews that other blacks did. Washington, who shared the conventional views of his southern contemporaries, began his career, as his biographer Louis Harlan put it, "full of misunderstandings about Jews," and as late as the 1890s a friend cautioned him to keep his little prejudices about the Jews out of his speeches. Washington seems to have thought of Jews as exploitative shopkeepers and usurious creditors and from time to time differentiated between the Jew and the white man. However, disparagement of the Jews was impolitic since a number of Jews made substantial financial contributions to black causes. As Harlan noted, "in [Washington's] effort to secure donations to his school . . . it was in his interest to drop his prejudice." And publicly he did so. Many of his twentieth–century writings, in fact, praise the Jews.[25]

W. E. B. DuBois also displayed hostility toward Jews which he would, in later years, repudiate. While on an ocean liner crossing the Atlantic in 1895 DuBois confided to his diary that although he had met two congenial Jews, the others of their ilk had "in them all that slyness, that lack of straight-forward openheartedness that goes straight against me."[26] In his major work, *Souls of Black Folk*, published in 1903, he relied on hearsay and folk tales to denigrate Jews, Yankees, and poor whites, but not "Southern

Gentlemen.''[27] Several of his fallacious comments about Jews were corrected in a 1953 edition of this classic work but for half-a-century DuBois let stand observations like:

> I have seen, in the Black Belt of Georgia, an ignorant, honest Negro buy and pay for a farm in installments three separate times, and then in the face of law and decency the enterprising Russian Jew who sold it to him pocketed the money and deed and left the black man landless, to labor on his own land at thirty cents a day.[28]

and:

> The rod of empire that passed from the hands of Southern gentlemen in 1865 . . . has never returned to them. Rather it has passed to those men who have come to take charge of the industrial exploitation of the New South—the sons of poor whites fired with a new thirst for wealth and power, thrifty and avaricious Yankees, shrewd and unscrupulous Jews. Into the hands of these men the Southern laborers, white and black, have fallen, and this to their sorrow.[29]

DuBois also wrote of the ''defense of deception and flattery, of cajoling and lying . . . which the Jews of the Middle Ages used and which left its stamp on their character for centuries.''[30]

Jewish leaders Jacob Schiff and Stephen Wise protested these prejudicial references and vainly tried to get DuBois to change them. ''I . . . continued to let the words stand as I had written them,'' DuBois wrote in 1953, ''and did not realize until the horrible massacre of German Jews, how even unconscious repetition of current folklore such as the concept of Jews as more guilty of exploitation than others, had helped the Hitlers of the world.''[31] At that point he not only changed phrases like ''the Jew is the heir of the slave-baron'' to ''immigrants are the heirs . . .,'' ''enterprising Jew'' to ''enterprising American'' and ''Jews of the Middle Age,'' to ''peasants of the Middle Age,''[32] but he candidly admitted as well:

> I am not at all sure that the foreign exploiters to whom I referred in my study of the Black Belt, were in fact Jews. I took the word of my informants, and I am now wondering if in fact Russian Jews in any numbers were in Georgia at the time.[33]

The hostility of Washington and DuBois, like that of other blacks, did not attract a great deal of attention until the depression of the 1930s. Before that time neither Jews, nor anyone else, paid much attention to the existing hostility. Few white people read black newspapers or cared what blacks were saying on any topic, and in any case many black attitudes toward Jews did not differ significantly from those held by white Christians, and where they were unique they were not considered particularly noteworthy by whites. Jews themselves had little interest in what blacks thought—they were primarily concerned with what the white Christian leaders were doing and saying.[34]

But after Hitler came to power in Germany, DuBois, now editor of the NAACP publication, *The Crisis,* caused a great many people to take notice when in September, 1933, he wrote:

> Nothing has filled us with such unholy glee as Hitler and the Nordics. When the only "inferior" peoples were "niggers" it was hard to get the attention of the *New York Times* for little matters of race, lynchings and mobs. But now that the damned include the owner of the *Times,* moral indignation is perking up.[35]

Other expressions of group feelings further conveyed black hostility toward Jews. *The New York Age* observed, "If the Jewish merchants in Germany treated the German workers as Blumsteins [a department store] treat the people of Harlem, then Hitler is right."[36] Many blacks opined that "the Jews can't be so bad off in Germany, they have all the money."[37] Lunabelle Wedlock, who surveyed the black press in the 1930s, concluded that most of the writers "are either indifferent to German anti-Semitism or view with evident pleasure the degradation of a minority group other than their own."[38]

The shrillness in tone can be accounted for in several ways. The most severe economic downturn in American history began in 1929 and blacks, as usual, suffered to a greater extent than whites. Half of the residents in Harlem in the 1930s were on relief. Blacks therefore gained some satisfaction in seeing another group—and one which they disliked—being persecuted as well. In addition, the 1930s were a period of more outspoken antisemitism in the United States than ever before. Over one hundred new antisemitic groups developed during the decade and demagogues like Father Coughlin became national media celebrities.[39]

Therefore blacks knew that attacking Jews was safe—even the whites were doing it quite openly while the more genteel Americans, who shared these prejudices but who voiced them in a more muted or subtle tone, did not object to outbursts against Jews. A third factor contributing to the intensity of feeling in the 1930s, as David Helwig pointed out in his essay, "Black Leaders and United States Immigration Policy, 1917–1929," was that during the 1920s blacks "internalized the ideology of Nordic supremacy"[40] and the belief in the inferiority of Jews, Italians, and other southern and eastern Europeans. Underscoring this adaptation of the xenophobia of the dominant culture, Wedlock wrote, "In general Negros subscribe to the white Gentile's concept of Jews, even to thinking of them in the light of the same stereotypes." She then noted that blacks added "deceitful" to "progressive, shrewd, ambitious, grasping, industrious, intelligent" when talking about Jews.[41]

The focal point of a good deal of the discontent centered on the lack of employment opportunities. With little or no income, blacks thought storekeepers' prices exorbitant. Jews owned many of the small stores frequented in the ghetto and extended credit to those unable to pay immediately, but blacks resented the merchants because they owed them money. Blacks were also angry that Jews hired relatively few of them as clerks until community pressure forced an alteration of that policy.[42]

Housing constituted another area of tensions. "A popular misconception in some urban ghettos where rent gouging was a constant irritant," Robert Wiesbord and Arthur Stein wrote, "was that *all* white landlords and shopkeepers were Jews." The image of the "fiendish Jewish landlord" and the "Shylock landlord" predominated in the ghettos of Chicago, New York, Detroit, Philadelphia, Pittsburgh, and other urban areas even when someone else owned the property. Independent studies concluded that blacks owned 75 percent of Harlem real estate in 1936 and that "Daddy" Browning, John D. Rockefeller, and the estate of John

J. Astor were among the largest single property holders in the area. But the facts seemed irrelevant to people's perceptions, and the passage of time did not lessen the prejudice. Three decades later *Time* magazine noted, "A Negro will frequently refer to his 'Jew landlord' even though the man's name may be O'Reilly, Kawolski or Santangelo."[43]

A third troublesome concern revolved around the employment of women in other people's homes. Black domestics preferred working for gentiles and a major expose in *The Crisis* in 1935, entitled "The Bronx Slave Market," exacerbated hostilities toward Jews. The article was not primarily an antisemitic piece. Nevertheless others perceived of it as such and it confirmed existing black prejudices because the street locations where blacks waited to sell their services were in heavily Jewish areas. Similar street markets existed in Chicago, Philadelphia, and other cities, and their origins could be traced to the Jacksonian era. They revived during the depression when desperate, unemployed women converged in particular spots and negotiated with lower middle class housewives for day labor. The sensational nature of "The Bronx Slave Market," and the legitimacy of the prospective domestics' complaints, led to the establishment of conveniently located employment agencies where employee and employer could contact one another in a more professional atmosphere. But the animosity created by the original report, and subsequent embellishments by women who worked for Jewish employers at their homes in the Bronx, added grist to the antisemitic mills.[44]

These frequent and negative contacts between blacks and Jews during the 1930s made both groups more wary of one another. Poor people found the Jews-as-scapegoat a satisfying target for blame. Thus one woman asked, "since the Jews controlled most of the money in the United States," why didn't they use "that financial power to better the condition of the Negro?" One scholar concluded: "To Harlem it had become a way of life to blame the Jew for discrimination and abuse."[45]

The coming of World War II ended the depression but had little effect on how blacks or whites perceived Jews. A December 1942, poll found that more Americans viewed Jews as a greater threat to this country than the Germans, Japanese, or fascists in our midst. White Catholics and Protestants alike displayed what *The Christian Register* (Unitarian) characterized as "vicious anti-Semitism." And in Massachusetts, Governor Leverett Saltonstall was forced by an exposé in new York's *PM* newspaper to establish a committee to investigate brutal attacks by Irish teen age gangs against Jewish boys.[46]

Similarly hostile attitudes toward Jews existed in the black community as well. In February 1942, *The Amsterdam News* observed, "There never has been such general anti-Semitic sentiment in Harlem as exists right now,"[47] and the following year the *Pittsburgh Courier* spoke of "the dangerous and disastrous spread of anti-Semitism among Negroes."[48] Race riots broke out in Detroit and Harlem, in 1943, and, unfortunately, many Jewish owners of small stores were often the targets. From that point on, Isabel Boiko tells us, "Jewish businessmen realized that there was no hope for the kind of peaceful co-existence they had envisaged because Negro bitterness toward the Jew appeared permanent."[49] Southern blacks shared the existing prejudices. "The Truth of the matter is," Tennessee's *National Baptist Voice* declared in May 1945, "Negroes are filled with Anti-Semitism. In any group of Negroes, if the white people are not around, the mention of the Jew calls forth bitter tirades." Ralph Bunche attempted to explain the reason for this pervasive hostility when he wrote, in 1941,

> In the home, the school, the church, and in Negro society at large, the Negro child is exposed to disparaging images of the Jew. . . . Negro parents, teachers, professors, preachers, and business men, who would be the first to deny that there is any such thing as "the Negro," or that there are "Negro traits," generalize loosely about "the Jew," his disagreeable "racial traits," his "sharp business practices," his "aggressiveness," "clannishness" and his prejudice against Negroes. There is an undercurrent of apparent resentment among many Negroes that the Jew is better off economically, politically and socially than the Negro; that the Jew is not so universally "Jim-Crowed" as his black brother in misery. The Jew is not disliked by Negroes because he is "white," but because he is a "Jew," as the Negro conceives the Jew.[50]

   After World War II antisemitism in the United States began to subside and antagonistic remarks about Jews, by both blacks and whites, became less frequent and more muted. Jewish and black civil rights groups and many of their leaders worked harmoniously with one another in an effort to obtain legal equality for all Americans. Some blacks, however, thought these efforts would be fruitless. "Top-crust Negroes and Jews are wasting time sitting in meetings agreeing on the evilness of Race Prejudice and thinking this agreement settles the problem," *The National Baptist Voice* observed. "Yes, for a few fortunate individuals, but the great masses of Negroes go right ahead nursing their grievances against the Jew, waiting for an opportunity to give vent to their pent-up wrath."[51]

   Jews and their organizations, however, sincerely believed in the efficacy of legal change and, more than any other white group in America, devoted themselves, from the late 1940s through the mid 1960s, to promoting equality of opportunity in this country. They supported the establishment of Fair Employment Practices Commissions in cities and states, were prime movers for the abolition of discriminatory policies among college admissions officers, and provided "friends of the court" briefs to the United States Supreme Court supporting the end to discrimination and segregation in America. They also supported antilynching bills in Congress, favored an end to the poll tax, and contributed lavish amounts of money and time to every cause designed to promote civil rights for all Americans. In fact, southern Jews often criticized their northern brethren in the 1950s and 1960s for being too conspicuous in the civil rights movement.[52]

   But Jewish activism did not eliminate existing prejudices. Blacks sensed a certain kind of hypocrisy in Jewish actions since they still engaged in discriminatory practices in employment, housing, and education (e.g., white liberals contributing to civil rights organizations while sending their own children to lily-white or only slightly integrated public and private schools). The Reverend James H. Robinson, a prominent black minister who traveled throughout the country in the 1950s, reported that "there is more anti-Semitism among Negroes than appears on the surface.

It increases as overall racial tension increases." Reverend Robinson ascribed this "increase" to southern blacks' resentment of the Jews' refusal to speak out there for civil rights, and the perception of northern blacks that Jews in the suburbs and better neighborhoods "are often as hostile as other whites, when Negroes attempt to move into a community."[53]

But even where Jews tried to be more involved in promoting democracy in the 1950s their efforts sometimes backfired. A Jewish agency professional in Detroit found that local NAACP leaders showed ambivalence in associating with them. The blacks wanted to be seen as the leaders of the Civil Rights Movement there, not as participants. In Chicago, Jews led the movement for a Committee Against Discrimination (CAD) but found it difficult to get any support from blacks. Blacks were, in fact, the weakest supporters. "There was some Negro distrust of the CAD," political scientist James Q. Wilson wrote,

> and suspicion of its heavily Jewish backing; allegations of Jewish "dictatorship" were made. Negro representatives were divided as to the stance the organization should take. Apparently, a degree of Negro chauvinism was also involved. Organizations to aid Negros should be led by Negros, some thought.

On the other hand, when the Federal government passed a weak civil rights bill in 1957, Richard Parrish, Secretary of the American Negro Labor Council, excoriated the NAACP leaders for " 'capitulating to phony liberal white Jews.' "[54]

In the 1950s Jewish leaders also tried to understand why blacks singled them out for attack but their studies unearthed little of value. A Pittsburgh Jewish agency professional indicated that blacks rarely said anything negative about white Protestant bankers, utility executives, and insurance men who engaged in discriminatory practices. "Even trained Negro workers seldom mention this invisible relationship which is never permitted to become an issue between" blacks and white Protestants.[55]

Not all of the articulate blacks, however, went along with the antisemitic rhetoric. Several writers tried to lend their influence to curbing the growing hostility that they perceived. Louis Martin of the *Chicago Defender* noted in 1958:

No other minority in American life including ourselves, has fought more vigorously nor more effectively against prejudice and bigotry than the Jews."[56]

The Pittsburgh Courier also cautioned readers to reevaluate their attitudes:

Not only have Jews stuck their necks out for us—they have fought gallantly and intelligently for social justice for everybody. The Jews are a people to be emulated, not despised.[57]

Similarly, Andrew W. Ramsey in his column, "Our Friends, The Jews," published in the *Indianapolis Recorder* in 1961, tried to get readers to see some incongruities in their beliefs:

The Negroes either reject the majority concept of the Negro while accepting the majority stereotypes regarding Jews or accept both evaluations.[58]

The opinions of these writers, however, had only a minimal effect since the negative attitudes that blacks maintained toward whites in general and Jews in particular did not change substantially. Black antisemitism, if anything, intensified during the 1960s. Beginning in 1961, and continuing for the next several years, Jews and blacks clashed in the labor movement, in schools, in areas of cultural and economic endeavors, and in their perception of what constituted the appropriate course of the civil rights movement once Congress passed the Civil Rights Act of 1964. What many Jews discovered, and what many blacks always knew, was that the goals of the two groups could not be the same because of unequal treatment of blacks and whites in this country, as well as different economic circumstances, cultural values, historical experiences, and levels of skills. Sociologist Nathan Glazer captured black sentiments exactly when he wrote in 1964, "The Negro anger is based on the fact that the system of formal equality produces so little for them."[59] Jews had been well educated, were perhaps the wealthiest ethnic group in America, and were positioned to benefit from equal opportunities in a wide variety of areas once they became available. But equality of opportunity for blacks did not significantly advance the group's position. Black spokesmen knew that their people had to make up for centuries of discrimination which had caused significant domestic and social problems, and that they needed additional education and training before most of them could take advantage of legal equality.

With the passage of the Civil Rights Act of 1964 most Jews believed that the fight for equality in America had been won. Most blacks disagreed. And after 1954 moderate black leaders, who had worked well with their Jewish counterparts, were displaced by a younger generation with different perspectives. No longer were black-Jewish relations tense only beneath the surface, they were out in the open. Black frustration at the failure of significant changes as a result of the passage of the civil rights legislation led them to alter their course of action.[60]

This a new breed of black militants, almost all young adults, challenged a variety of sacred cows. They were impatient with their older and more moderate leaders. Some espoused the Muslim rather than the Christian faith, and adopted Arab attitudes toward Israel as their own. Almost all recognized that blacks had to take charge of their own destiny and thus cut their ties with whites in the Civil Rights movement. Jews were faulted for failing to help blacks move up the economic ladder. And the "super-competence of the Jewish organizers and intellectuals," Andrew Kopkind wrote in 1969, "made the young blacks realize quite clearly that they had to master the techniques of their own revolution."[61]

Because the passage of the Civil Rights Acts of 1964 and 1965 failed to provide the hoped for changes in black lives, other avenues for improvement were explored. The militants focused more sharply on economic and political goals, particularly on institutions that limited their opportunities, such as schools.[62] The idea of small community controlled school districts appealed to civil rights supporters, idealists, and people of good will—black and white—because the public schools in the city had not been particularly successful in educating black children. In the Fall of 1967 one black school teacher, John Hatchett, had written:

> We are witnessing today in New York City a phenomenon that spells death for the minds and souls of our black children. It is the systematic coming of age of the Jews who dominate and control

the educational bureaucracy of the New York Public School system and their power starved imitators, the Black Anglo-Saxons.[63]

The experimental new school board in Ocean Hill-Brownsville, established in 1967, seemed to be a promising step toward greater control by blacks of their destinies.

But the new school board found itself locked in with a set of tenured teachers who belonged to the American Federation of Teachers (AFT) union. In an attempt to reorganize the district, Rhody McCoy, the chief school board administrator, dismissed several of the old-timers, most of whom were Jewish, and replaced them with younger people, 40 percent of whom were also Jewish. Those fired sought union protection, the head of the teachers' union, Albert Shanker, accused the Ocean Hill-Brownsville school board of antisemitism, and New York City's teachers went out on strike in the Fall of 1968. What originally had appeared as an attempt by blacks to control the local school district, and as an employer-employee conflict to union members, escalated into the most vicious and visible black-Jewish confrontation in the history of the United States. The strike polarized the city and made national headlines. No provocative statement made by either side remained unpublicized. The teachers' union took the remarks of perhaps half a dozen vicious antisemites and circulated thousands of copies of the most defamatory remarks. Parents and others in the district paraded with signs reading, "Jew Pigs," and calling Hitler the "Messiah." Jews were accused of practicing "genocide" on black children, and Jewish teachers received notes reading "Watch yourself, Jew, crossing streets, drinking tea, etc. You have been marked for elimination." The numerous insults and glares exchanged by both sides intensified mutual hostility.[64]

McCoy and the governing board of the Ocean Hill-Brownsville district went on record as opposing antisemitism, but the actions of the teachers' union and several of the black militants exacerbated the conflict. Although the school strike finally ended on November 18, 1968, with places found elsewhere in the system for the fired teachers, its repercussions lasted for years. Many teachers who experienced that incident still have vivid memories of it. For many blacks, the behavior of the Jewish teachers and their union confirmed long held prejudices. The New York Civil Liberties Union later condemned Shanker for "proving" accusations of antisemitism during the strike with "half-truths, innuendoes, and outright lies," while the Anti-Defamation League observed in its report of the same conflict:

> anyone familiar with the events of the last few years would know that this [conflict] has been building up and has been waiting for an incident to release the mounting wrath, and ... the planned and calculated incitement of Blacks against Jews.[65]

Three other incidents in New York City in 1968-69 lent support both to the views of the Jews who believed blacks were becoming increasingly more antisemitic, and to blacks who were persuaded that Jews controlled the media and other power points in American society. The first concerned John Hatchett's appointment as director of the New York University's Afro-American Center. Hatchett, a militant black teacher, had accused the Jews of controlling and dominating the New York City school system. Many Jews, therefore, felt uncomfortable with NYU's decision and tried, unsuccessfully, to get it reversed. But after only a few months on the job, in the Fall presidential campaign, Hatchett accused the respective Democratic and Republican presidential nominees, Hubert H. Humphrey and Richard M. Nixon, of being, along with Albert Shanker, "racist bastards." The use of such language in describing these men led NYU to terminate his contract. However, supporters of Hatchett, a *New York Times* reporter noted, "see him now as a victim of racism and question whether the fear of losing contributions by wealthy Jews was behind N.Y.U.'s action in dismissing him."[66]

The Hatchett affair was eclipsed by the ending of the teachers' strike in November and an inflammatory poem read over the air of a small New York City FM radio station in December. A black school teacher, Leslie Campbell, hesitated to quote the verse of one of his students while being interviewed on a radio talk show because he feared the public relations consequences of doing so. However, Julius Lester, the program's host, prevailed upon him to go ahead. Dedicated to Albert Shanker, it began

Hey, Jew boy, with that yarmulke on your head
You pale faced Jew boy—I wish you were dead.

Campbell's reading evoked no immediate response but when two weeks later, on January 16, 1969, *The New York Times* carried the story, the Jewish defense agencies called for the revocation of the radio station's license.[67]

Two days later, on January 18, 1969, an exhibit entitled "Harlem on My Mind" opened at the Metropolitan Museum of Art. Intended as a tribute to blacks and their cultural accomplishments, it created a furor because of some of the comments a sixteen year old girl wrote in the introduction to the exhibit's catalog. Without pausing to consider the context and the limitations of an adolescent's perspective, knowledge, or sense of the appropriate, critics zeroed in on her sentences:

> Behind every hurdle that the Afro-American has yet to jump stands the Jew who had already cleared it. Jewish shopkeepers are the only remaining survivors in the expanding black ghettos. The lack of competition allows the already exploited black to be further exploited by Jews.

Many Jews, and Jewish organizations, demanded that these remarks be expunged from the catalog and any other suggestion of antisemitism be immediately eliminated from the exhibit. The catalog, however, had already been published and the exhibit organizers argued that the girl's remarks reflected cultural values and beliefs and were not designed as attacks on anyone. Nevertheless, the protests were so strong that the catalog was withdrawn at the end of the month.[68]

The events of 1968 and 1969 frightened American Jews. They viewed them as the most overt manifestations of bigotry in the United States since the end of World War II. While some Jews were bitter, and reacted by reducing their financial support of civil rights causes, others believed that Jewish welfare was tied to the improvement of all minorities.

In the 1970s, leading black and Jewish organizations wanted to heal existing ruptures and to some extent did so, but one overriding issue—affirmative action—prevented a complete rapprochement. Both groups wanted to bring more blacks into industry at skilled levels, and also into professional positions. Both favored training and education for those formerly denied quality assistance. But blacks also wanted specific numerical goals while most Jews interpreted that stipulation as "quotas"—something that historically white Christians had used against them. Jews had been working the entire century for equal opportunity based on individual merit; they were not willing to negate their advances in this sphere by acceding to the demands of group rights.[69] Moreover, many non-Jewish whites also favored some kind of "affirmative action" which did not stipulate specific numerical goals.

This issue did not have universal agreement from Jewish organizations, however. When in 1974 the University of Washington passed over an individual, Marco De Funis, for admission to law school and accepted another candidate with lower test scores but from a different cultural background, de Funis sued on the grounds of reverse discrimination. Both the National Council of Jewish Women and the Union of American Hebrew Congregations stood with the National Urban League in filling *amicus curiae* briefs with the courts, supporting the university's contention that test scores alone were an inadequate criteria for admission. The case went into federal courts but the University of Washington subsequently admitted De Funis to law school before the United States Supreme Court had the opportunity of rendering a judgment on the matter.[70]

Another case, however, that of Allan Bakke, a white Christian of Norwegian ancestry, did get to the Supreme Court and in 1978, by a slender 5–4 verdict, the majority ruled against race alone being an acceptable criterion for determining school admissions.[71] Although polls showed that 77 percent of white people approved of the Court's decision and only 12 percent disapproved, among blacks the figures were practically reversed. "By 74–15 percent," a Lou Harris survey concluded, "a majority of blacks tend to feel that 'unless quotas are used, blacks and other minorities just won't get a fair shake.' "[72] This real conflict over affirmative action and quotas might have strained black-Jewish relations but would not have caused or aggravated antisemitism, however, if underlying hostility did not exist.

The same might be said for another incident: Andrew Young's resignation as United States Ambassador to the United Nations in 1979. The State Department forced the Ambassador out because he had met secretly with representatives of the Palestinian Liberation Organization (PLO) and misinformed officials in Washington about the meeting. But blacks assumed that American Jews had been responsible for the resignation, and tensions between blacks and Jews rose once again. One minister complained: "Our people had been amazed that the Jews had such political clout with the President and that they cause [sic] the resignation of our Ambassador."[73]

The Bakke case and the Young affair brought anti-Jewish attitudes to the fore but the earlier rise of the Black Muslim movement in the 1960s and 1970s also reflected hostility. The Black Muslims explicitly despised Jews, and their leading spokesman in the 1980s, the Reverend Louis Farrakhan, found a responsive audience among some blacks in America when he referred to Judaism as a "dirty religion" and Hitler as a "great man."[74]

Other blacks did not speak out against Farrakhan because too many people within the community endorsed the man and his views. When Vernon Jordan, Executive Director of the National Urban League, however, praised Jews for their support in the Civil Rights movement and stated that "Black-Jewish relations should not be endangered by ill-considered flirtations with terrorist groups devoted to the extermination of Israel," he found a coalition of "Grassroots Leaders" camped in front of the Urban League offices denouncing him for his blasphemy. "No longer must our Black leaders attack our people for the Jews," they proclaimed. On the other hand, a black minister in Harlem received roaring approval when he told his congregation that he favored Palestinians over the Israelis in the Middle East and the Reverend Jesse Jackson did not lose his constituency within the black community when he proclaimed that supporting the PLO marked "Black America's finest hour."[75]

During the Reverend Jesse Jackson's 1984 campaign for the Democratic presidential nomination, his reference to Jews as "Hymies," his comment that "certain members of the Jewish community [were] persecuting" him, and his attachment to Farrakhan did not significantly alter his standing in the black community. "Many Black leaders were reportedly appalled by Jackson's association with Farrakhan but would not criticize him publicly," a newspaper story concluded. But in 1986 historian John Hope Franklin observed that Jackson's candidacy had "a positive effect on American politics";

> For the first time White America saw a Presidential candidate who spoke out on all of the issues, not just black issues. Jesse showed that he could discuss any subject. He held his own with the other candidates and, in many circumstances, bested them. It was a marvelous experience for whites.[76]

Obviously, careless remarks which were interpreted as antisemitic by many whites, were insufficient reasons for many blacks to withdraw their support of Jackson's candidacy.

Trying to analyze the reasons for black antisemitism and its manifestations at crucial moments in the past half century reveal the complexity of the problem. There can be no doubt that religious teachings and economic stereotypes contributed significantly to the elixir of resentment and hatred which we have observed in recent decades. But there are other historical factors which suggest a more complicated analysis than merely adding up the two factors of Christianity and money. Hostility toward Jews has been common in Christian societies for centuries and it has been especially intense during periods of economic and social crises or at the height of nationalistic fervor. In the United States, the worst outbreak of antisemitism before the twentieth century occurred during the Civil War. In Europe, nationalistic and anti-semitic movements coincided with the attempt to unify the Slavs at the end of the nineteenth century (Pan-Slavism), appeared in the new nations carved out of the Austro-Hungarian empire after World War I, and became especially destructive in Nazi

Germany.[77] To a lesser extent, antisemitic feelings developed among black nationalists in the United States during the 1960s.

There are still other explanations for the hostility that many blacks have displayed toward Jews with increasing sharpness since the 1930s. Whereas some blacks originally may have become antisemitic because of Christian teachings or commonly held attitudes in American society about a Jewish Shylock, psychological factors have also come into play. Until the 1960s, when the impact of the Civil Rights Movement began to make whites less hostile to Jews and blacks more so (see appendix on polls), antisemitic feelings among blacks may have been stimulated unconsciously as a way of identifying with the dominant culture and coping with an inferior status in the United States. Sociologists B. Z. and May L. Sobel underscored this point when they wrote in 1966,

> the Jew is really the only "dislike" the Negro can legitimately feel in common with his white Christian brethren . . .; anti-Jewish feeling *can* be viewed as a key to in-group participation. It does indeed offer a real way to identify with the dominant group, and . . . it may very well help him to gain inner group security. Dubious as might be his other claims to sharing in the general culture, the Negro can join in the use of anti-Semitism as a pretext for the release of aggression as he cannot more readily do with more powerful or accepted groupings.[78]

Another psychological factor, which Robert Gordis emphasized in his 1967 article, "Negroes Are anti-Semitic Because They Want a Scapegoat," was also articulated by Ralph Bunche a generation earlier. "Negroes are an oppressed, frustrated people," Bunche noted in 1942. "Such a people hit always upon the simplest and most convenient explanation of its troubles. It pounces on a scapegoat as a means of psychological escape." And since the Jews' "powers of retaliation are less great than are those of the Gentile whites," they are a safer target to attack.[79]

Psychiatrists Sidney Furst and Curtis Kendrick expanded on these points in the 1970s. Furst observed that "Jews present a convenient [scapegoat] on which troubled people can project their particular difficulties," while Kendrick noted that antisemitism among blacks is, in the main, "an instance of the projection onto someone else of the disowned, negative aspects of the self." He added that "the unconscious feelings that one is bad as bigots say join with other unconscious, reprehensible feelings the person wants to displace on to someone else, and add a special power to the resulting prejudice."[80] Jewish actions, which are often cited erroneously as causes for black hostility, may in fact have contributed to the maintenance of those prejudices. Sociologist Richard Simpson has argued that "contact between members of different groups, where one is subordinate to the other, is more likely to intensify any sterotypes and hostilities which exist."[81] Jews have been extraordinarily mobile and successful in the United States. Their encounters with blacks have almost always been those of the shopkeeper to customer, landlord to tenant, employer to employee, civil rights leader to follower, financial assistant to financial beneficiary, teacher to student, welfare worker to client, and so forth. One can easily see, therefore, how Simpson's analysis might be confirmed. Not until the nation, as a whole, dedicates itself to the eradication of poverty and the end to hostility between and among different groups is it likely that black animosity toward Jews will diminish.

Until black equality in the United States is achieved, however, many blacks will continue scapegoating Jews. Existing anti-Jewish attitudes seem resistant to change. There is probably nothing Jews can do to alter entrenched feelings because the perceptions that many blacks have of Jews have been carelessly adopted. As one scholar pointed out,

> Stereotypes tend to reinforce themselves because people are likely to expose themselves only to messages they want to hear; they interpret messages to coincide with their own preconceptions; and tend to remember only what they want to remember. Logic, reason, understanding, education have little impact. We are moved by those facts that bolster our stereotypes.[82]

Jewish actions are often viewed as either paternalistic or colonial. Any help provided, as Rabbi Robert Gordis pointed out in 1967, "inevitably breeds ill will, ingratitude and a sense of inferiority."

This point was illustrated during one of the social upheavals in Harlem during the 1960s when one black opined, "You know all those Jews in the civil rights marches and going down South—you know why they do it? They do it to take the heat off themselves. They've got a bad conscience because they live on black dollars. We had the riots because of the Jews." Benign neglect, on the other hand, brings charges of indifference. In 1966 Will Maslow argued that even if all of the Jews left Harlem, "the image of the Jew as Shylock and Christkiller would still persist" among blacks.[83] Rational policies and programs are not usually successful in combatting deep-seated prejudices. Jews must continue to behave as they think right; blacks will continue to respond to Jews as they think appropriate.

Appendix on Polls

Much of the aforementioned discussion is based on impressionistic assessments of black antisemitism garnered from scholarly works, newspaper and magazine articles, and reports buried in the files of Jewish organizations. Existing poll data, however, substantiate most of these evaluations of black attitudes toward Jews. The percentages of blacks judged to be antisemitic seems greater than the percentage of whites who fall into that category, at almost every comparable period of time.

Information from polls by itself is confusing. The wording of questions, the nature of both the people being interviewed and the people doing the interviewing, and the context of the times in which the surveys are taken all affect the statistical results. Thus polls alone, or any individual poll, must be analyzed from a broad perspective, weighing other relevant factors. Having made these caveats, however, certain observations are permissible. Significant percentages of blacks at every level of society and of both sexes have been adjudged antisemitic during the past half century and surveys taken in the 1980s have found two out of five blacks, compared with one out of five whites, antisemitic. Earlier assessments also found great percentages of blacks to be prejudiced. One poll in the 1940s adjudged 70 percent of blacks to be antisemitic; a 1950s survey found two-thirds of black women compared with one-quarter of black men hostile to Jews; and tests of black college students in both the 1930s and 1960s showed that they had stronger negative feelings about Jews than did whites. Black attitudes toward Jews, except for the one measuring attitudes of white and black college students in the late 1930s, do not seem to have been the subject of separate polls until the 1960s. Therefore comparing black and white attitudes before that time is quite risky. Nonetheless, Charles H. Stember, who studied polls reflecting white attitudes toward Jews between 1937 and 1962, wrote in 1966:

> The South, as noted earlier, is one of the subgroups whose responses probably are distorted in our statistics because the samples representing it in the early polls were highly select. The early studies, in which the South appeared less anti-Semitic than other areas, contained virtually no Negroes, since respondents were drawn from the voting population, and Negroes then were almost totally disenfranchised in most of the region. In the 1962 survey, with Negroes represented in their true proportion, Southern attitudes toward Jews strongly resembled those in the rest of the country, except for slightly more hostility toward Jewish businessmen and Jews as employees. It is at least conceivable that this change may reflect a level of anti-Semitism among Negroes that is higher than among whites. We have no statistical data showing the former to be more hostile toward Jews than the latter, but a number of informal investigators have reported fairly widespread anti-Semitism among Negroes in recent years.[83]

At one time it was believed that antisemitism among blacks decreased as their educational attainments increased but since the 1960s a variety of polls have found that younger, militant, and better educated individuals are the most antisemitic members of their groups. In 1964 Gertrude Selznick and Stephen Steinberg found that 17 percent of white people under age 35 were antisemitic in contrast to 49 percent of the blacks in that category. In 1979, a Lou Harris poll found national black leaders, presumably those who had been under 35 in 1964, more antisemitic than their followers. Moreover, Harris found the blacks to be more antisemitic than white corporate leaders in 1978. He reported:

> by 54–36%, a majority of [white] corporate leaders feel that "Jews are irritating because they are too aggressive," a view shared by an even higher 65–23% of national black leaders. And when asked if they agreed with the charge that "when it comes to choosing between people and money, Jews will choose money," corporate leaders divided by the narrowest of margins, 49–48%, that they disagree. A 67–19% majority of national black leaders feel that "most of the slumlords are Jewish." They also feel by 81–13% that most Jews will choose money over people, and by 50–39% that "Jews are more loyal to Israel than to America."[84]

In one area, the association of Jews with money, pollsters have found substantial black agreement with those opinions offered by other blacks all the way back to the nineteenth century. Gary Marx, whose conclusions were based on interviews conducted in New York, Chicago, Atlanta, and Birmingham in 1964, found that 54 to 62 percent of those questioned agreed that "Jews are more willing than others to use shady practices to get what they want," while 39 to 50 percent of the respondents also supported the statement, "Jewish businessmen are so shrewd and tricky that other people don't have a fair chance in competition." In all, Marx asked nine questions and responses indicated that 64 percent of the blacks harbored some degree of antisemitic feeling. But he decided that "for an individual to be considered anti-Semitic, he had to have agreed to five or more items,"[85] and thus the author concluded that only 24 percent of blacks were antisemitic. (Although a quick look at the following table indicates what whites in the North with some high school and/or college education are much less antisemitic than blacks in that region, arithmetic errors by Marx in the tables listing whites with some high school education and blacks with some college education make it impossible to make an accurate assessment.) It is noteworthy, I think, that people could be adjudged not antisemitic or low on antisemitism even though they found Jews, in general, "somehow unethical—or unfair in their business practices." And, as Marx pointed out, "even a great many of those with scores of only two or three on the index held such beliefs."[86] Yet even though Marx's data and explanations demonstrated the existence of antisemitism among blacks, careless observers adopted his conclusions and were quick to minimize the problem. One wrote, "As for the generally held concept that Blacks have a special dislike for Jews, Marx's study shows this opinion to be completely erroneous."[87]

Marx's study showed no such thing. In fact the following summary columns of his conclusions do not necessarily substantiate his position, especially since both his totals of antisemitic and non-semitic whites with some high school education, and of blacks with some college education add up to 110 percent.[88]

Table 11.1 Anti-Semitism of Whites and Negroes by Region and Education[a]

	North		South	
	Whites	Negroes	Whites	Negroes
Grammar school				
Non-anti-Semitic	36%	25%	32%	36%
Low on anti-Semitism	34	45	32	52
High on anti-Semitism	21	23	12	8
Very high on Anti-Semitism	9	7	24	4
High plus very high	30%	30%	36%	12%
Total	100%	100%	100%	100%
Number	(195)	(43)	(25)	(25)
At least some high school				
Non-anti-Semitic	39%	42%	48%	21%
Low on anti-Semitism	51	41	28	51
High on anti-Semitism	12	11	12	21
Very high on anti-Semitism	8	6	12	7
High plus very high	20%	17%	24%	28%
Total	100% [sic]	100%	100%	100%
Number	(454)	(62)	(58)	(28)
At least some college[b]				
Non-anti-Semitic	64%	47%		
Low on anti-Semitism	28	47		
High on anti-Semitism	5	11		

Very high on anti-Semitism	3	5
High plus very high	8%	16%
Total	100%	100% [sic]
Number	(215)	(19)

[a]Based on data from national study only.
[b]For the South, there were too few cases to make comparisons.

Another poll, taken within months of Marx's survey in 1964, reached somewhat different conclusions. The authors, Gertrude Stark and Stephen Steinberg, compared the attitudes of blacks and whites toward Jews on eleven items; in eight of them, blacks were more prejudiced than whites, as the following table shows:

Table 11.2 Acceptance of Individual Anti-Semitic Beliefs by Race[89]

	Whites	Blacks	Ratio of Black Acceptance
Jews			
care only about their own kind	24%	43%	180
use shady practices to get ahead	40	58	145
control international banking	28	40	143
are shrewd and tricky in business	34	46	135
are not as honest as other businessmen	27	35	129
always like to head things	53	60	113
have a lot of irritating faults	40	44	110
are more loyal to Israel than America	30	32	107
stick together too much	53	48	90
have too much power in the U.S.	11	9	82
have too much power in the business world	31	19	61

Still other surveys, taken by the National Opinion Research Center (1964), Louis Harris Associats (1974 and 1978), and Daniel Yankelovich Associates (1981), confirm that more blacks than whites agree with the statement: "When it comes to choosing people and money, Jews will choose money," and "Jews are more willing than others to use shady practices to get what they want." Both of these questions found support from blacks in 36 to 58 percent of the cases. The conflicts and confusions of the polls, and the varying statistics listed, should not obscure, however, the

conclusion reached by Lou Harris in 1978 and confirmed by the
Yankelovich survey of 1981: "Blacks tend to be more anti-Jewish
than any other group."[90]

Ironically, however, Jews are less anti-black than are Catholics or Protestants. Surveys taken in the 1940s, 1950s, and 1960s
reached substantially the same conclusions: of all the major religious groups in this country Jews were the least prejudiced, Catholics the most.[91] Nevertheless Jews were held to a higher standard
than the others. At a 1967 meeting of the Angry Black Young Men
held in New Haven, Connecticut, and attended by perhaps 600
people (75 percent of whom were estimated to be black), the
speaker attacked Jews, Irish, Italians, and Poles. A report on the
audience response to the talk indicated that "no part of his pres-
entation received as much applause as his anti-Jewish diatribes."[92]
It took the editors of the *Catholic World* to point out in 1969 what
many Jews themselves felt:

> For some reason the American public seems to expect a more
> passive standard of behavior from Jews than from Christians. In
> protesting against open housing, Poles and Italians and Irish have
> engaged in violence against the blacks and the public was not
> unsympathetic. Other ethnic groups can overreact but when Jews
> do so, they are said to be hypersensitive.[93]

It is also interesting to note that blacks who come in conflict with
Italians, Irishmen, or Poles categorize these people as white,
whereas in their dealings with Jews, Jews are singled out for
castigation.

Notes

1. Henry L. Feingold, "Finding a Conceptual Framework for the Study of American
Antisemitism," *Jewish Social Studies* (Summer-Fall, 1985), 47:308.

2. Ann G. Wolfe, "Negro Anti-Semitism: A Survey," unpublished paper, March 15,
1966, located in American Jewish Committee Archives, New York City; Shlomo Katz, ed.,

Negro and Jews: An Encounter in America (New York: Macmillan, 1967), p. 96; Roi Ottley, *"New World A-Coming"* (Boston: Houghton Mifflin, 1943; reprinted by Arno Press, 1968), p. 123; Kenneth B. Clark, "Black Power and Basic Power," *Congress Bi–Weekly* (January 8, 1968), 35:8; David Riseman, "The Politics of Persecution," *Public Opinion Quarterly* (Spring 1942) 6:49; Hasia R. Diner *In the Almost Promised Land: American Jews and Blacks, 1915–1935* (Westport, Conn: Greenwood Press, 1977), p. 238; see also Nicholas C. Polos, "Black Anti-Semitism in Twentieth Century America: Historical Myth or Reality?" *American Jewish Archives* (1975) 27:23.

3. James Baldwin, "Negroes are Antisemitic Because They're Antiwhite," and Robert Gordis, "Negroes Are Antisemitic Because They Want a Scapegoat," in Leonard Dinnerstein, ed., *Antisemitism in the United States* (New York: Holt, Rinehart and Winston, 1971), pp. 116–131.

4. Abraham G. Duker, "On Negro-Jewish Relations—A Contribution to a Discussion," *Jewish Social Studies* (January 1965), 27:23; Lunabelle Wedlock, *The Reaction of Negro Publications and Organizations to German Anti-Semitism* (Washington, D.C.: The Howard University Studies in the Social Sciences, volume 3, (2), 1942; foreword by Ralph Bunche) p. 116: Katz, *Negro and Jews*, p. 96; Isabel Boiko Price, "Black Responses to Anti-Semitism: Negroes and Jews in New York, 1880 to World War II" (Ph.D., Department of History, University of New Mexico, 1973), p. 50.

5. Richard Wright, *Black Boy* (New York: Harper, 1945; Perennial Classic edition, 1982), p. 70.

6. Clifton F. Brown, "Black Religion—1968," in Patricia W. Romero, ed., *In Black America: 1968, the Year of Awakening* (Washington, D.C.: United Publishing co., 1969), p. 351.

7. Arnold Shankman, *Ambivalent Friends* (Westport, Conn: Greenwood Press, 1982), p. 115.

8. Joseph P. Weinberg, "Black-Jewish Tensions: Their Genesis," *CCAR Journal* (Spring, 1974), 21:33.

9. Ibid., p. 34; Shankman, *Ambivalent Friends*, p. 134.

10. Robert G. Weisbord and Arthur Stein, *Bittersweet Encounter: The Afro-American and the American Jew* (Westport, Conn: Negro Universities Press, 1970), p. 71, note 15; see also Thomas Wentworth Higginson, "Negro Spirituals," *Atlantic Monthly* (1867), 19:688.

11. Wright, *Black Boy*, p. 70.

12. *Harper's Magazine* (1859), 19:859–60.

13. Horace Mann Bond, "Negro Attitudes Toward Jews," *Jewish Social Studies* (January 1965), 27:3–4.

14. James Baldwin, "The Harlem Ghetto: 1948," *Commentary* (February 1948), 5:168.

15. Shankman, *Ambivalent Friends*, pp. 34–35.

16. "Jew In War on Ridicule," *New York Age*, September 25, 1913, p. 4.

17. David J. Hellwig, "Black Images of Jews: From Reconstruction to Depression," *Societas* (Summer 1978), 8:212; Shankman, *Ambivalent Friends*, p. 144; "Letters from Washington, DC," *The Weekly Louisianan* (New Orleans), October 4, 1879, p. 1; "The Pursuit of Business," *The Freeman* (Indianapolis), December 21, 1895, p. 1; "Persecution of the Jews," editorial, *Washington Bee*, August 18, 1899; "Charity Begins at Home," *Colored American* (Washington, D.C.), June 20, 1903, p. 8; Jessie Fortune, "Among the Children of the East Side Jews," *New York Age*, February 8, 1905, p. 4; Arthur Abernathy, *The Jew a Negro* (Moravian Falls, N.C.; Dixie Publishing Co., 1910), pp. 107–8; Weisbord

and Stein, *Bittersweet Encounter,* p. 75; Bunche, "Foreword," *Reaction of Negro Publications,* p. 9.

18. "The Hebrew Race In America," *The Voice of the Negro* (Atlanta) (January 1906), 3:20; Shankman, *Ambivalent Friends,* pp. 115, 116, 117, 118, 119, 127, 130; Hellwig, "Black Images," p. 126; Price, "Black Responses," p. 139; "A Lesson From the Jews," *Colored American,* July 5, 1902, p. 8; Booker T. Washington, *The Future of the American Negro* (New York: Haskell House, 1968; originally published 1900), pp. 182–83.

19. Hellwig, "Black Images," p. 207.

20. *New York Age,* July 20, 1905, p. 4.

21. Steven Bloom, "Interactions Between Blacks and Jews in New York City, 1900–1930, as Reflected in the Black Press," (Ph.D. diss. Department of History, New York University, 1973), p. 97; James Weldon Johnson, "Views Reviews," *New York Age,* February 3, 1916, p. 4; James Weldon Johnson, "The Negro and the Jew," *New York Age,* February 2, 1918, p. 4.

22. "The Jew Shows Us How In Many Ways," *Norfolk Journal and Guide,* May 22, 1926, p. 14.

23. Quoted in Seymour S. Weisman, "Black-Jewish Relations in the USA, II," *Patterns of Prejudice* (January 1981), 15:49.

24. Lawrence W. Levine, *Black Culture and Black Consciousness (New York: Oxford University Press, 1977), p. 305;* Shankman, *Ambivalent Friends,* p. 141, fn. 29; Daryl Cumber Dance, *Shuckin' and Jivin': Folklore from Contemporary Black Americans* (Bloomington: Indiana University Press, 1978), pp. 151 ff; Nathan Hurvitz, "Blacks and Jews in American Folklore," *Western Folklore Quarterly* (October, 1974) 33:324–325; Richard M. Dorson, "Jewish-American Dialect Stories on Tape," in Raphael Patai, ed., *Studies in Biblical and Jewish Folklore* (Bloomington: Indiana University Press, 1960), p. 116; Richard M. Dorson, ed., *Negro Folktales in Michigan* (Cambridge: Harvard University Press, 1956), pp. 75, 76–77; Jack Nusan Porter, "John Henry and Mr. Goldberg: The Relationship Between Blacks and Jews," *Journal of Ethnic Studies* (Fall 1960) 7:75–76; Lucy S. Davidowicz, "Can Anti-Semitism Be Measured?" Commentary (July 1970) 50:42; Richard M. Dorson, "More Jewish Dialect Stories," *Midwest Folklore* (Fall 1960) 10:138.

25. Louis R. Harlan, "Booker T. Washington's Discovery of Jews," in J. Morgan Kousser and James M. McPherson, eds., *Religion, Race, and Reconstruction* (New York: Oxford University Press, 1982), pp. 269, 270, 275, 276; Louis R. Harlan, *Booker T. Washington: The Wizard of Tuskegee, 1901–1915* (New York: Oxford University Press, 1983), p. 260; Louis R. Harlan, et al., eds., *The Booker T. Washington Papers* (11 volumes; University of Illinois Press, 1972–), 3 (1889–1895):412.

26. Francis L. Broderick, *W. E. B. DuBois—Negro Leader in a Time of Crisis* (Stanford University Press, 1959), fn. on pp. 26–27.

27. W. E. Burghardt DuBois, "The Relation of the Negroes To The Whites in The South," *Annals of the American Academy of Political and Social Science* (1901) 18:126.

28. W. E. B. DuBois, *The Souls of Black Folk* (Chicago: A. C. McClurg and Co., 1903), p. 170.

29. Ibid., p. 169.

30. Ibid., p. 204.

31. W. E. B. DuBois, *The Souls of Black Folk* (Milwood, N.Y.: Kraus-Thomson Organization, Ltd., 1973), pp. 42–43.

32. Herbert Aptheker, "The Souls of Black Folk: A Comparison of the 1903 and 1952 Editions," *Negro History Bulletin* (1971) 34:16.

33. DuBois, *Souls of Black Folk* (KTO, 1973), p. 41.

34. David H. Pierce, "Is The Jew a Friend of the Negro?" *The Crisis* (August, 1925) 30:184.

35. "As The Crow Flies," *The Crisis* (September, 1933) 40:197.

36. Price, "Black Responses," p. 230.

37. Wedlock, *Reaction of Negro Publications*, p. 16.

38. Ibid., p. 83.

39. Donald S. Strong, *Organized Anti-Semitism in America* (Washington, D.C.: American Council on Public Affairs, 1941), p. 146; Minutes of the Executive Committee of the American Jewish Committee (1932) 6:178, Blaustein Library, New York City.

40. Price, "Black Responses," pp. 177, 180; David J. Hellwig, "Black Leaders and United States Immigration Policy, 1917–1929," *Journal of Negro History* (Summer, 1981) 66:121.

41. Wedlock, *Reaction of Negro Publications*, p. 29; see also Hellwig, "Black Images," p. 212 and Davidowicz, "Can Anti-Semitism Be Measured?" p. 42.

42. James J. Weinstein, "Behind the Harlem Riots," *Jewish Frontier* (May, 1935) 2:13.

43. Weisbord and Stein, *Bittersweet Encounter*, p. 41; Wedlock, *Response of Negro Publications*, p. 169; Price, "Black Responses," pp. 197, 201; American Jewish Committee Memo, June 11, 1941, folder, "Report of Committee on 'Street Corner Markets,' "; Nathan Zuckerman, ed., *The Wine of Violence* (New York: Association Press, 1947), p. 322; Weinstein, "Behind the Harlem Riots," p. 121; "The Black and the Jews: a Falling Out of Allies," *Time* (January 31, 1969) 93:57.

44. Robert G. Weisbord and Arthur Stein, "Negro Perception of Jews Between the World Wars," *Judaism* (1969) 18:435; Wedlock, *Response of Negro Publications*, pp. 24, 116; "Letters From Readers: Jew Hatred Among Negroes," *The Crisis* (April 1936) 43:122; Harold Orlansky, "A Note on Anti-Semitism Among Negroes," *Politics* (August 1945) 2:251; Riesman, "Politics of Persecution," p. 49.

45. Edward L. Israel, "Jew Hatred Among Negroes," *The Crisis* (February 1936) 43:50; Price, "Black Responses," p. 339; Wedlock, *Response of Negro Publications*, p. 182.

46. "The New Wave of Anti-Semitism," *New Currents* (June, 1943) 1:3; "Not In New England Alone," *The Christian Register* (Unitarian) (May 1945) 124:175; Arnold Beichman, "Saltonstall Orders Anti-Semitic Attacks Investigated," *PM*, October 20, 1943, p. 4; Beichman, "Christian Front Hoodlums Terrorize Boston Jews," *PM*, October 18, 1943, p. 5.

47. *Amsterdam News*, February 14, 1942, as quoted in Price, "Black Responses," p. 318.

48. *Pittsburgh Courier*, October 23, 1943, as quoted in Zuckerman, *Wine of Violence*, p. 315.

49. Price, "Black Responses," p. 267.

50. "The Jew and the Negro," *National Baptist Voice* (Nashville, Tennessee) (May 15, 1945) 38:1; Bunche, "'Foreword," p. 8; see also Weisbord and Stein, "Negro Perceptions," p. 444.

51. "The Jew and the Negro," *National Baptist Voice*, May 15, 1945, p. 1.

52. William Frankel, "The Bakke Case Legacy," *The New Statesman and Nation (December 22, 1978) 96:855;* Tom Brooks, *"Negro Militants, Jewish Liberals, and the Unions,"* Commentary (September 1961) 32:29; Ellen Hume, "Falling Out: Blacks and Jews Find Confrontation Rising Over Jesse Jackson," *The Wall Street Journal*, May 29, 1984, pp. 1,

18; Weisbord and Stein, *Bittersweet Encounter*, pp. 134–135; Nathan Glazer, "Jews and Blacks: What Happened to the Grand Alliance?" in Joseph R. Washington Jr., ed., *Jews in Black Perspectives: A Dialogue* (Rutherford, N.J.: Fairleigh Dickinson University Press, 1984), p. 105; Claybourne Carson, Jr., "Blacks and Jews in the Civil Rights Movement," ibid., pp. 115–16; Bill Kovack, "Racist and Anti-Semitic Charges Strain Old Negro-Jewish Ties," *The New York Times*, October 23, 1968, p. 32; Peter I. Rose, "Blacks and Jews: The Strained Alliance," in *The Annals of the American Academy of Political and Social Science* (March, 1981) 454–55, 61; Murray Friedman, "Virginia Jewry in the School Crisis: Anti-Semitism and Desegregation," in Leonard Dinnerstein and Mary Dale Palsson, eds., *Jews in the South* (Baton Rouge: Louisiana State University Press, 1973), pp. 341, 349; Isaac Toubin, "Recklessness or Responsibility," *Southern Israelite* (February 27, 1959), p. 13.

53. James H. Robinson and Kenneth B. Clark, "What Negroes Think About Jews," *Anti-Defamation League Bulletin*, December, 1957, p. 7; see also Will Maslow, "Negro-Jewish Relations, in the North," in folder, "Jewish-Negro Relations, Tensions, Race-Rel., Negroes 38–60, Will Maslow, 'Negro-Jewish Relations in the North,' " box 258, American Jewish Committee Mss., YIVO, New York City.

54. Ibid., folder, "Jewish-Negro Relations, Tensions, AJC, Study Comments, Race Rel. Negroes 58–59, Letter from B. M. Joffe of Jewish Community Council of Detroit to S. Andhil Fineberg, 1/22/59"; ibid., folder, "Race Rel. Negroes 52–60," memo from Harry Fleischman to Murray Friedman re: "Negro-Jewish Relations and *Pittsburgh Courier*," June 13, 1960; James Q. Wilson, *Negro Politics: The Search for Leadership* (New York: Free Press, 1960), pp. 160–161.

55. ACJ Mss., YIVO, box 258, folder, "Jewish-Negro Relations . . . 58–59," letter from Lillian A. Friedberg of Pittsburg Jewish Community Relations Council to S. Andhil Fineberg, January 20, 1959; see also folder "Jewish–Negro Relations . . . 38–60."

56. Louis Martin, "Dope and Data," *Chicago Defender*, April 5, 1958.

57. "Let Us Fight This Beast," *The Pittsburgh Courier*, January 16, 1960, p. 12.

58. Clipping, Andrew W. Ramsey, "Our Friends, The Jews," *The Indianapolis Recorder*, January 11, 1961, in folder, "Jewish-Negro Relations. . . . 41–62," box 257, AJC Mss., YIVO .

59. Nathan Glazer, "Negroes and Jews: The New Challenge to Pluralism," *Commentary* (December 1964) 38:32.

60. Clark, "Black Power and Basic Power," p. 9.

61. Alvin F. Poussaint, "Blacks and Jews: An Appeal for Unity," *Ebony* (July, 1974) 39:127: Gordis, "Negroes Are Antisemitic Because," p. 137; Carson, "Blacks and Jews in the Civil Rights Movement," p. 119; Trude Weiss-Rosmarin, "Black-Jew Hatred in Historical Perspective," *Jewish Spectator* (January 1969) 34:3; Andrew Kopkind, "Blacks v. Jews," *New Statesman* (February 7, 1969) 77:175.

62. Kovach, "Racist and Anti-Semitic Charges," p. 32.

63. Strober, *American Jews*, pp. 120-121.

64. Kovach, "Racist and Anti-Semitic Charges," p. 32; Carson, "Blacks and Jews in the Civil Rights Movement," p. 28; *The New York Times*, September 6, 1968, p. 42; January 26, 1969, p. 58; A. Mazrui, "Negritude, the Talmudic tradition and the intellectual performance of Blacks and Jews," *Ethnic and Racial Studies* (January 1978) 1:29; Fred Ferretti, "New York's Black Anti-Semitism Scare," *Columbia Journalism Review* (Fall 1969) 8:28; Brown, "Black Religion," p. 351; Marie Syrkin, *The State of the Jews* (Washington, D.C.: New Republic Books, 1980), p. 279; Nat Hentoff, ed., *Black Anti-Semitism and Jewish Racism* (New York: Richard W. Baron, 1969), pp. 56–57; Polos, "Black Anti-Semitism," 19–20.

65. "The Black and the Jew: A Falling Out of Allies," *Time* (January 31, 1969) 93:55, 58; *The New York Times*, November 20, 1968, p. 1; Ferretti, "New York's Black Anti-Semitism Scare," p. 24; David Polish, "The Jewish-Negro Confrontation," *The American Zionist*, (April, 1969) 54:19.

66. Kovach, "Racist and Anti-Semitic Charges," p. 32.

67. Talk by Julius Lester, "Blacks, Jews and the Media," presented at conference on Black-Jewish Relations in the United States (Washington, D.C.), November 19, 1985; *Time*, January 31, 1969, p. 56; "The WBAI Incident," *Columbia Journalism Review*, (Fall 1969) 8:28; "New York: How Free the Air?" *Newsweek* (February 10, 1969) 73:25; *The New York Times*, January 16, 1969.

68. *The New York Times*, January 12, 1969, section II, p. 25; *Time*, January 31, 1969, p. 56; Gerald S. Strober, *American Jews: Community in Crisis*, (Garden City, N.Y.: Doubleday, 1974), p. 127; Rose, "Blacks and Jews," p. 67.

69. Vernon E. Jordan, Jr., "Together!" *The Crisis*, 81 (October, 1974), 282.

70. Ibid; Vernon E. Jordan, Jr., "Black and Jewish Communities: An Address to the Atlanta Chapter of the American Jewish Committee," *Vital Speeches* (August 1, 1947) 40:630; *The New York Times*, February 27, 1974, p. 15.

71. *The New York Times*, June 29, 1978, p. 1.

72. Louis Harris and Associates, Inc., *A Study of Attitudes Toward Racial and Religious Minorities and Toward Women* (New York: National Conference of Christians and Jews, 1978), p. 46.

73. William Safire, "Of Blacks and Jews," *The New York Times*, September 27, 1979, p. A 19; Syrkin, *The State of the Jews*, p. 279; Hume, "Falling Out," p. 18; Carl Gershman, "The Andrew Young Affair," *Commentary* (November, 1979) 68:25; Charles Silberman, "Jesse and the Jews," *The New Republic* (December 29, 1979) 181:13; Clipping, folder 1, "Jews and Negroes, 1975–," Schomberg Clipping File, Schomberg Collection, New York Public Library.

74. Will Maslow, "Negro-Jewish Relations," in Alan Westin, ed., *Freedom Now! The Civil-Rights Struggle in America* (New York: Basic Books, 1964), p. 300; Bond, "Negro Attitudes," p. 8; *The New York Times*, October 8, 1985, p. B3.

75. Peter Noel, "Urban League Beseiged," *New York Amsterdam News*, October 27, 1979, p. 4; clipping, folder "Jews and Negroes," Schomberg Collection.

76. Hume, "Falling Out," p. 18; clipping, folder, "Jews and Negroes," Schomberg Collection; Ron Chepesiuk, "Spokesman for Civil rights," *Modern Maturity* (April–May, 1986) 29:63.

77. M. Ginsberg, "Anti-Semitism," *The Sociological Review* (Worcestershire) (January–April 1943) 35:5, 7.

78. B. Z. Sobel and May L. Sobel, "Negroes and Jews: American Minority Groups in Conflict," *Judaism* (Winter 1966) 6:10.

79. Bunche, "Foreword," in *The Reaction of Negro Publications*, p. 9.

80. Daniel Goleman, "Anti-Semitism: A Prejudice That Takes Many Guises," *The New York Times*, September 4, 1984. See also, Eugene B. Brody and Robert L. Derbyshire, "Prejudice in American Negro College Students," *Archives of General Psychiatry* (December 1963) 9:626.

81. Richard L. Simpson, "Negro-Jewish Prejudice: Authoritarianism and Some Social Variables As Correlates," *Social Problems* (1959), 7:145.

82. Price, "Black Responses," p. 3; Rose, "Blacks and Jews: The Strained Alliance," p. 64; Irving Weingarten, "The Image of the Jew in the American Periodical Press, 1881–1921" (Ph.D. diss., School of Education, Health, Nursing, and Arts Programs, New York

University, 1979), p. 199; Gordis, "Negroes Are Antisemitic Because They Want a Scape-goat," p. 137; Leonora E. Berson, *The Negroes and the Jews* (New York: Random House, 1971), pp. 8–9; Will Maslow, "Negro-Jewish Relations in America: A Symposium," *Midstream* (December 1966) 12:64; see also Ann G. Wolfe, "Negro Anti-Semitism: a Survey" (unpublished paper, March 15, 1966, in American Jewish Committee Archives, New York City).

83. Geraldine Rosenfield, "The Polls: Attitudes Toward American Jews," *Public Opinion Quarterly* (Fall 1982) 46:433; Hume, "Falling Out," p. 1; Leo Laufer, "Anti-Semitism Among Negroes," *The Reconstructionist* (October 29, 1948) 14:10, 17; Simpson, "Negro-Jewish Prejudice," *Social Problems* (1959) 7:144–45; Brody and Derbyshire, "Prej-udice in American Negro College Students," pp. 619, 628; James A. Bayton, "The Racial Stereotypes of Negro College Students," *Journal of Abnormal and Social Psychology* (January 1941) 36:98 ff.; Charles Herbert Stember, *Jews in the Mind of America* (New York: Basic Books, 1966), p. 225.

84. Carolyn Olivia Atkinson, "Attitudes of Selected Small Samples of Negroes Toward Jews and Other Groups," a study prepared for the American Jewish Committee, 1968, pp. 73–74, in AJC Archives: Gertrude J. Selznick and Stephen Steinberg, *The Tenacity of Prejudice* (New York: Harper and Row, 1969), p. 122; Ronald Tado Tsukashima and Darrel Montero, "The Contact Hypothesis: Social and Economic Contact and Generational Changes in the Study of Black Anti-Semitism," *Social Forces* (September 1976) 55:161; Ronald T. Tsukoshima, *The Social and Psychological Correlates of Black Anti-Semitism* (San Francisco: R&E Research Assoc., 1978), p. 10; folder, "Race Relations: Negro-Jewish," Columbia Univ. Study ("BGX"), American Jewish Committee Archives; Harold E. Quinley and Charles Y. Glock, *Anti-Semitism in America* (New York: The Free Press, 1979), 70; Ronald Tadao Tsukashima, "The Social and Psychological Correlates of Anti-Semitism in the Black Community' (Ph.D. diss., Department of Sociology, UCLA, 1973), p. 189; Silberman, "Jesse and the Jews," p. 12; Lou Harris Associates, *A Study of Attitudes*, p. 115; see also, Chaim I. Waxman, "The Fourth Generation Grows Up: The Contemporary American Jewish Community," in *The Annals of the American Academy of Political and Social Science* (March 1981) 454:79 and Murray Friedman, "Black *Commentary* (October 1979) 68:31.

85. Gary T. Marx, *Protest and Prejudice: A Study of Belief in the Black Community* (New York: Harper and Row, 1967), pp. 128–29.

86. Ibid., p. 133.

87. Polos, "Black Anti-Semitism," p. 27.

88. Marx, *Protest and Prejudice*, p. 146.

89. Selznick and Steinberg, *The Tenacity of Prejudice*, p. 119.

90. Rosenfeld, "The Polls," p. 440; Lou Harris, *A Study of Attitudes*, p. xvii.

91. Kenneth R. Berg, "Ethnic Attitudes and Agreements With a Negro Person," *Journal of Personality and Social Psychology* (August 1966) 4:215; Gordon W. Allport and Bernard M. Kramer, "Some Roots of Prejudice," *The Journal of Psychology* (1946) 22:27; Sam Wells, "The Jewish Elan," *Fortune* (February 1960) 61:160, 164; Andrew M. Greeley, "Ethnicity and Racial Attitudes: The Case of the Jews and the Poles," *American Journal of Sociology* (1975) 80:909.

92. Minutes of the American Jewish Committee's Board of Governors, November 8, 1967, p. 4.

93. John B. Sheerin, C.S.P., "The Myth of Black Anti-Semitism," *Catholic World* (May 1969) 209:51.

Part IV.
Bibliographical Essay

The Historiography
of American Antisemitism

Although antisemitism is part of American cultural baggage, it has attracted the interest of few American historians. War, politics, and diplomacy were the stapes of the professionals until social history came into fashion in the 1950s and 1960s. Since then ethnicity has been one of the chic topics of this "new social history," and American Jewish history and antisemitism are subdivisions of this recently discovered territory. Before the 1970s, however, only one non–Jewish historian, John Higham, delved deeply into the subject. During the past decade or so, however, both Jewish and non–Jewish historians have explored different areas of the American Jewish past and have addressed the issue of antisemitism.

Prejudice against Jews properly belongs to both old and new approaches to American history because it repeatedly occurs in all kinds of analyses. Relatively latent in ordinary times, antisemitism intensifies in periods of social and economic crises such as the Civil War, the depressions of the 1890s and 1930s, and the anxieties provoked by the two World Wars. In our own time it regularly surfaces among blacks as evidenced by their reactions to the New York school strike of 1968, the resignation of Andrew Young as U.S. Ambassador to the United Nations in 1979, and the more recent political campaign of the Reverend Jesse Jackson in 1984.

Perhaps the worst period of American antisemitism occurred in the twentieth century between the ends of the two world wars. Neither respectable people nor fanatics like Henry Ford, members of the Ku Klux Klan, the Silver Shirts, Father Coughlin, members of the Christian Front, et al. had any use for Jews. The more genteel people shunned Jews quietly (Frederick Jackson Turner's biographer, Ray Billington, tells us that he never found a Jew with whom he was socially comfortable[1]) and Jewish academics were about as abundant as blacks in the Reagan administration. Educated Jews knew the odds against them and generally avoided the academic world; history, especially, offered few opportunities.[2] Consequently, hardly anyone in the profession cared to write about American Jewry or the problems Jews faced because of bigotry.

For American Jews, on the other hand, historical research could counteract antisemitism by showing how patriotic their brethren had been, how welcome they had been in colonial America (which was untrue), and how they had contributed to the growth and prosperity of the United States.[3] So much of what had been written by Jews was in the realm of filiopietism that, in order to get some real understanding of the American Jewish experience, *Commentary* sponsored a conference on the writing of American Jewish history in May 1948. The participants, mostly historians, other scholars, and members of the American Jewish Committee's professional staff, discussed why Jews had generally been excluded from the writings on American history (one of the reasons was that most minorities had been excluded as a matter of course) and what kinds of analyses were needed to inform other Americans about Jewish activities in the past. Harvey Wish, however, noted the agenda and commented, "there is a dimension in general American history which we have tended to ignore, perhaps through a conspiracy of silence. That dimension involves the role of anti-Semitism in American history, not particularly with regard to its importance as far as the Jew is concerned, but its importance in American development."[4]

Wish touched a raw nerve. Antisemitism had been rampant during the previous three decades and the last thing Jews wanted to do was to bring attention to the fact that they were so disliked and ostracized by other Americans. Jews wanted to convey only positive images in the hope that they would convince the antisemites that they were worthy members of society.

But two books, both of which appeared in 1947, brought national attention to the existing prejudice. Carey McWilliams' *A Mask for Privilege* (Boston: Little, Brown, 1947) tried to help the Jews when he argued that antisemitism was a product of the rapacious and reactionary entrepreneurs who had benefited from the industrial revolution and had thereby made a shambles of American democratic traditions. Laura Z. Hobson's novel, *Gentleman's Agreement* (New York: Simon and Schuster,

1947), explained the subject much better. Gentiles simply did not like Jews. Respectable people preferred not to live, work, attend school, socialize, or relax with people thought to be Jews. None of the Gentile characters in Hobson's novel were mean, vicious, unpleasant, demented, or otherwise deranged. They were the pillars of the community whom one pointed to as "fine people." Hobson's novel made more of an impact than McWilliams' book. It was significant because it suggested how pervasive and ingrained antisemitism was in American society.

Most Jewish organizations were concerned about the causes of antisemitism and how the prejudice might be combatted. Beginning in 1944 with the establishment of the Community Relations Councils, massive efforts were made by Jewish organizations to fight antisemitism and, if possible, eliminate it from the American scene. As part of the effort, it was thought appropriate to commission scholars to examine the roots of the problem with the hope that by understanding the nature of the prejudice it would be easier to eradicate. As a result the American Jewish Committee sponsored a series of sociological and psychological analyses which culminated in the publication of Leo Lowenthal, *Prophets of Deceit* (New York: Harper, 1949), Bruno Bettleheim and Morris Janowicz, *Dynamics of Prejudice* (New York: Harper, 1950), T. W. Adorno, et al., *The Authoritarian Personality* (New York: Harper, 1950), and Nathan Ward Ackerman and Marie Jahoda, *Anti-Semitism and Emotional Disorder* (New York: Harper, 1950).

In the 1960s, in a renewed effort to examine the problem, the Anti-Defamation League gave money to the University of California for a major sociological study of antisemitism. These books, which found the largest numbers of antisemites among the Protestant fundamentalists, blue collar workers, and least educated Americans, include Charles Y. Glock and Rodney Stark, *Christian Beliefs and Anti-Semitism* (New York, 1966), Gertrude Selznick and Stephen Steinberg, *The Tenacity of Prejudice* (New York, 1969), and Rodney Stark, et al., *Wayward Shepherds: Prejudice and the Protestant Clergy* (New York, 1971). The series findings are summarized in Harold E. Quinley and Charles Y. Glock, *Anti-Semitism in America* (New York, 1979).

In American history, however, the first postwar scholarly analysis came from the pen of Oscar Handlin, who published "How U.S. Anti-Semitism Really Began," *Commentary* (June 1951) and "American Views of the Jews at the Opening of the Twentieth Century," *Publications of the American Jewish Historical Society* (June 1951) 40:323–344. Handlin believed that a philo-Semitic attitude prevailed in the United States through the 1890s and that the few slurs, the negative stereotyping on the stage, and the occasional slight really constituted "no hostility, no negative judgment." But he did note some anger toward Jews in those areas of the country "strongly moved by radicalism," and he acknowledged that in some areas of the country the idea entrenched itself that Jews "controlled the great fortunes of the world" and were somehow responsible for the economic plight of the the dispossessed in this country. The stereotype of the strange and mysterious Jew who was somehow responsible for crucifying mankind on a cross of gold took hold and later became the basis for the development of antisemitism in this country after 1913.[5]

Four years later, in *The Age of Reform* (New York: Knopf, 1955), Richard Hofstadter reflected on Handlin's theme and although he qualified his own argument by writing that "it would be easy to misstate the character of Populist anti-Semitism or to exaggerate its intensity," he suggested that "the Greenback-Populist tradition activated most of what we have of modern popular anti–Semitism in the United States."[6]

Hofstadter's rather casual comments on the subject spawned a decade of historiographical controversy about alleged Populist antisemitism. Perhaps the best argument against it was Walter Nugent's *The Tolerant Populists* (Chicago: University of Chicago Press, 1963), but before the debate ended there were articles by Norman Pollack, Oscar Handlin, and Irwin Unger expanding upon the subject in *Agricultural History* (1965) 39:59–85). Pollack defended the democratic ideals of the Populists, Handlin restated his position that the Populists were neither more nor less antisemitic than other Americans, but Unger, agreeing that not all Populists were antisemites, did point out that

> some Populists clearly disliked foreigners and Jews, and for reasons, in the latter case, that were uniquely Populistic. To Populists, the Jew was a "non–producer," a mere manipulator of money, a parasite, and at the same time representative of the sinister and forbidding power of international finance. "In these evil conditions, made by bad laws, the Jews alone thrive," wrote Ignatius Donnelly. "The reason is they deal only in money; they have no belief in farming, manufacturing, or any other industry; they are mere money-managers. As everything else goes down, money rises in value and those who control it become masters of the world."

I find Unger's argument quite convincing, but John Clymer, writing in 1971, did not. "The Handlin-Hofstadter thesis regarding anti-Semitism has been seriously questioned," he wrote, "and it is doubtful if feeling against the Jews was nearly as deep or as widespread as was once thought."[7] My own research, on the other hand, convinces me that antisemitic feeling in this country was deeper and more widespread than any historian has ever suggested. Fred Jaher and I are in the process of preparing a book on antisemitism in the United States and Oxford University Press will publish it once we produce the manuscript.

Going back to the 1950s, one must now discuss the works of John Higham. No other American historian has written as deeply or as extensively about antisemitism in the United States. In a major book, *Strangers in the Land*, a series of articles in the 1950s and 1960s, and then a compilation of those articles in *Send these to me.* . . , Higham's studies have been consistently thoughtful, detailed, and complex. His research indicated that both positive and negative stereotypes of the Jew existed simultaneously in nineteenth-century America and that they focused on both economic and religious matters. In the last third of the nineteenth century he saw both increased acceptance and rejection of Jews and without singling out the Populists *per se* he indicated that antisemitism was "strongest in those sectors of the population where a particularly explosive combination of social discontent and nationalistic aggression prevailed."[8]

Naomi W. Cohen and Michael Dobkowski have expanded upon the arguments presented by Handlin, Hofstadter, and Higham. Cohen and Dobkowski presented information that proved antisemitism was much more pervasive than any of the other three historians suggested and they provided ample documentation to substantiate these views. Dobkowski, in a summary of his book *The Tarnished Dream* (Westport, Conn., Greenwood Press, 1979), claimed that antisemitism pervaded every area of American society and that Handlin, Hofstadter, and Higham had overlooked much of the bigotry displayed in the contemporary press, in literature, and on the stage.[9] Cohen pointed out that "Christian religious teachings always constituted a significant component of antisemitism," and that the Anglo-Jewish press had been detailing hostile attitudes toward Jews in the United States at least as far back as 1840. Moreover, Jews felt threatened by a proposed constitutional amendment in the 1860s and 1870s which attempted to have the United States acknowledge the authority of God, Jesus, and the Scriptures.[10]

My own position is that antisemitism always existed in America and that it has often been ignored or overlooked because so little has been written on the subject. But one doctoral thesis, produced at the City University of New York by Louise A. Mayo ("The Ambivalent Image:

The Perception of the Jew in Nineteenth Century America," 1977), spent almost five hundred pages cataloguing both positive and other stereotypes of the Jew in America. Although short on analysis, it is long on detail and no one who reads it would question the depth and breadth of antisemitism in America long before the 1890s. But even a cursory study of American history points to the fact that Jews were disfranchised in colonial times and often prohibited by law from becoming physicians or attorneys. Morris U. Schappes, "Anti-Semitism and Reaction, 1795–1800" *(Publications of the American Jewish Historical Society* (December 1948) 38:109:137) has not been followed up on by other historians, and his collection of antisemitica in *A Documentary History of the Jews in the United States, 1654–1875* (New York: Citadel Press, 1950) should convince even the most skeptical observer that the field is worthy of historical study.

There are several other nineteenth-century studies which touch on or delve more deeply into antisemitism in nineteenth-century America. Jonathan Sarna's *Jacksonian Jew* (New York: Holmes and Meier, 1981) showed how Mordecai M. Noah tried to bridge two cultures; Maxine Sellers' "Isaace Leeser: A Jewish-Christian Dialogue in Antebellum Philadelphia" *(Pennsylvania History* [July 1968] 35:231–242) describes how the Rabbi tried to get Gentile Americans to appreciate and understand Jews and their heritage; and Bertram W. Korn's *American Jews and the Civil War* (Philadelphia: Jewish Publication Society of America, 1951) includes a chapter on savage antisemitism in both the North and the South during that conflict.

During the past decade Jews have felt secure enough in this country to explore other areas of antisemitic manifestations in the American past. We have thus learned that antisemitism existed in Detroit before the Civil War (Robert A. Rockaway, "Anti-Semitism in an American City: Detroit, 1850–1914," *American Jewish Historical Quarterly* [September 1947] 64:42–54), and that early American credit bureaus discriminated against Jews (Stephen G. Mostov, "Dun and Bradstreet Reports as a Source of Jewish Economic History: Cincinnati, 1840–1875," *American Jewish History* [March 1983] 72:333–353, and David A. Gerber, "Cutting Out Shylock: Elite Anti-Semitism and the Quest for Moral Order in the Mid-Nineteenth Century American Market Place," *Journal of American History* (December 1982) 69:615–637.

Much of my own work has focused on American antisemitism: *The Leo Frank Case* (New York: Columbia University Press, 1968) analyzed the episode in its historical context and assessed the impact of antisemitism upon the Atlanta community's response; subsequently, to understand the antecedents of antisemitism in the South, I wrote "A Note on Southern Attitudes Toward Jews," *(Jewish Social Studies* [January 1979] 32:43–49) and "A Neglected Aspect of Southern Jewish History," *(American Jewish Historical Quarterly* [September 1971], vol. 61.) Together with Mary Dale Palsson I then edited *Jews in the South* (Louisiana State University Press, 1973). Studying about Jews in the South convinced me that Southern antisemitism was more extensive than any historian save Bertram Korn had ever before suggested. More recently Louis Schmier's probing account of "The First Jews of Valdosta" (*Georgia Historical Quarterly* [Spring 1978] 62:32–50) offered additional insights.

But there are other historical works which expose the nature of American antisemitism. Saul Friedman's *The Incident at Massena* (New York: Stein and Day, 1978) discusses a case in up–state New York in which Christians suspected that Jews kidnapped a child to kill her and then use her blood for religious purposes. A number of books indicated Franklin D. Roosevelt, the State Department, and the American public for their callousness toward the sufferings of European Jewry during World War II. Arthur Morse's *While Six Million Died* (New York: Random House, 1967) was the first of these publications, but David Wyman's *Paper Walls* (Amherst: University of Massachusetts Press, 1968), *The Abandonment of the Jews: America and the Holocaust, 1941–1945* (New York: Pantheon Books, 1984), and Henry Feingold's *The Politics of Rescue* (New Brunswick: Rutgers University Press, 1970) are the best.

A topic which few historians have explored but about which there is enough literature to begin is black antisemitism. I think Kenneth Clark's "Candor About Negro-Jewish Relations," *(Commentary* [February 1946] 1:8–14) is the finest but James Baldwin's "The Harlem Ghetto," *(Commentary* [February 1948] 15:165–170) and "Negroes Are Anti-Semitic Because They're Antiwhite" *(The New York Times Magazine,* April 16, 1967), Eugene I. Bender's "Reflections on Negro-Jewish Relationships," *Phylon* (Spring 1969) 30:59–65, Robert G. Weisbord and Arthur Stein, *Bittersweet Encounter* (Westport, Conn.: Greendwood Press, 1970), Oscar R. Williams, Jr., "Historical Impressions of Black-Jewish Relations Prior to World War II," *Negro History Bulletin* (July–August 1977) 40:728–731, Louis R Harlan's "Booker T. Washington's Discovery of Jews," in J. Morgan Kousser and James M. McPherson, eds., *Region, Race, and Reconstruction* (New York: Oxford University Press, 1982), Horace Mann Bond's, "Negro Attitudes Toward Jews," *Jewish Social Studies* (January 1965) 27:3–9, Fred Ferretti, "New York's Black Anti-Semitism Scare," *Columbia Journalism Review* (Fall 1969) 8:18–29, and Carl Gershman,

"The Andrew Young Affair," *Commentary* (November 1979) 68:25–33, are also informative. David J. Hellwig's "Black Images of Jews: from reconstruction to depression," *Societas,* (Summer 1978) 8:205–223, is a gem.

Space considerations prevent me from discussing much of the good literature available on antisemitism in academia, Henry Ford, the Ku Klux Klan, the German-American Bund, the Silver Shirts, Father Coughlin, the Christian Front, the America First movement, antisemitism during World War II, and other topics, but items on these subjects are listed in the bibliography. One outstanding work, however, that was written after this essay originally appeared, is Dan A. Oren's methodical *Joining the Club:* A History of Jews and Yale (New Haven: Yale University Press, 1985). It is without question one of the finest analyses ever done on any aspect of American antisemitism.

As I bring this essay to a close, I want to mention some of the more promising scholars in the field. Leo Ribuffo has done an outstanding analysis of antisemitism in *The Old Christian Right: The Protestant Far Right From the Great Depression to the Cold War* (Philadelphia: Temple University Press, 1983), and "Henry Ford and *The International Jew"* *(American Jewish History* [June 1980] 69:437–477). If his superior scholarship in this field continues, he will be among the leading historians of American antisemitism. Jonathan Sarna's excellent "Anti-Semitism and American History" *(Commentary* [March, 1981] 71:42–47) is the first historiographical article on the topic. Although I do not always agree with Sarna's observations made in other works, he is now both the most prolific and the most provocative historian in the field of American Jewish History and whatever he writes on the subject is worth considering. David A. Gerber is a third person whose work on antisemitism is quite good. His edited collection, *Anti–Semitism in American History* (Urbana: University of Illinois Press, 1986), contains some of the newest insights into the subject.

Two collections of articles on antisemitism are Leonard Dinnerstein, ed., *Antisemitism in the United States* (New York: Holt, Rinehart and Winston, 1971) and Naomi W. Cohen's special issue on the subject for *American Jewish History* (September 1981), vol. 71.

The best bibliography of the entire topic is Robert Singerman, *Antisemitism: An Annotated Bibliography and Research Guide* (New York: Garland Publishing Co., 1982). Melvin M. Tumin's *An Inventory and Appraisal of Research on American Antisemitism* (New York: Freedom Books, 1961) covers mostly sociological analyses.

Source Notes

1. Ray Allen Billington, *Frederick Jackson Turner* (New York: Oxford University Press, 1973), p. 437.

2. L. S. Feuer, "Stages in the Social History of Jewish Professors in American Colleges and Universities," *American Jewish History.* (June 1982) 71:455, 460. See also, Sidney Hook, "Anti-Semitism in the Academy: Some Pages of the Past," *Midstream* (January 1979) 25:49–54. In his 1962 presidential address to the American Historical Association, Carl Bridenbaugh fondly recalled his rural boyhood outside of Philadelphia in which he and his fellows "gathered and sold chestnuts, fished, and trapped muskrats along the banks of a broad creek." He then went on to comment about "the discouraging prospect that we all, teachers and pupils alike, have lost much of what this earlier generation possessed, the priceless asset of a shared culture. Today imaginations have become starved or stunted, and wit and humor, let alone laughter and a healthy frivolity, are seldom encountered. Furthermore, many of the younger practitioners of our craft, and those who are still apprentices, are products of lower middle class or foreign origins, and their emotions not infrequently get in the way of historical reconstructions. They find themselves in a very real sense outsiders on our past and feel themselves shut out." He went on to admonish those responsible for graduate student admissions to select only those people who could show evidence of "a broad and ranging general culture." Finally, in case any of his audience had any doubt about which group he wanted excluded from the profession, he added, "We must find ways to make the past a living past. . . . This will be particularly difficult for most of the urban-bred scholars of today if their work is to show any real, perceptive comprehension of the workings of human nature. The deficiency is environmental, for in former times such understanding was vouchsafed to historians who were raised in the countryside or in the small town. . . ." Carl Bridenbaugh, "The Great Mutation," *The American Historical Review* (January 1963) 68:317, 322–23, 328.

3. Marshall Sklare, "Problems in the Teaching of Contemporary Jewish Studies," *American Jewish Historical Quarterly* (June, 1974) 63:362; Jonathan D. Sarna, "Anti-Semitism and American History," *Commentary* (March 1981) 71:42.

4. Oscar Handlin, "Report on a Conference on the Jewish Experience in America Held at Hotel Warwick, New York City, N.Y., May 22–23, 1948," unpublished ms., Blaustein Library, American Jewish Committee, New York City, p. 42.

5. Oscar Handlin, "How U.S. Anti-Semitism Really Began," *Commentary* (June 1951) 11:541–548, *passim.*

6. Richard Hofstadter, *The Age of Reform* (New York: Knopf, 1955), pp. 80–81.

7. Kenton J. Clymer, "Anti-Semitism in the Late Nineteenth Century: The Case of John Hay," *American Jewish Historical Quarterly* (June 1971) 60:344.

8. John Higham, "Anti-Semitism in the Gilded Age: A Reinterpretation," *Mississippi Valley Historical Review* (March 1957) 43:572; all of Higham's essays on antisemitism appear in John Higham, *Send these to me . . .* (New York: Atheneum, 1975; 2 ed., The Johns Hopkins University Press, 1984).

9. Michael N. Dobkowski, "American Anti-Semitism: A Reinterpretation," *American Quarterly* (1977) 29:167. Some of the passages of Michael Dobkowski's *The Tarnished Dream* seem to have been taken verbatim, and without acknowledgement, from the writings of John Higham. As a result of this Greenwood Press has withdrawn *The Tarnished Dream* from the market. This does not mean, however, that all of the arguments and

substantiation of antisemitism made by Dobkowski should be ignored. The book has merit and serious scholars of antisemitism should be familiar with what Dobkowski has to say.

    10. Naomi W. Cohen, "Antisemitism in the Gilded Age: The Jewish View," *Jewish Social Studies* (Summer/Fall 1979) 41:190, 192 ff.

Bibliography

Of Additional Items Not Mentioned in Either Text or Notes

Baltzel, E. Digby. *The Protestant Establishment.* New York: Random House, 1964.

Bayor, Ronald. *Neighbors in Conflict:* The Irish, Germans, Jews and Italians of New York City, 1929–1941. Baltimore: The Johns Hopkins Press, 1978.

Berman, Hyman. "Political Antisemitism in Minnesota During the Great Depression." *Jewish Social Studies* (Summer/Fall 1976) 38:247–267.

Bloore, Stephen. "The Jew in American Dramatic Literature (1794–1930)," *Publications of the American Jewish Historical Society,* (June 1951) 49:345–360.

Boxerman, Burton A. "A Reaction of the St. Louis Jewish Community to Anti-Semitism." Ph.D. thesis, St. Louis University, 1967.

Brinkley, Alan. *Voices of Protest.* New York: Knopf, 1982.

Erens, Patricia B. "The Image of thee Jew in the American Cinema: A Study in Stereotyping." Ph.D. thesis, Northwestern University, 1981.

Flower, Edward. "Anti-Semitism in the Free Silver and Populist Movements and the Election of 1896." M.A. thesis, Columbia University, 1952.

Friedman, Murray. "Black Anti-Semitism on the Rise." *Commentary* (October 1979) 68:31–35.

Greenberg, Leonard A. "Some American Anti-Semitic Publications of the Late 19th Century." *Publications of the American Jewish Historical Society* (1947) 37:421–425.

Holmes, William F. "Whitecapping: Anti–Semitism in the Populist Era." *American Jewish Historical Quarterly* (March, 1974) 63:244–261.

Levinger, Lee J. *Anti-Semitism in the United States.* New York: Block Publishing Co., 1925.

Marcus, Sheldon. "Social Justice: The History of a Weekly Journal, 1936–1942." Unpublished Ed. D., Yeshiva University, 1970.

Masters, Nick Arthur. "Father Coughlin and Social Justice." Unpublished Ph.D. thesis, University of Wisconsin, 1955.

Mosley, Charlton. "Latent Klanism in Georgia, 1890–1915." *Georgia Historical Quarterly* (Fall 1972) 53:365–387.

Rapp, Michael G. "An Historical Overview of Anti-Semitism in Minnesota, 1920–1960." Unpublished Ph.D. thesis, University of Minnesota, 1977.

Sable, Jacob M. "Some Organizational Efforts to Combat Anti-Semitism in America, 1906–1930." Ph.D. thesis, Yeshiva University, 1964.

Schwartz, Henry. "The Uneasy Alliance: Jewish-Anglo Relations in San Diego, 1850–1860." *Journal of San Diego History* (Summer 1974) 20:52–60.

Scholnick, Myron Israel. "The New Deal and Anti-Semitism in America." Ph.D. thesis, University of Maryland, 1971.

Stark, Rodney and Stephen Steinberg., "Jews and Christians in Suburbia." *Harper's Magazine* (August 1967) 235:73–78.

Stember, C. H. *Jews in the Mind of America.* New York: Basic Books, 1966.

Strong, Donald S. *Organized Anti-Semitism in America.* Washington, D.C., 1941.

Synnott, Marcia G. *The Half-Opened Door.* Westport, Conn.: Greenwood Press, 1979.

Wechsler, Harold S. *The Qualified Student.* New York: John Wiley, 1977.

Weingarten, Irving. "The Image of the Jew in the American Periodical Press, 1881–1921." Ph.D. thesis, New York University, 1980.

Index